The
Writer's Loop

A Guide to College Writing

The Writer's Loop

A Guide to College Writing

Lauren Ingraham
University of Tennessee at Chattanooga

Jeanne Law Bohannon
Kennesaw State University

 bedford/st.martin's
Macmillan Learning

Boston | New York

For Bedford/St. Martin's

Vice President, Editorial, Macmillan Learning Humanities: Edwin Hill
Executive Program Director for English: Leasa Burton
Senior Program Manager: Laura Arcari
Marketing Manager: Vivian Garcia
Director of Content Development, Humanities: Jane Knetzger
Development Manager: Caroline Thompson
Senior Digital Content Project Manager: Ryan Sullivan
Lead Digital Asset Archivist and Workflow Manager: Jennifer Wetzel
Production Supervisor: Brianna Lester
Associate Media Project Manager: Emily Brower
Director of Media Editorial, Humanities: Adam Whitehurst
Editorial Services: Lumina Datamatics, Inc.
Composition: Lumina Datamatics, Inc.
Text Permissions Manager: Kalina Ingham
Photo Permissions Editor: Angela Boehler
Photo Researcher: Brittani Morgan, Lumina Datamatics, Inc.
Director of Design, Content Management: Diana Blume
Text Design: Claire Seng-Niemoeller
Cover Design: William Boardman
Printing and Binding: LSC Communications

Manufactured in the United States of America.

1 2 3 4 5 6   24 23 22 21 20 19

For information, write: Bedford/St. Martin's, 75 Arlington Street, Boston, MA 02116

ISBN 978-1-319-31454-5 (Paperback)
ISBN 978-1-319-25919-8 (Loose-leaf Edition)

Acknowledgments

Text acknowledgments and copyrights appear at the back of the book on pages 347–48, which constitute an extension of the copyright page. Art acknowledgments and copyrights appear on the same page as the art selections they cover.

Preface

Welcome to *The Writer's Loop*. We're grateful to be your partners in teaching your students, and we've designed this text to speak directly to them.

In past writing classes, students might have heard the phrase "writing is a process," and perhaps their instructors offered opportunities to brainstorm, write rough drafts, and revise before the final draft. But many students haven't always had that opportunity. And even if they have, that linear writing process can sometimes feel quite rigid and, frankly, unproductive. Students know that writing projects have a starting point and an ending point, and often they assume that the way to get from beginning to end is to march forward in a straight line without ever looking back. They might brainstorm on Monday, draft on Tuesday, revise on Wednesday, edit on Thursday, and turn in a final draft on Friday, without fully engaging with the ideas they're writing about. Of course, instructors know that most successful writers don't work that way. *The Writer's Loop* asks students to think about and practice writing as a recursive, looping process that more authentically reflects best practices for drafting and revising.

In our teaching, and in *The Writer's Loop*, we invite students to understand that they have their own individual writing processes that shift from project to project. Often, students enter our classes unable to imagine themselves as writers who can use their skills to enact change. We've learned over the years that the best support we can offer them is to help them believe in their ability to grow as writers. In *The Writer's Loop*, we acknowledge that writing can be hard—even for professional writers who work at it every day—and we offer plenty of low-stakes writing and reflection activities to help students find a point of engagement that works for them. The consistent learning framework in each chapter helps students strategically "loop" through their writing process, discovering the unique writing habits that will be most productive for them. We see validation that this approach works in the reflective statements that open students' final portfolios. They'll often comment on their fear or worry about writing early in the semester, then marvel at how much more confident they feel about their writing. Others reflect on the improved quality of the writing itself, noting that adopting a looping process allowed them to step away from an emerging draft, develop perspective, and be willing to address what wasn't working. Our message to students throughout this book is that taking the time to dig deeper into those early drafts is time well spent. It helps them produce higher-quality writing they can be proud of.

Features of *The Writer's Loop*

Strong writers pause often, reflect on what they've written, and loop backwards and forwards throughout the writing process to rethink and revise their plans. All the features of *The Writer's Loop* are designed to support students in this recursive process, helping them loop back frequently to improve their writing in big and small ways.

A consistent, scaffolded learning framework

To teach students to develop and embrace a looping, recursive process—and become a better writer as a result—we're bringing them a model that has worked well for our students. Within the chapters, each numbered section is organized in a four-part framework:

1. First, students engage with new concepts by reading about them.

2. Next, a Reflect activity prompts them to write about how these new concepts connect to their past experiences with writing or to an assignment they're currently working on.

3. An Understand section follows, diving deeper into the concepts through extended examples, often in the form of videos, annotated readings, or annotated student essays.

4. Then, an Apply activity prompts students to try out the new strategies they've learned in their own writing. These assignments range from asking students to write a brief paragraph to asking them to produce a full draft of a writing project.

The low-stakes Reflect and Apply activities in each chapter build toward the Chapter Project, a higher-stakes writing assignment. The thirteen Chapter Projects call for a range of common types of writing including personal essay, literacy narrative, reflection, evaluation, rhetorical analysis, argument, public writing, annotated bibliography, and researched writing.

Dynamic, multimedia format with customizable content

We conceived and designed *The Writer's Loop* to be a digital writing guide that is available with a printed companion text. To fully take advantage of its interactive features, customizable content, and powerful writing tools, use *Achieve with Ingraham and Bohannon, The Writer's Loop* (see **macmillanlearning.com** for details). Achieve puts student writing at the center of your course and keeps revision at the core, with a dedicated composition space that guides students through draft, review, source check, and revision. In Achieve, students can read the complete text of *The Writer's Loop,* watch the integrated videos, complete the Reflect and Apply activities, get feedback from peers, and work on the multi-draft Chapter Projects. Through emphasis on feedback and revision, the writing tools in Achieve reinforce *The Writer's Loop*'s focus on helping students embrace a recursive writing process. To provide support when students are offline, the printed edition of *The Writer's Loop* contains the complete text of the chapters and assignments.

Videos that help students develop confidence

Seventeen animated videos throughout the text follow four student characters as they work through some of the writing processes, strategies, and concepts we introduce. These inviting videos give students confidence to tackle their own writing challenges as they work through similar assignments. The four characters—Gabby, Jay, Li, and Meg—provide a relatable lens through which to learn about the writing process. Each video is no more than three minutes long, making them great icebreakers for class discussion. Videos can be viewed within the e-book in *Achieve with Ingraham and Bohannon, The Writer's Loop.* Watch the introductory video to meet the characters.

Video: Meet the Characters

Clear, concise treatment of key rhetorical concepts

We strive to maintain a friendly and engaging tone throughout the text, with the goal of providing straightforward explanations and relatable examples of important rhetorical concepts. We have taken care to keep the text brief while offering plenty of step-by-step guidance for using a recursive, looping writing process.

Chapters 1–4 serve as a bridge to college writing for students. Chapter 1, "Being an Academic Writer," acknowledges that students are often worried about their transition from high school to college—or returning to college as an adult student. In that chapter, we invite students and instructors to acknowledge that many students embarking on this journey are taking on something new and we offer tools to help bridge that transition. Chapter 2 introduces students to the term "rhetoric" in a way that's different from how they've likely experienced it in their communities as a negative political term. Chapter 3 introduces students to the central idea of this text, that writing is a recursive process, by challenging them to see beyond a linear writing process that marches through brainstorming, drafting, revising, and editing. Chapter 4 helps students understand how to use feedback to revise their work in this recursive process.

Chapter 5 builds on Chapters 1–4 to invite students to move from understanding a recursive writing process, including taking feedback into account, to focus on using outside readings in their writing. It offers students a productive three-step process of reading texts. Chapter 6 then focuses specifically on writing academic arguments, and Chapter 7 introduces students to writing in multimodal spaces.

Beginning with Chapter 8, we introduce students to a research process that can evolve into a research project that's developed in Chapters 8–12. In those chapters, we show students how to develop a research question; locate and annotate relevant, credible sources; refine a thesis; incorporate source material responsibly; and revise a draft that effectively addresses counterclaims. Finally, in Chapter 13, we show students how to create a final course portfolio that includes their best work and reflects their learning.

While we've sequenced the chapters in a way that makes sense to us, you can assign chapters in any order you like or skip chapters you don't need. For example, we believe strongly in portfolio pedagogy to help students develop as writers without being distracted by disappointing grades early in a course. But if you prefer to grade each writing project independently throughout the course, you can opt out of Chapter 13. Similarly, if your course does not include a research project, you might choose to use Chapter 10 (on developing and revising a thesis) and Chapter 12 (on tightening an argument) in conjunction with Chapter 6 (on composing academic arguments).

Writing assignments that encourage a looping process

To consistently prompt students to engage in a recursive process, the major writing assignments in the text are designed as multi-draft assignments, and some can be used in sequences across chapters. For example, the Apply activities in Chapter 3 invite students to write three successive drafts of the Chapter 3 Project, a literacy narrative. The Chapter 6 Project asks students to write an academic argument, then the Chapter 7 Project invites them to rewrite that argument for a public, digital space. For the Chapter 10 Project, students produce a thesis statement that can be used in a non-research-based assignment or revised as they work on the Projects in Chapters 11 and 12, which ask them to write successive drafts of a research paper. You can edit and customize the assignments as needed in Achieve.

Real sample essays for students to model and critique

Twelve sample essays throughout the text provide models for students to learn from and critique. Written by real students in our courses and in those of our colleagues, these examples demonstrate many of the concepts introduced in the text. We offer them not as perfect examples but as realistic models of student writing that demonstrate the benefits of a looping writing process.

A Student's Companion for The Writer's Loop

Authored by Elizabeth Catanese (Community College of Philadelphia), this supplement offers thorough support for students taking a corequisite or ALP course alongside first-year composition. The text includes coverage of college success strategies; activities to support the assignments in *The Writer's Loop*; and additional practice in correcting writing problems, from revising topic sentences and developing paragraphs to correcting fragments. This handy resource can be found in the book's Achieve and can be packaged with the text as a print supplement.

Acknowledgments

We are grateful to the following instructors who served on our editorial advisory board as we developed *The Writer's Loop*:

Fernando Benavidez, Delaware County Community College

Erin Breaux, South Louisiana Community College

Brian Dickson, Community College of Denver

Clark Draney, College of Southern Idaho

Anneliese Homan, State Fair Community College

Michael Morris, Eastfield College

C. Cole Osborne, Guilford Technical Community College

Tony Russell, Central Oregon Community College

Andrea Sheridan, Orange County Community College

Matt Teorey, Peninsula College

We are also grateful to the many instructors who participated in focus groups, offered feedback on the table of contents, and reviewed drafts of manuscript throughout our writing process: Domenick Acocella, Borough of Manhattan Community College; Troy Appling, Florida Gateway College; Jenny Billings Beaver, Rowan Cabarrus Community College; Mara Beckett, Glendale Community College; Robert Brandon, Cleveland State Community College; Traci Bryan, Ivy Tech Community College; Howard Cox, Angelina College; Jason Dockter, Lincoln Land Community College; Jennifer Eble, Cleveland State Community College; Ming Fang, Florida International University; Allison Fetters, Chattanooga State University; Cheryl Finley, California State University; Lucy Johnson, Washington State University; Lilia Joy, Henderson Community College; Kevin Knight, Cape Fear Community College; David Leitner, Lincoln Land Community College; Janet Maher, Nassau Community College; Stephanie Masson, Northwestern State University; Sara McCurry, Shasta College; Brian Mosher, Chemeketa Community College; Vicki Moulson, College of the Albemarle; Stacy Oberle, Lone Star College–Fairbanks Center; Holly Pappas, Bristol Community College; Jennifer Royal, Santa Rosa Junior College; Jessica Saxon, Craven Community College; Nathan Shank, Oklahoma Christian University; Eric Smith, Kent State University; Matt Teorey, Peninsula College; and Cheli Turner, Greenville Technical College.

We thank the following instructors and their students, who class-tested the content: Lamya Mohamed Almas, Alabama State University; Laura Lee Beasley, University of West Georgia; Erin Beaver, Colorado Mountain College; Clint Burhans, Delta College; Nicholas Goodwin, Evergreen Valley College; Peter Huk, University of California, Santa Barbara; Rick Iadonisi, Grand Valley State University; Rachel Luria, Florida Atlantic University; Robert Morrison, South Piedmont Community College; Dauvan Mulally, Grand Valley State University; and Brandi Spelbring, Southern Arkansas University. Finally, we thank the dozens of additional survey respondents and class testers who shared their insight on the chapters and videos.

We thank the students who generously granted us permission to use their work: Mujtaba "MJ" Aljutel, Jora Burnett, Carson Cook, Jared Glidden, Kristjan Grimson, Nia Hale, Amy Johnson, Rebekah Jones, Eddie Kihara, Henry Law, William Lewis, and Carson Long.

We are so grateful for colleagues at Bedford/St. Martin's who have supported this project for years. Thank you, Leasa Burton, who was at the first pitch and appreciated the concept. Our original development editor, Mara Weible, helped us dream big and imagine *The Writer's Loop* as a wholly digital guide. Molly Parke provided important leadership in the early years and made some necessary difficult decisions that helped move the project forward. Laura Arcari and Carrie Thompson came on board in the later stages of development and led us to the finish line. Thank you, all! Thanks, too, to Azelie Foster and Vivian Garcia for your marketing work; Adam Whitehurst for your expertise with the digital platform; Suzanne Chouljian for overseeing the videos; and Ryan Sullivan and Emily Brower for seeing the project through production.

Lauren Ingraham writes: I would like to thank my husband and son, Jim and William, who gave up lots of time with me so I could complete this project. I also had support from amazing colleagues at the University of Tennessee at Chattanooga who teach in the first-year writing program. Thank you to all who shared assignment examples and student work. Thanks specifically to April Green, Tiffany Mitchell, Jeff Drye, Rowan Johnson, Tracye Pool, Oren Whightsel, and Sheena Monds. Thanks, too, to Yvonne Artis, for providing important administrative support. Finally, I thank Jeanne Bohannon, who has been a perfect match as a collaborator. Her work on the videos transformed this project, and her feedback always made my work stronger.

Jeanne Law Bohannon writes: I would like to thank my husband, Chuck, and my son, Duncan, who read so many video scripts and watched countless edits of animations to offer his Digital Native perspectives. I am also grateful for my beloved goldendoodle, Jax, and best feline friend, Bear, who steadfastly sat with me every day as I wrote. My dear Bear, you didn't make it to see the fruits of your emotional labor, but you are as much a part of this work as I am. Special thanks also to colleagues at Kennesaw State, who provided indispensable advice on the pedagogies and scholarly framing of the videos and student work examples. Thanks especially to student colleagues for their opinions and feedback, and to my chair, Sheila Smith McKoy, who gave me both the encouragement and space to complete my work. Ultimately, without Lauren's vision, her years of work, and her infinite expertise, none of this would have come to fruition. Thank you for the opportunity to write with you, my friend; I'm glad the universe brought us together!

In closing

The most important thing we want you to know is that we're on your side. We're rooting for you at every step, and we've designed *The Writer's Loop* with you and your students in mind. Let's get started!

Lauren Ingraham

Jeanne Law Bohannon

Bedford/St. Martin's puts you first

From day one, our goal has been simple: to provide inspiring resources that are grounded in best practices for teaching reading and writing. For more than thirty-five years, Bedford/St. Martin's has partnered with the field, listening to teachers, scholars, and students about the support writers need. We are committed to helping every writing instructor make the most of our resources.

How can we help *you*?

- Our editors can align our resources to your outcomes through correlation and transition guides for your syllabus. Just ask us.
- Our sales representatives specialize in helping you find the right materials to support your course goals.
- Our *Bits* blog on the Bedford/St. Martin's English Community (**community .macmillan.com**) publishes fresh teaching ideas weekly. You'll also find easily downloadable professional resources and links to author webinars on our community site.

Contact your Bedford/St. Martin's sales representative or visit **macmillanlearning.com** to learn more.

Achieve with Ingraham and Bohannon, The Writer's Loop

Achieve with Ingraham and Bohannon, The Writer's Loop puts student writing at the center of your course and keeps revision at the core, with a dedicated composition space that guides students through draft, review, source check, and revision. See **macmillanlearning.com** to learn more.

Print and Digital Options for *The Writer's Loop*

Choose the format that works best for your course, and ask about our packaging options that offer savings for students.

Print

- **Paperback.**   To order the paperback edition packaged with *Achieve with Ingraham and Bohannon, The Writer's Loop*, use ISBN 978-1-319-33414-7.
- **Loose-leaf edition.**   This format does not have a traditional binding; its pages are loose and hole-punched to provide flexibility and a lower price to students. To order the loose-leaf packaged with Achieve, use ISBN 978-1-319-33545-8.
- *A Student's Companion for The Writer's Loop.*   Our new corequisite course supplement is available in Achieve. For print packaging options, contact your Macmillan sales representative.

Digital

- *Achieve with Ingraham and Bohannon, The Writer's Loop.*   For details, visit **macmillanlearning.com**.
- **Popular e-book formats.**   For details about our e-book partners, visit **macmillanlearning.com/ebooks**.
- **Inclusive Access.**   Enable every student to receive their course materials through your LMS on the first day of class. Macmillan Learning's Inclusive Access program is the easiest, most affordable way to ensure all students have access to quality educational resources. Find out more at **macmillanlearning.com/inclusiveaccess**.

Your Course, Your Way

No two writing programs or classrooms are exactly alike. Our Curriculum Solutions team works with you to design custom options that provide the resources your students need. (Options below require enrollment minimums.)

- **ForeWords for English.**   Customize any print resource to fit the focus of your course or program by choosing from a range of prepared topics, such as Sentence Guides for Academic Writers.
- **Macmillan Author Program (MAP).**   Add excerpts or package acclaimed works from Macmillan's trade imprints to connect students with prominent authors and public conversations. A list of popular examples or academic themes is available upon request.
- **Bedford Select.**   Build your own print handbook or anthology from a database of more than 900 selections, and add your own materials to create your ideal text. Package with any Bedford/St. Martin's text for additional savings. Visit **macmillanlearning.com/bedfordselect**.

Instructor Resources

You have a lot to do in your course. We want to make it easy for you to find the support you need—and to get it quickly.

Instructor's Manual for The Writer's Loop is available as a PDF that can be downloaded from **macmillanlearning.com** or viewed in *Achieve with Ingraham and Bohannon, The Writer's Loop*. In addition to chapter overviews and teaching tips, the instructor's manual includes suggestions for using the videos, classroom activities, sample syllabi, and a correlation to the Council of Writing Program Administrators' Outcomes Statement.

About the Authors

Lauren Ingraham is a professor and Director of General Education at the University of Tennessee at Chattanooga. Specializing in writing program administration and rhetoric and composition studies, Dr. Ingraham teaches both undergraduate and graduate students. Her current research focuses on ways to improve high school students' readiness for college writing and building more high-impact practices into undergraduate education. She has been a consultant for the National Council of Teachers of English, and she's published in *Composition Studies*, *WPA*, and the edited collection *The Framework for Success in Postsecondary Writing: Scholarship and Applications* (2017).

Jeanne Law Bohannon is an associate professor of English at Kennesaw State University. Her work with first-year writers focuses on creating digital and dialogic learning spaces, where students cultivate their writerly ethos through community engagement and public humanities. She is the director of the #ATLStudentmovement Project and a coprincipal investigator for the Learning Information Literacy Across the Curriculum (LILAC) initiative.

How *The Writer's Loop* Supports WPA Outcomes for First-Year Composition

This chart aligns with the latest WPA Outcomes Statement, ratified in July 2014.

WPA Outcomes	Most Relevant Features of *The Writer's Loop*
Rhetorical Knowledge	
Learn and use key rhetorical concepts through analyzing and composing a variety of texts.	• Chapter 2 defines rhetoric, introduces five key rhetorical concepts, and offers advice for understanding the rhetorical situation. • Readings integrated throughout the chapters provide opportunities for students to analyze a variety of texts, including multimodal texts. • Apply activities and Chapter Projects call for students to compose a variety of texts.
Gain experience reading and composing in several genres to understand how genre conventions shape and are shaped by readers' and writers' practices and purposes.	• Readings integrated throughout the text represent a range of genres, including essays, arguments, news articles, blog posts, posters, videos, and press releases. • Chapter Projects call for a range of genres, including personal essay, literacy narrative, rhetorical analysis, argument essay, proposal, annotated bibliography, and researched essay.
Develop facility in responding to a variety of situations and contexts calling for purposeful shifts in voice, tone, level of formality, design, medium, and/or structure.	Chapter 2 guides students to consider five key aspects of the rhetorical situation—purpose, audience, context, genre, and tone—and other chapters frequently return to these concepts.

(Continued)

WPA Outcomes	Most Relevant Features of *The Writer's Loop*
Understand and use a variety of technologies to address a range of audiences.	The various texts and technologies students interact with in the print text and in Achieve help them understand the range of technologies they can use to address their own audiences.
Match the capacities of different environments (e.g., print and electronic) to varying rhetorical situations.	• Chapter 2 helps students consider which genres (print or electronic) are most appropriate for their rhetorical situation. • Chapter 7 helps students consider the multimodal genres that are useful in public, digital spaces.

Critical Thinking, Reading, and Composing

Use composing and reading for inquiry, learning, critical thinking, and communicating in various rhetorical contexts.	• Chapter 8 encourages an inquiry-based approach to research writing. • Chapters 5 and 9 cover critical reading. • Reflect activities throughout the text provide low-stakes writing-to-learn opportunities.
Read a diverse range of texts, attending especially to relationships between assertion and evidence, to patterns of organization, to the interplay between verbal and nonverbal elements, and to how these features function for different audiences and situations.	Many of the readings and sample essays throughout the text are annotated to point out main ideas, claims and support, patterns of organization, transitions, and other rhetorical moves of writers.
Locate and evaluate (for credibility, sufficiency, accuracy, timeliness, bias, and so on) primary and secondary research materials, including journal articles and essays, books, scholarly and professionally established and maintained databases or archives, and informal electronic networks and internet sources.	Chapter 8 offers guidance for finding relevant sources and evaluating them for currency, reliability, authority, and purpose or point of view.

WPA Outcomes	Most Relevant Features of *The Writer's Loop*
Use strategies—such as interpretation, synthesis, response, critique, and design/redesign—to compose texts that integrate the writer's ideas with those from appropriate sources.	• Chapter 6 shows students how to support their arguments with a variety of evidence. • Chapter 11 focuses on the many reasons to use sources (to provide context, showcase evidence, and address counterclaims) and why and how to integrate quotations, paraphrases, and summaries.
Processes	
Develop a writing project through multiple drafts.	• A strong emphasis on recursive writing throughout the book encourages and supports students in writing multiple drafts. • Apply activities in each chapter build recursively toward the Chapter Project. • Chapter Projects are designed as multi-draft assignments.
Develop flexible strategies for reading, drafting, reviewing, collaborating, revising, rewriting, rereading, and editing.	• Chapter 3 explains writing as a recursive process and guides students to develop their own looping process. • Chapter 4 focuses on revising and editing with peer feedback. • Chapter 12 shows students how to revise to tighten an argument.
Use composing processes and tools as a means to discover and reconsider ideas.	• Reconsidering ideas is the heart of the looping process that *The Writer's Loop* advocates. The entire guide and the writing tools in Achieve support this goal by encouraging rereading, reflection, and revision. • Reflect and Apply activities frequently build on one another to guide students to reconsider their initial responses. • Chapter 10 offers unique, in-depth coverage of crafting and revising a thesis, pushing students to reconsider ideas and evidence in the process.

(Continued)

WPA Outcomes	Most Relevant Features of *The Writer's Loop*
Experience the collaborative and social aspects of writing processes.	• Chapter 4 focuses on gathering and using peer feedback throughout the writing process. • Videos throughout the text show student characters working together, demonstrating effective collaborative processes.
Learn to give and to act on productive feedback to works in progress.	• Chapter 4 focuses on gathering and using peer feedback throughout the writing process. • Writing tools in Achieve help students create revision plans based on peer and instructor feedback.
Adapt composing processes for a variety of technologies and modalities.	The range of texts and technologies students interact with in the print text and in Achieve and the range of texts they are asked to produce in the Chapter Projects give them practice in developing and adapting their own writing processes.
Reflect on the development of composing practices and how those practices influence their work.	• Reflect activities in each chapter prompt students to reflect on their past practices and currently developing writing processes. • Chapter 13 guides students to develop a reflective course portfolio.
Knowledge of Conventions	
Develop knowledge of linguistic structures, including grammar, punctuation, and spelling, through practice in composing and revising.	• Chapter 4 includes help for addressing common sentence-level problems. • Editing Marks in Achieve make it easy for instructors to offer feedback on common errors with built-in links to additional instruction. • LearningCurve activities in Achieve provide game-like quizzing on grammar, punctuation, and mechanics.
Understand why genre conventions for structure, paragraphing, tone, and mechanics vary.	Emphasis on rhetoric throughout the text encourages critical thinking about variations in structure, style, and tone.
Gain experience negotiating variations in genre conventions.	The various genres represented in readings and writing assignments give students practice with a range of conventions.

WPA Outcomes	Most Relevant Features of *The Writer's Loop*
Learn common formats and/or design features for different kinds of texts.	• Chapter 1 explains expectations for academic writing and the typical structure and style of academic essays. • Annotated student writing throughout the text demonstrates common formats for academic writing. • The text-only and multimodal readings throughout the text familiarize students with a broad range of design features and choices.
Explore the concepts of intellectual property (such as fair use and copyright) that motivate documentation conventions.	• Chapter 1 explains the importance of developing an academic ethos that includes giving credit to sources. • Chapter 9 focuses on managing sources and avoiding plagiarism. • The Appendix explains citation as a central part of academic writing.
Practice applying citation conventions systematically in their own work.	• The Appendix shows students how to cite sources in MLA and APA styles. • Sample student essays throughout the book demonstrate the correct use of MLA style for citing sources.

Brief Table of Contents

Videos

Detailed Table of Contents

7 Writing for Public, Digital Spaces 183

Goal: To effectively adapt academic writing skills to public, digital spaces.

10   Crafting a Thesis for a Substantial Writing Project   251

Goal: To develop a robust, rhetorical thesis for a researched essay.

10.1   Explore thesis options in response to your research question   251

10.2   State a specific type of claim and support it   257

12 Tightening Your Argument 294

Goal: To revise the first draft of your research essay to create a tighter argument, possibly by including more effective sources.

The
Writer's Loop

A Guide to College Writing

1

Being an Academic Writer

≋ Achie√e *If your instructor has assigned them, you can watch the videos for this chapter, complete the Reflect and Apply activities, and work on the Chapter Project in Achieve.*

1.1 Develop an academic ethos

You're probably familiar with the word *academic*. It's a word that refers to school-related activities in general. But *ethos* may be a new term for you. It means behaving, working, or communicating in a way that builds credibility with an audience. For example, medical doctors develop their ethos with patients by listening to their patients' concerns and treating them with compassion and empathy. Auto mechanics develop their ethos with car owners by knowing how to decipher the strange noise the car is making and repairing the car in a reasonable time frame and for a fair price. In this section, you'll learn how to develop an academic ethos and how it relates to your personal ethos.

Examining key features of an academic ethos

When we talk about developing your ethos in academic writing, we want to help you find ways to build credibility as a scholar in your college environment. As a college scholar, you will interact often with other people, ideas, and texts. Some of these interactions will come with perspectives and experiences that are similar to yours, while others may seem unfamiliar or even unbelievable. Knowing some features of a scholarly ethos can help you communicate effectively in this arena.

When building your own academic ethos, do the following:

Be open to new ideas and ways of thinking.   Be curious and welcome different perspectives. Treat opposing views fairly and with an open mind. Being open to new ideas doesn't mean automatically accepting them. Rather, it means being willing to thoughtfully consider them before deciding how to respond.

Collaborate.   Value the exchange of ideas and recognize that we make stronger arguments by sharing our initial ideas and gathering feedback from other people and texts. We sometimes "loop in" feedback from peers and instructors and apply it to our work in progress. At other times, we incorporate research and acknowledge this borrowed content by giving credit to the original source.

Provide evidence.   Support your claims with solid evidence. Drawing on facts, logical thinking, informed opinion, and relevant personal experience, writers with an academic ethos support claims with plenty of evidence to create a persuasive case. Likewise, readers with an academic ethos evaluate the evidence a text includes to see if it effectively supports the text's claims.

Reflect on and admit your limitations.   Pause from time to time to consider new ideas and different perspectives more deeply. Having an academic ethos means being ready to admit that your own perspective has some limitations or built-in biases. Acknowledging these limits boosts your ethos because it helps your audience see you as a thoughtful, reasonable writer and scholar.

Connecting your academic ethos to your personal history

When you think about it, you've probably been practicing elements of an academic ethos even without knowing the term. Let's consider how the features of an academic ethos might already be part of your daily life.

- **Being open to new ideas and ways of thinking.** When has a friend, family member, or coworker said something that at first seemed odd, but later, when you thought about it, you could see where they were coming from? If we slow down a bit and listen openly to others, we can respond thoughtfully.
- **Collaborating.** As much as we may love our independence, often we'll solve a problem more easily if we include others in the problem-solving.

For example, when planning a big holiday meal, one family member may be the host or considered "in charge," but often other family members are asked to contribute various dishes or help with cleanup.

- **Providing evidence.** In a disagreement with a friend, you may have brought up evidence that made them reconsider their position. Or, you may have changed your own opinion based on evidence your friend pointed out. This recently happened to us. We were convinced that we were getting the best deal possible with our current Internet service provider, but when a friend actually showed us her bill from a different provider to demonstrate that we could save money if we switched providers, we were forced to pay attention to that evidence and consider switching providers.

- **Reflecting on and admitting limitations.** Every time we acknowledge that we haven't lived through what someone else has, we forge a deeper connection with that person. Adopting a bit of humility goes a long way. For example, perhaps a friend is complaining to you about being treated rudely in his job as a kitchen line cook even though you've never done that job. Even without that personal experience, you can listen and try to understand why he feels belittled.

Of course, it's also possible that you have limited experience with being open to new ideas, collaborating, providing evidence, or admitting your limitations. That's OK. As you develop your academic ethos, you'll get better at it.

REFLECT

Consider your process of developing an academic ethos

The questions below invite you to reflect on your process of developing your emerging academic ethos. As you think about how your personal history contributes to this process, we also invite you to consider the kinds of courses you'll take in college, what you already know about discussions in college classes, what kind of writing you may have composed or will compose, and which labs you may need to complete or have already completed.

1. **When have you been open to new ideas and ways of thinking?** When and how have you encountered a new idea or way of thinking? Did ▶

this happen before you got to college or after you got there? How did you respond to that situation? How open were you to it? What can you learn from this experience about engaging with new ideas and approaches?

2. **When and how have you collaborated?** Either before or during college, when have you had to work with others to develop your ideas? When have you learned something by hearing another's thoughts or perspectives?

3. **When have you provided evidence to support an idea?** Have you made or heard claims that lack sufficient evidence to support them? Has anyone challenged you or others to back up a claim with evidence? When, in college or elsewhere, have you taken a position and supported it? Describe the scenario and explain how you dealt with it.

4. **When has admitting your limitations helped you connect with an audience?** How have you observed people taking intellectual risks or encouraging others to do so? Sometimes this might include statements like "Just work with me for a minute" or "Just hear me out" or "This isn't a perfect example, but…" or "Can you say more about that?" When have you taken risks like this or admitted that your ideas or claims have limitations? If you've never been in this position, consider why that might be.

UNDERSTAND

Watch Gabby reflect on developing her academic ethos

Now that you've thought about what it means for you to develop your own academic ethos, watch as a student reflects on the same process. In this video, Gabby discovers she has already begun developing her academic ethos in other areas of her life. Now, she needs to think about how to use that mindset to grow into an effective college writer.

Video: Developing an Academic Ethos

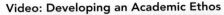

APPLY

Write about the benefits and challenges of adopting an academic ethos

The opportunity to cultivate an academic ethos can be exciting. It's a chance to expand your ways of interacting with the world and embrace new possibilities. But it can also be daunting because it may feel completely unlike the way you're used to interacting with people and texts. Many of us come from families and communities where most of our family and friends see the world just as we do. Our home communities aren't necessarily open to new ways of thinking or may value individual accomplishments more than collaborative achievements. As such, they may seem incompatible with an academic ethos. Students sometimes feel like they have to choose between their existing ethos and a new academic one, but we believe both can coexist and benefit each other. The perspectives you bring to college from your home community can provide important and valuable contributions to discussions you'll have with peers and others at college who also bring their own perspectives that may be very different from your own. ▶

Write a few paragraphs about developing your own academic ethos, focusing on what is exciting and what is challenging about this process. In your response, consider the key characteristics we discussed: being open to new ideas and ways of thinking, collaborating, providing evidence, and reflecting on and admitting your limitations.

1.2 Learn how to build and refine a thesis

One of the most important building blocks for developing an academic ethos is the ability to write a clear thesis for an essay, the type of academic writing most first- and second-year college students are asked to compose most often.

Understanding what a thesis is

The *thesis* (or thesis statement) is a sentence that states the main point or central idea of your essay. Sometimes, it also previews for the reader how your essay will be organized. In that way, it's like a road map for your essay. Your thesis basically says to an audience: here's where I want to take you, and this is how I'm going to take you there. Think of it like the little blue ball on a maps app. You plug in the beginning and end point, and the ball tracks your path to your destination. And when you veer off the path you established, you have to recalculate your route. So, the thesis helps you stay on your path to an effective essay. Even better, when you write a well-crafted thesis, it helps you—the writer—plan your essay.

A strong thesis has additional features:

- **It reflects your take on an idea or issue.** A thesis is based on your perspective, whether that comes from your own experience or from outside evidence you've gathered. For example, if you were writing an informative essay about being in the school band and you enjoyed your band experience, your thesis might look like this: "Being in the school band taught me much more than simply how to play the trumpet."

- **It defines the scope of the draft.** A well-crafted thesis addresses only a portion of a larger conversation. This focus helps you go into more depth with your support while staying within the parameters of your assignment. So, in an essay about how chimpanzees communicate with each other, your thesis would indicate that you will be writing only about chimps—and not orangutans or spider monkeys. For example: Scientists have discovered that chimpanzees "talk" to each other using dozens of gestures.

- **It appears early in the draft.** In academic essays, the thesis usually appears early in the draft, often in the first paragraph. Most of the time, your essay needs to start with a little background information for context before leading into the thesis. Sometimes, though, making the thesis your first sentence makes sense. Including your thesis early in the essay will help your readers understand your perspective and the scope of your essay.

In an *academic argument*, the term *thesis* means something more specific, as you'll see when you get to Chapter 6. For now, let's stick to general guidelines for a thesis.

Thinking and reading before composing a working thesis

When you're deciding on a thesis, it's helpful to go through a process that includes questioning your own perspective and considering other sources of information.

Acknowledge your gut opinion.   When presented with a problem that needs a solution, most people have a general idea of how to solve it based on past experience. This is your starting point, but it shouldn't be your stopping point. Know that you may eventually present a very different thesis, but it's OK to start with your initial idea of what you plan to argue in your essay.

Gather relevant information.   Once you have a gut opinion, it's time to look outside yourself for other ideas. Some assignments require you to carefully read one or more texts so that you can write about them effectively. Other assignments may require you to consult published research or various groups or individuals—students on your campus, people in your community, or individuals who outwardly disagree with you—as part of your information gathering. All of these sources can provide valuable information as you begin forming your working thesis.

Consider the evidence.   Once you've gathered additional information, think it through. What pieces of information contradict your original gut opinion? Which ones support it? What offers you a new way of thinking about a solution? Because you'll be using evidence to support your thesis, let the evidence guide you as you continue thinking about what you will say in your essay.

Question your original assumptions.   Here you loop back to your original gut opinion and apply all you've learned through this process to test your original idea. Does the evidence you've gathered support your gut opinion? How does it suggest you need to alter your position? Remember, it's OK to revise your opinion based on the information you've gathered.

Composing a working thesis

Once you've considered your perspective on a topic, gathered additional information about it, and looped back to adjust your main point to reflect your thinking, you're ready to compose a working thesis. Here's a way to get started.

- **Begin with the general idea your essay will address.** Sometimes your instructor will tell you what your essay must address. For example, if your class has been reading a short story, your instructor might ask everyone to write about an important character in the story. Sometimes, you have more freedom to choose a topic. Let's say you are assigned to write an essay about a community issue that interests you. You decide to write about your town's new program that allows high school students to complete summer internships with the city government.

  General topic: high school summer internships with city government

- **Consider your interest in this topic.** Once you have a general topic for your essay, think about why you're really interested in it. What's your personal connection to it? Is it something you've experienced yourself or observed from a distance by reading or hearing about it? After brainstorming about your interest in your topic, you're ready to say more about it. Using our summer internship example, you've realized you want to say more about a positive change in a friend who completed one of these internships.

  Interest in the topic: seeing firsthand the positive impact on a friend who completed an internship

- **Gather more information about the topic to develop new insight.** For some essays, including personal essays, "gathering more information" could mean simply taking time to search your memory and make notes. For other essays, you might interview others involved or do some research online. Once you've gathered and thought about this additional information, you'll have new insights to share with your readers. In our internship example, you've learned through talking with others who completed a city internship that the experience was valuable to more people than just your friend.

New insight: The internship program is a valuable experience that has benefitted many students.

When you combine your interest in the topic and the new insight you want to leave with readers, you have a formula for a thesis.

THESIS = Interest in the topic + New insight for readers

So, a good working thesis for our essay about a community issue would be this:

Working thesis: The city of Springfield's summer internship program offers valuable experience to local high school students that they otherwise wouldn't be able to gain.

Remember that you will need to revise your working thesis as you learn more about your topic and use that information to shape your thinking.

REFLECT

Reflect on your experience of composing a thesis

In your years of schooling, you've probably had to compose essays and exams that included a thesis or main point. Here we invite you to reflect on your past experiences with creating thesis statements. Write a paragraph in which you describe the "rules" for writing a thesis—or stating a main point—that you've followed in the past and the challenges you may have had coming up with a thesis for a writing assignment.

UNDERSTAND

Learn how to improve a thesis

As you have seen, a thesis starts with your gut opinion about a subject and changes as you gather more information about it. Once you get to a rough draft of your thesis, it's time to refine and improve it even further. Below are some strategies for tightening your thesis as you loop back through it. Just as we saw with strategies for developing an academic ethos, you may not need all of these strategies all of the time. Use the strategies that make the most sense for your individual thesis and process.

Move beyond stating existing facts.   A thesis needs to start a conversation, not present ideas that everyone already knows. The statement "Flight delays have many causes other than bad weather" includes an informed position and an insight, but it's not a conversation worth having. It's just a fact. Ask yourself if your thesis is limited to presenting a fact. If so, consider ways to move beyond that fact to a thesis that presents a conversation starter.

> **Just a fact:** The first 24-hour cable news channel, CNN, went on the air in 1980.

> **Better thesis:** Because it creates information overload, round-the-clock cable news is detrimental to democracy.

Consider the "So what?" question.   Your thesis will need a specific purpose and plan in order to reach a specific audience. When readers encounter your thesis, you want them to get interested and to keep reading. If instead readers think "So what?" then you're off to a shaky start. Ask yourself the "So what?" question to figure out if you have a rhetorical thesis.

> **Working thesis:** Because it creates information overload, round-the-clock cable news is detrimental to democracy.

SO WHAT?

> **Better thesis:** A thriving democracy requires people to be informed and thoughtful, qualities they can never maintain when round-the-clock cable news keeps them in a state of information overload.

Add qualifiers.   You can strengthen a thesis by adding *qualifiers*—words that limit the scope of what you're saying. Consider using qualifying words such as *might, sometimes, in some cases,* and *often* to put important limits on statements you make in a thesis. If your working thesis includes or implies absolutes such as *must, always, never,* or *everyone,* you risk alienating your audience. A good part of academic ethos to remember here is acknowledging limitations.

> **Working thesis:** A thriving democracy requires people to be informed and thoughtful, qualities they can never maintain when round-the-clock cable news keeps them in a state of information overload.

> **Better thesis:** A thriving democracy requires people to be informed and thoughtful, qualities ~~they can never~~ *that are difficult to* maintain when round-the-clock cable news keeps them in a state of information overload.

Replace vague terms with concrete terms.   Thesis statements sometimes use words like *society, culture,* and *people* that really don't communicate specific ideas to an audience. To make a thesis more effective, scale down terminology to refer to specific people your essay addresses. Instead of an all-encompassing "society," think about the specific group who is the real subject of your essay, such as high school seniors, Americans living in poverty, aggressive drivers, or nonviolent drug offenders. The key here is to be specific and clear with your terms.

> **Working thesis:** A thriving democracy requires people to be informed and thoughtful, qualities that are difficult to maintain when round-the-clock cable news keeps them in a state of information overload.

> **Better thesis:** A thriving democracy requires ~~people~~ *citizens* to be informed and thoughtful, qualities that are difficult to maintain when round-the-clock cable news keeps them in a state of information overload.

UNDERSTAND

Watch Gabby improve a working thesis

To understand how you might take steps to revise a working thesis, take a look at the following video. In it, Gabby works with Jay to question a working thesis and revise it to make it more effective. Notice how she uses the specific strategies we've discussed to produce her revised thesis.

Gabby's revised thesis: The town of Springfield should ~~not remove~~ *continue fluoridating its* ~~fluoride from our drinking~~ water because research shows that *, even though it costs $20,000 a year,* ~~fluoride in drinking~~ water is a safe, cost-effective~~, and equitable~~ *fluoridated* *equitable, and* way to improve dental health ~~for children and adults.~~ *residents'* .

Video: Improving a Working Thesis

APPLY

Practice revising sample working thesis statements

Below are three thesis statements that need work. Revise them to transform them into stronger, more effective thesis statements. You may change, add, or delete as many words as you like to create your improved thesis statements. Following each, briefly explain the problems you addressed.

1. Everyone needs to be tested for sexually transmitted infections every six months.

2. Social media is causing problems in our society.

3. There is a shortage of health care providers in America's rural communities.

1.3 Understand expectations for academic writing

You've just learned how a thesis works in academic writing. Now, we'll turn to additional elements of academic writing you'll practice as a college writer.

Seeing academic writing as one of many rhetorical styles

Every type of communication has its own style, ranging from extremely informal to extremely formal. On the extremely informal end, think about tweets and text messages: they use abbreviations, invented spelling, and are often irreverent. On the extremely formal end, think about the "Terms and Conditions" agreements from our web browsers and social media platforms. Most of us agree to them, even though we might not follow the legal jargon they use. Popular writing and academic writing land somewhere in the middle of this continuum of rhetorical styles, with popular writing tilting toward the informal end and academic writing tilting toward the formal end.

Extremely Informal Writing	Popular Writing	Academic Writing	Extremely Formal Writing
Tweets, text messages, conversations with friends and family	Novels, magazines, informational websites, newspapers	College essays, lab reports for a biology course, case studies for a finance class	Legal contracts, sacred texts

Considering the typical structure of an academic essay

Understanding how academic essays are structured can help you compose your assignments more effectively. Academic essays have four main components: a title, an introduction, additional paragraphs, and a conclusion.

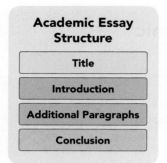

Academic Essay Structure

- Title
- Introduction
- Additional Paragraphs
- Conclusion

Title.   Because the title is the first part of your essay readers encounter, it serves as an invitation to engage. The title announces your topic and reveals something about your position in relation to your topic. In this way, the title is like an abbreviated version of the thesis. Even though a title begins an essay (from a reader's perspective), you don't need to come up with a title early in your writing process. Many writers wait until they have a complete draft before deciding on a title.

Introduction.   The introduction leads an audience into an essay by providing context and a "hook"—a question or interesting statement that captures the audience's attention and prompts them to read further. In many academic essays, the last sentence of the introduction paragraph is where we find the thesis.

Additional paragraphs.   The paragraphs between the introduction and conclusion support the thesis or explore the main point in a variety of ways, including providing historical or other context, telling a story that illustrates one of your points, and using evidence to support your ideas. An essay can include as many supporting paragraphs as you need to develop your ideas effectively.

Conclusion.   The final paragraph wraps up the essay, often by telling readers why your thesis is worth considering or taking into account. In this way, it revisits the "So what?" question. The conclusion might also suggest next steps readers can take concerning your ideas. What should the audience do with the information you've delivered? Should they take a certain action? Think differently about your topic? Presenting the audience with potential next steps is a way of making sure your message is not only understood but acted on.

Understanding the typical style of academic writing

While essays are likely to be the most common form of academic writing you complete early in college, as you progress toward graduation you might be asked to compose a variety of print and multimodal texts, such as lab reports, market analyses, business proposals, presentations, posters, websites, or research reports. While the formats vary, academic writing is defined by a typical style.

Academic writing relies on evidence.   Evidence takes different forms, including statistics, personal stories, information sources, and expert statements. Academic writers always use some sort of evidence to support their theses, even if it is their own experience or quoted passages from a text they are analyzing.

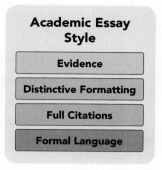

Academic writing has distinctive formatting.   Formatting issues, such as page numbering, headings, fonts, and font size are often based on instructors' preferences. Different fields of study and different genres have their own guidelines for formatting. Always read your writing assignments carefully to determine your instructor's expectations for formatting your essay. Be sure to ask your instructor if you still have formatting questions after reading the assignment thoroughly.

Academic writing requires full citations.   A citation in this context is a formatted statement of where and when outside source material was published and who wrote it. Even if an academic text is published online, it uses complete citations for all outside sources it references. Unlike other forms of online writing that embed links to sources as a shorthand way of citing them, academic writing includes full lists of sources at the end of the text, as well as in-text citations in the essay itself. There are different types of academic citation styles; ask your instructor which ones to use for specific assignments.

Academic writing uses formal language.   As you have learned, academic writing style leans toward formality. You can use a few strategies to reach that formal style as you revise your writing. Avoid slang and informal conversational language. Steer clear of contractions (instead of *don't*, spell out *do not*). Use correct grammar and punctuation.

Keep in mind that academic writing evolves. Like many other types of writing, academic writing is in flux, and some of its formality is relaxing. For example, it used to be a given that the first-person point of view (using *I, my, we,* and *our*) was considered inappropriate in academic writing. Now, it's much more common. Academic genres are expanding, too. Online texts like researched blogs and TEDTalk presentations are now frequently used by scholars to present their work. As you progress through college, check with your instructors about their individual preferences for academic writing.

To see an example of a more formal style of academic writing, consider the following essay by our student Mykaela Harris. In the essay, she explores her process for developing an academic ethos.

Mykaela Harris

Professor Ingraham

ENGL 1010

12 November 2018

Connecting My Personal History with

My Academic Ethos

The essay is formatted according to instructor guidelines, including name, date, title, and double-spaced text.

When I first arrived at college and started writing for a college audience, I learned that there are many different ways people can enhance their writing, such as providing evidence, taking constructive criticism from others, and acknowledging the weaknesses of the ideas presented. These beneficial writing strategies are all ways to strengthen something called an *academic ethos*, something I'd never heard of. To me, having a strong academic ethos means that a writer has developed a sense of credibility, which typically leads to a more engaged audience. This concept intimidated me at first because I didn't think I brought a lot of credibility to college discussions. Some of my usual ways of dealing with things seemed incompatible with having an academic ethos. However, I soon realized that many of the skills I needed to develop a strong academic ethos were things that were already part of my daily life.

The thesis appears at the end of the first paragraph.

Where I grew up, everyone had a pretty similar worldview. Most people had similar interests, acted in similar ways, and had similar opinions on things like politics, religion, and other social issues. However, we were taught not to talk about these issues in public in case someone did hold a different view and might be upset by our comments or hold our opinions against us. When I came to college, this all changed. I was constantly surrounded by people with many different points of view due to their life experiences. They didn't hold back their opinions—at

Harris 2

all. At first I was surprised by their openness and surprised that people on the receiving end of their comments weren't offended. They just treated it as a back-and-forth conversation. I found myself making friends with people of all backgrounds, and this made me more open to hearing new ideas and opinions and helped me develop my own core beliefs.

I'm learning that being open to new ideas is an incredibly important part of the writing process. So much of my writing process consists of seeking out opinions and information on a topic so I can have material to write about. If the only viewpoints I consider are the ones that align with mine, I will ultimately end up with writing that seems extremely biased and incomplete. This is one of the hardest skills to master, as most people—including me—can be extremely stubborn when it comes to their core beliefs. However, college provides countless opportunities to practice this, and my experiences of learning from other people have made my writing richer and more accessible. This has been an important part of developing my academic ethos.

Other parts of my background prepared me to understand how to develop an academic ethos. When I played sports in high school, coaches would often observe my performance during my tennis matches or soccer games and come to me afterwards with notes on how to improve my performance in the future. This not only helped me become a better athlete, but also prepared me to appreciate this type of constructive criticism. When writing for college classes, early drafts of my papers are often read by my professors and peers. The feedback that I receive from them can be incredibly helpful, as they typically catch mistakes and issues that I did not originally notice while writing. This collaboration has been an extremely

Mykaela uses evidence to support her point.

Harris 3

crucial part of developing my academic ethos, and I have found that it is one of the skills that transferred very easily from my personal life to my academic work.

Ways that I interact with my family have also affected my developing academic ethos, especially when it comes to how I provide evidence. There have been many occasions when I have been in a disagreement with a family member over something insignificant like a TV show or the specifics of something someone said. There is no better feeling than rewinding the show or pulling up an old text message and proving that I was right all along. In any situation, having evidence to back up an argument gives my ideas some credibility and feels immensely satisfying, and this translates to college writing. A huge part of a strong academic ethos is being able to provide evidence to support my ideas. Adding a few facts and statistics in key parts of a paper to support my points can add a sense of legitimacy that would otherwise be lacking. In my experience, finding the perfect piece of evidence to persuade my audience is one of the most exciting and fulfilling parts of writing.

Another connection between my regular life and developing an academic ethos deals with how I've tried to resolve differences between family members. I have some opinions that differ from those that my family have, and we often will try to have calm discussions about our differences to try to get the other person to see the other point of view. However, if none of us backs down from our viewpoints, these sometimes devolve into shouting matches, and nobody wants that. I have found that when I acknowledge the imperfections of my argument and the strengths of theirs, the person I am talking to will be much more likely to consider the words I am

Personal experience can be effective evidence in an essay.

Formal language is used instead of something more casual.

Harris 4

saying. Although this is a very difficult skill to master, it has greatly benefitted me in not only my personal life, but also when it comes to my writing quality. I've learned that if I pretend that my arguments are flawless, then they will come across as stubborn and extremely biased. It might seem like a mistake to admit where your argument is weak, but it will actually add integrity to your writing and make you seem more rational.

When I first began writing in college, developing a strong academic ethos seemed impossible. However, once I started having conversations with classmates and other new college friends, I started to reconsider my previous habit of keeping my opinions to myself and not asking others for their opinions. I wanted to know more about what they thought. I've also come to understand that many of the skills needed for developing an academic ethos were skills I was constantly using in my daily life. I think I'm on my way to establishing an academic ethos and becoming an effective college writer.

Because she is writing a personal essay, Mykaela uses the first-person point of view ("I" language) to tell her story.

REFLECT

Consider your entrance into academic writing

As a student who may be new to academic writing, you may wonder if you can handle this more formal type of writing. We're here to say: "Yes, you can!" We invite you to compare your understanding of academic writing with other types of written communication you produce regularly. What similarities do they share and how are they different from one another? For example, how is academic writing similar to or different from writing a tweet or updating your Facebook status? As you consider your response, think back to the typical style of academic writing: it relies on evidence, uses specialized formatting, requires full citations, and uses formal language.

UNDERSTAND

Watch Jay identify the features of an academic essay

Understanding the expectations of academic writing is a challenge without some actual academic writing to examine. In the following video, take note of the way Jay studies an essay by student Henry Law to practice identifying various features of academic writing. You can read Henry's essay below, in which he makes an argument about genetically modified organisms (GMOs).

Video: Recognizing Features of an Academic Essay

Law 1

Henry Law

Professor Ingraham

English 101

23 March 2018

    Stop Worrying, Start Reading: How Genetically Modified

    Organisms Are Necessary and Good for Our Food Supply

    Are Genetically Modified Organisms (GMOs) that bad?

Many people, even some scientists, would like us to think that

Law 2

GMOs are the worst thing for our natural food supply since the Industrial Revolution. However, many other scientists argue that GMOs have been a safe part of our food system for many years. In fact, GMOinside.org notes that man-made DNA first surfaced from labs in 1973, and the first GMO patent was issued in 1980 (Karimi). Taking this history into account, I argue that GMOs are a vital part of our food system because their use allows crops to resist natural pests, to yield food with higher nutrient values, and to combat famine worldwide.

Unlike non-GMO crop products, GMOs can be engineered to be resistant to natural pests, such as insects. In a tutorial written for North Carolina State's agricultural program, John R. Meyer writes, "insects consume or destroy around 10% of gross national product in large, industrialized nations and up to 25% of gross national product in some developing countries." Crops are constantly destroyed by insects such as locusts. GMOs can be used to create resistance to these natural predators. By doing this, GMOs also reduce the amount of herbicides used to protect plants from insects by traditional methods. In addition to providing plants with protection, GMOs can also produce more nutrition than non-GMO crops.

Many people in the U.S. and around the world do not obtain the proper nutrients to keep them healthy and long-lived. Use of GMOs can produce products that have more nutrients and vitamins, satisfying the hungry stomachs of people in need. This means that science can give the world more bite for its buck. According to an article from The Center for Science in the Public Interest, "using biotechnology to make food has great potential: safer pesticides and less harm to wildlife, more nutritious foods, and greater yields to help feed the world's hungry nations" ("Genetically Engineered Foods"). GMOs provide more nutrition

Law 3

than non-GMO foods, and this can solve hunger all around the world. GMOs can also provide greater crop yields to help feed people in developing countries with too much population growth.

World hunger is a major issue currently and will be in the future. In a quarter of a century, there will be an estimated 8.3 billion people worldwide to feed (Borlaug). Scientists agree that, good or bad, GMO crops do produce greater amounts of food. For example, in the U.S. we have genetically engineered corn and soybeans that can be grown faster and in more seasonal cycles, while yielding a lot more crops for human consumption. This type of food production could lead to the eradication of hunger for billions of people worldwide.

As we know, scientists rarely come to a 100% consensus on any issue, and GMO production is no different. However, I believe that GMOs are an important part of our food system's future because they make crops resistant to predators, they yield food with high nutritional value, and they can help feed the world. Like them or not, GMOs provide too much good for human civilization for us to ignore them, or even worse, ban their use.

Law 4

Works Cited

Borlaug, Norman. "Ending World Hunger: The Promise of
    Biotechnology and the Threat of Antiscience Zealotry."
    Plant Physiology, Oct. 2000, doi: 10.1104/pp.124.2.487.

"Genetically Engineered Foods: Are They Safe?" *Nutrition
    Health Letter*, Center for Science in the Public Interest, 2001.

Law 5

Karimi, Shireen. "GMO Timeline: A History of Genetically
    Modified Foods." *GMOInside.org*, Green America,
    10 Mar. 2013, www.greenamerica.org/blog/gmo-timeline
    -history-genetically-modified-foods.
Meyer, John R. "Impact of Insects." General Entomology, North
    Carolina State University, 24 Mar. 2016, projects.ncsu.edu/
    cals/course/ent425/library/tutorials/importance_of_insects/
    impact_of_insects.html.

APPLY

Write about your comfort level with academic writing

At the end of Section 1.1, you wrote a few paragraphs about what's exciting and challenging about developing your own academic ethos. Now that you've learned more about the nature of academic writing—including the role of a thesis and expectations for content and style—think about how you feel about your ability to compose academic writing. Use the visuals below to review the typical structure and style of an academic essay.

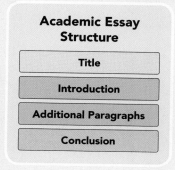

Academic Essay Structure

- Title
- Introduction
- Additional Paragraphs
- Conclusion

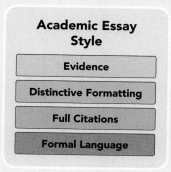

Academic Essay Style

- Evidence
- Distinctive Formatting
- Full Citations
- Formal Language

Depending on your background and high school experience, the features of academic writing we've discussed may or may not be familiar to you. Write a few paragraphs discussing how you feel about composing academic writing.

Chapter 1 Project
Write an essay about developing your academic ethos

In Chapter 1, you've learned that being an academic writer means practicing some new mindsets and skills, including developing an academic ethos, building and refining a thesis, understanding the structure of an academic essay, and recognizing expectations for academic writing.

In Section 1.1, you wrote a few paragraphs about the benefits and challenges of developing an academic ethos. In Section 1.3, you wrote a few paragraphs to capture your current thoughts about composing academic writing. To complete the Chapter 1 Project, return to your notes and use them to write an academic essay that focuses on your current thoughts about combining your existing personal ethos with your emerging academic ethos. You should feel free to use some of your original sentences "as is," use edited versions of them, or write new content that helps your essay be coherent and clear.

To plan your essay, review our instruction about what an academic essay includes: a title (which can be written after the essay is complete), an engaging introduction with a thesis that captures your main idea, additional paragraphs that help tell your story, and a conclusion that wraps up the essay and leaves readers with a sense of why your perspective matters.

As you write, aim for an essay of between 500–750 words. To see an example of how another student responded effectively to this prompt, look back at Mykaela Harris's essay in Section 1.3.

2

Understanding Rhetoric

≈ Achieve *If your instructor has assigned them, you can watch the videos for this chapter, complete the Reflect and Apply activities, and work on the Chapter Project in Achieve.*

2.1   Understand what rhetoric really is

Even if you've encountered the word *rhetoric*, it's probably not a word you use regularly. These days, it's often used when people are unhappy about the words someone has chosen. For example, when a politician talks about something he or she will accomplish, a political opponent might say, "That's just empty rhetoric!" In this sense, rhetoric has a bad reputation. Too often, rhetoric is associated with someone using language to unjustly elevate their own position or to make their opposition look bad.

In truth, rhetoric is by itself neither innocent nor powerful. What matters is how people use it. Rhetoric is the practice of conveying an effective message to an audience. Sounds simple, right? Well, it is and it isn't. Rhetoric allows people to express themselves clearly, understand one another, and find solutions to common problems.

Examining the inspirational power of rhetoric

Why do you need to know what rhetoric is and why it can be powerful? Because we all communicate messages every day of our lives. Even if you don't consider yourself a *rhetor*—someone who uses rhetoric—you are. You write emails, texts, social media posts, game chats, papers for school, and countless other messages at home, at work, and at play. When you use rhetoric in each of these situations, you try to reach an audience and achieve a purpose. Maybe that purpose is to convince a friend that one approach to solving a problem is better than another. Maybe you're just exploring a different perspective on a social issue. Or maybe you're just trying to create a connection with someone. Transferring these communication skills you already have to college reading and writing is another strategy to use as you make meaning in the world around you.

We've said rhetoric is the practice of conveying an effective message to an audience. To consider just how meaningful that is and to see how people

Video: Neil Gaiman Addresses the Class of 2012

University of the Arts

create connections with rhetoric, let's check out some examples of rhetoric in action.

Neil Gaiman gives a powerful commencement speech. Speaking to the graduating class of 2012 at the University of the Arts in Philadelphia, writer Neil Gaiman encourages aspiring artists to "make good art" regardless of what life throws at them. He specifically connects to his audience—budding artists—by elevating and valuing the work they want to pursue after graduation. With a good balance of humor and seriousness, he says,

> Husband runs off with a politician? Make good art. Leg crushed and then eaten by a mutated boa constrictor? Make good art . . . Someone on the Internet thinks what you're doing is stupid or evil or it's all been done before? . . . Do what only you can do best. Make good art.

Watch the video of this part of his speech and listen to how well his remarks were received by his audience.

Hannah Brencher writes uplifting letters to strangers. After graduating from college, Hannah Brencher fell into a depression. To heal herself, she began writing letters to strangers whom she believed also needed support—even if that support came from a stranger. She'd leave the letters all over town—on park benches and subway trains—hoping that people would find them and their day would be brighter. Eventually, she started a nonprofit organization called The World Needs More Love Letters (www.moreloveletters.com) that sends bundles of handwritten letters to people nominated by their friends and family. On YouTube, you can find videos of Brencher talking about the project and videos of people receiving their letter bundles.

Read the following excerpt from Brencher's book *If You Find This Letter* to see how her mother's letter-writing habit taught Brencher about the power of receiving a supportive love letter.

> As we waited for the train, I watched my mother wedge something into the belly of my suitcase, with the hope I wasn't looking. I tried to force myself to forget it was there. I fidgeted and folded my ticket, waiting to leave. I knew it was a letter. It was always a letter.
>
> My mother is a nostalgic creature. There are three things you should know about my mother: The first is that she is always, somehow, the life of every party. The second is that any person my mother has ever loved could tell you the exact way a kazoo sounds when it's left in a voice mail on your

birthday. It's nailed tight to my memories of growing up—watching her flip through the pages of her address book and find the name of whoever it was she'd marked on her calendar. I remember hearing the dialing of the cordless phone. My mother would wait. And then the sound of a kazoo being played to the tune of "Happy Birthday" would stream throughout the house.

The third thing to know about my mother is that she's a nostalgic creature and I have to believe she made me into one too. She's hidden love letters for me to find all my life. There was a note tucked on top of a piece of chocolate cake when heartbreak visited my freshman dorm room for the first time. There was a card left on my dashboard the day after Whitney Houston died. Confetti fell out from the inside. Musical notes skittered across the front. She wrote six words to me in red Sharpie: *And I will always love you.* I am the product of my mother's bread crumb trails of love letters.

Every coming and going we've ever shared has been built up with letters, notes, trinkets, and the like, as if tiny wedges of paper and confetti could keep a person always coming back. She'd trailed tiny clues four years earlier as we moved me into my first dorm room. I found letters tucked in plastic Tupperware bins and notes within books I hadn't even opened yet. Pieces of my mother would pop up and appear throughout the semester. In random classes. At staff meetings. On retreats. My mother is an expert at leaving evidence she was here in the lives of everyone around her.

One of the notes she mailed to me in my first week of college included a long quote she'd copied from *O, The Oprah Magazine* while sitting in a waiting room of a doctor's office. The quote was about a mother and a daughter. The final point of release. The girl was leaving, marching into adulthood without her mother's steady hand to hold. The girl turned at the door and the mother went to reach out, wanting to tell her daughter one last thing, but she pulled back instead. It was that moment when the mother finally had to say, "I've given everything I can and I have to trust it is enough. She must go out there and see and feel and understand the rest on her own."

The breath fell out of me when I read that quote for the first time. I kept reading it out loud. I felt bare and exposed through my mother's scratchy handwriting whenever I read it. The card with the quote inside of it somehow got lost and my mother couldn't remember what issue of *O* she found it within. I spent the next summer going through every *O* magazine at the town library, looking for any last evidence the paragraph ever existed, but I never found it. I'm still looking.

The letters from my mother kept coming throughout college. I was one of the only students who had a reason to go to their PO box at the end of the day, and that was mainly because my mother didn't have a cell phone or text messaging or any kind of social network to check into. I'd told her a bunch of times she should get a cell phone but she only ever said the same thing back to me: "I've gone over fifty years without anyone needing to find me. Why start now?"

President Obama connects with Vietnamese rapper.   When world leaders make diplomatic trips overseas, they typically meet with officials and host public appearances that include public speeches. When President Barack Obama traveled to Vietnam in 2016, he hosted a town hall for the country's youth. From the audience, a twenty-six-year-old rapper, a woman named Suboi, asked a pointed question about women producing hip-hop music that criticized certain parts of Vietnamese society. Their exchange included Suboi asking a question about free speech and rap music in a country with strict free speech laws. President Obama answered her with, "Before I answer your question, why don't you give me a little rap? Let's see what you got." This communication exchange conveyed a message from President Obama that free speech was important and conveyed a message from Suboi that she was a voice for free speech. Take a look at the rest of their exchange in the following video.

Video: President Barack Obama and Suboi

Pool/AP Images

Look for rhetoric in your everyday communication

Now that you've seen that rhetoric exists all around us, think about the many ways you communicate in your everyday life. When speaking face to face, you use nonverbal expressions and physical gestures that give clues about your intended message. When you text, abbreviations and emojis can be a shared language. Even updating your status on Facebook or other social media sites is practicing rhetoric.

Write a paragraph explaining the variety of ways you communicate in a typical day. How effective are those communications? How do you know?

Experience the power of rhetoric

Videos are multimodal forms of communication demonstrating how powerful rhetoric can be. In September 2014, the rapper Prince Ea posted his video "Can We Auto-Correct Humanity?" on YouTube. Within three and a half years, it had more than twenty million views. And as TechTimes.com reported, "it garnered more than 150,000 shares within hours of its posting."

The video is Prince Ea's commentary on what he calls "media overstimulation." In the video, he laments that "touchscreens can make us lose touch" and suggests that Facebook ought to be called an "antisocial network" because it sometimes prevents people from having true, human connections.

Many who shared the video commented that it was an optimistic, uplifting message. It didn't motivate them to unplug from technology completely, but they claimed it made them reconsider their relationship to technology.

As you watch the video, think about what makes its message so attractive to viewers.

Video: Prince Ea, "Can We Auto-Correct Humanity?"

Prince Ea

APPLY

Plan a rhetorically effective message

Now it's your turn to put your understanding of rhetoric into practice. If you wanted to communicate your thoughts about the "Can We Auto-Correct Humanity" video Prince Ea produced, you would have to think through a number of decisions:

1. What message would you want to convey? Would it be completely supportive, completely unsupportive, or a mixture of both messages?

2. You'd need to think about the audience you'd want to reach. Who needs to hear your message? Why that person or group?

3. What kinds of words and tone would you use?

4. You'd need to consider the form you'd want your message to take and how you would communicate your message. Ask yourself: If you're trying to communicate with Prince Ea directly, is adding a comment to the thousands of comments already on the YouTube site the best way to reach him? Should you tweet him? Should you research his management to get a mailing address and write a formal letter to him?

Write a paragraph or more explaining the message you would convey, the audience you'd hope to reach, and the medium or form you'd use to reach that audience. Then explain your rationale for those choices.

2.2 Understand five key components of rhetoric

Practicing rhetoric means you create texts in a particular way. You're now composing not only with an eye to what the text says but also to *how* the text works. *How* would a magazine article you write engage its readers? If you owned a small business, *how* would you want to think about creating a successful ad campaign? *How* would an award-winning blogger decide what to write about for a specific blog post? *How* does an activist raise awareness of a social cause? Writers use many strategies to create and polish their messages, but to be effective, all writers must work with five key components of rhetoric: purpose, audience, tone, genre, and context.

Considering purpose, audience, tone, genre, and context

The five components of rhetoric work like individual pieces of a puzzle. Alone, they're not very useful. But when they are assembled well, they work together to create an effective rhetorical message.

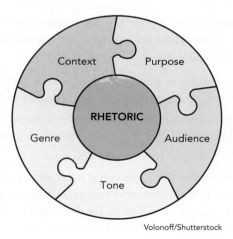

Volonoff/Shutterstock

- **Purpose** refers to the reason for creating a text and the goal the writer intends to achieve. People create texts for a wide array of purposes, including to make an argument, to offer social commentary, to entertain, to reflect on an experience, and to conduct business.

- **Audience** refers to the intended or anticipated recipient(s) of the text or message. Audience and purpose go hand in hand because the purpose can be achieved only if the message gets to the appropriate audience.

- **Tone** refers to the attitude the text conveys: grateful, hostile, condescending, playful, indifferent. Effective texts have tones that suit their purpose and audience.

- **Genre** refers to the form the text takes. Formal letters, blogs, magazine articles, emails, text conversations, and even tweets are all examples of genres. For your writing to be rhetorically effective, it should appear in a genre that will appeal to the targeted audience and allow the text to achieve its purpose.

- **Context** refers to all the situations and backstories swirling around the text, including recent events and previous exchanges between the author and this audience.

Using the five components of rhetoric to understand a text

Rhetorically approaching a text — and by "text," we mean any kind of written communication — involves asking a lot of questions about it. It's a bit like seeing an illusionist pull off a mind-blowing trick, then spending the rest of the evening asking your friends who were also at the show how he did it.

When you encounter a text and are trying to figure out its message, you have to consider all five components of effective rhetoric and start asking questions. Answering these questions will help you not only engage with a text but understand its rhetorical effectiveness in conveying a message. Then, when you compose a message, you will be able to ensure it is rhetorical.

- **What's the text's *purpose*?** What is this text trying to achieve? Why does it exist? What's it trying to accomplish? What does it want the audience to do or think after engaging with it? How can I tell? What about the text clues me in to its purpose? What can I learn about the purpose from the title or subheadings? What can I learn about the purpose from the content of the text itself?

- **Who is the text's *audience*?** How can understanding the purpose give me clues about who the specific audience might be? Who is this text appealing to? How can I tell? Is the probable audience hostile, friendly, or indifferent? What in the text gives me clues? Does anything in the text — such as "My fellow Americans" or "Hi Facebook peeps!" — identify specific audience members?

- **What is the text's *tone*?** Given the purpose and audience you've identi-fied, what kind of tone would be appropriate? Formal? Casual? Hostile? Friendly? Considering those expectations can help you look deeper into the tone to see if it matches your expectations. How does word choice or formatting help set the tone? Do some words have a strong emotional res-onance? If so, what emotions do they evoke? Does the text include visual elements that contribute to the tone, such as written words in ALL CAPS or images that reinforce the text's message?

- **What is the text's *genre*?** Remember that genre is the form a message takes, like a meme, a text message, a web page, an academic essay, or a newspaper article. What's the genre of the text you're encountering? What are some features of that genre? How do written words generally appear? How are the words formatted? How are visuals typically used? What kinds of visuals are typically used?

- **What's the *context* surrounding the text?** What's going on in the world or in the community that may have prompted the writer to write? To what is the writer responding? What larger conversation is going on that this text might contribute to?

REFLECT

Think about the five components of rhetoric

We've encouraged you to think about rhetoric as having five key compo-nents: purpose, audience, tone, genre, and context. We've suggested that you approach a text by asking questions to understand how these five compo-nents function together in a text. But we don't expect all this to come easily.

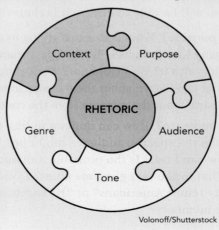

Volonoff/Shutterstock

What component of rhetoric seems most difficult to grasp at this point? Reflect on this component and write a short response about your concerns. What about this component of rhetoric is confusing or makes you wonder how you'd incorporate it in your own writing?

UNDERSTAND

See how the five components of rhetoric work together in a text

Now let's take a look at how we can study a text to determine its purpose, audience, tone, genre, and context. Later, you can use those skills to compose your own rhetorically effective writing. We've annotated the following article to show you how it contains all five of the key components of rhetoric. As you read, think about which parts of rhetoric you don't yet deeply understand, then look to see how the author uses them.

Growing Social Movements through Reason, Not Disruption

ED KROMER

The following article was published in 2015 on the Faculty Research page of the website of the Foster School of Business, University of Washington. The purpose of the site is to promote the school and to share news of faculty research with the university community and the general public. This article focuses on research by assistant professor Abhinav Gupta, who had recently published a study on social activism in a scholarly journal.

When campaigning for social change, disruptive protests may win a few battles, but efforts to educate are more likely to win the war.

This according to new research by Abhinav Gupta, an assistant professor of strategic management at the University of Washington Foster School of Business.

Audience: The writer states the main point of Gupta's research up front, in language that will be understood by the general public.

Gupta's study of the effectiveness of activist efforts indicates that disruptive tactics such as protests and sit-ins can yield some immediate, localized success, but they do little to expand the objectives of a cause more broadly.

Evidence-backed education efforts, on the other hand, prove more potent at persuading even leaders of organizations *not* targeted by activists. By appealing to their rational decision-making processes, activists can generate a spillover effect in their campaign for change.

This "contagion" can multiply their impact and grow a movement exponentially.

"Disruption plays a role in terms of raising attention and bringing awareness to an issue," says Gupta. "But if it's used exclusively, it can turn off a lot of people and be very limited in its effectiveness. We find that evidence-based education proves more effective at achieving a campaign's larger goals."

Act Locally, Think Globally

Racial equality. Environmental protection. Same-sex marriage. Gender pay equity. A living wage. The list of causes that inspire people to organize for change is long and unending.

But the resulting campaigns for social change—often described as "grassroots" efforts—typically have far fewer resources and capabilities than the organizations they endeavor to influence.

So activists are forever calculating the way to maximally multiply their impact. Gupta says that they often target a few influential organizations—universities, corporations, government agencies—that are likely to set the standard for peer institutions.

A textbook example of this strategy is the "Rein in Russell" campaign engineered by a group called United Students Against Sweatshops (USAS) in 2009.

To make progress toward its ultimate goal of improving working conditions in developing countries, the group went after the apparel manufacturer Russell Athletic which had

Purpose: This paragraph hints at the article's purpose: to explain Gupta's research to people interested in the topic.

Genre: The writer follows typical conventions of news articles, stating the most important information in the opening paragraphs and using short paragraphs with interesting quotations.

Context: The writer acknowledges the larger social context that makes Gupta's research relevant and timely.

recently closed a manufacturing facility in Honduras after efforts to unionize its 1,300 workers. To pressure Russell to reopen a fully unionized plant, USAS targeted the company's biggest organizational customers: universities. Not all of them, but a select group of influencers.

Rein in Russell achieved success quickly. Within a year, the campaign reached critical mass. More than 75 major universities pledged to cut ties with Russell if it didn't reopen the unionized factory. And the company gave in to growing financial pressure.

Tone: The writer remains neutral and objective while describing events, as is appropriate for a news article.

Hearts and Minds

Gupta's interest in Rein in Russell began while he was in graduate school at Pennsylvania State University, where the campaign was born.

What he found most intriguing was that so many of the universities that got on board came to this decision without even being targeted by activists.

How did they do it? What tactic triggered this spillover effect, this contagion to change policies?

To find out, Gupta and co-authors Forrest Briscoe and Mark Anner analyzed the strategy and tactics of the campaign, and interviewed activists and university administrators—from both targeted and untargeted schools.

They learned that the USAS activists deployed two very different tactics to rein in Russell: disruption and evidence-based education. They first tried disruption, acting on what Gupta calls a longstanding intuition that localized protests expand impact by prompting organizations to surrender pre-emptively.

So the students fomented protests and sit-ins, which persuaded a few of the targeted universities to drop Russell. But they found that disruption and the threat of disruption did not lead to anything like the domino effect they desired.

"We found that those tactics didn't have a positive spillover effect," Gupta says. "They were effective where they were deployed. But peer universities that weren't protested did not join the cause. Their administrators would say that other universities did not make their decision rationally, that they caved in to intimidation."

What did get the ball rolling across the nation's major universities was a change in tactics. USAS organizers brought workers from Russell's shuttered factory on a limited campus tour to share their stories of abuse.

This new approach, Gupta says, was "purely intended to change minds and values."

And it was hugely effective.

Know Your Target

Why did it work?

Gupta says the evidence-based tactics appealed to the sense of reason that drives organizational decision making.

"Instead of justifying decisions in terms of right versus wrong, which is a question of values and morality, organizational decision makers—university administrators and corporate executives—work by the principle of rationality," he says. "This is to say that there should be a reason that you can justify for its service to organizational goals."

Those goals may be maximizing profits or galvanizing reputation or recruiting the best employees.

Gupta believes that knowing how to speak to these organizational goals is the key for would-be agents of social change to multiply their local actions into global results.

He adds that organizations, for their part, can avoid some of the bad publicity and lost productivity that are byproducts of disruptive demonstrations by proactively giving audience to activist groups, hearing their concerns and communicating the reasoning behind organizational policies and behaviors.

The Place for Protest

Though the study finds that education is one of the most effective social activist tactics in the long term, Gupta says it also reveals that disruptive tactics have a role to play as well.

First, disruption can apply enough pressure to be locally effective. Beyond that, protests and other disruptions can serve as a precursor for more broadly effective demonstrations of education and reasoning. By drawing attention and raising awareness to the cause (if not universal sympathy), they can pave the way for more rational messages to convince organizational decision makers to change their policies.

"There is a place for disruption," Gupta says. "Evidence-based tactics and disruption-based tactics have a kind of good cop/bad cop dynamic. Disruption gets attention. Evidence and persuasion change minds."

"Social Activism and Practice Diffusion: How Activist Tactics Affect Non-targeted Organizations" was published in the June 2015 issue of *Administrative Science Quarterly*.

APPLY

Practice rhetorical analysis

In Section 2.2, we've asked you to think about how purpose, audience, tone, genre, and context work together to contribute to a text's meaning and effectiveness. We've also showcased some of the ways the article "Growing Social Movements through Reason, Not Disruption" demonstrates these key elements of rhetoric.

Now we invite you to apply your new knowledge and skills to a different text on a similar topic. Read the following article and answer the questions that follow about how the writer uses the five components of rhetoric. (The notes you make here will help you complete the Chapter 2 Project.)

Today's Protests Rely on the Masses

SHARON COHEN

> *Sharon Cohen is a reporter for the Associated Press. Based in Chicago, she writes frequently about issues of criminal justice, police misconduct, gun violence, and legal matters. This story originally appeared on AP News in June 2018.*

▶

The Rev. Martin Luther King Jr. marching arm-in-arm with other civil rights activists. Cesar Chavez hoisting a picket sign in a farm workers' strike. Gloria Steinem rallying other feminists for equal rights.

During the 1960s and into the 1970s, amid the turbulence of protests for civil rights and against the Vietnam War, every movement seemed to have a famous face—someone at a podium or at the front of a march who possessed a charismatic style, soaring oratory and an inspiring message.

Not so today.

The new wave of political activism, marked by protests in the nation's capital and cities across America, looks more anonymous.

Since the presidential election of Donald Trump, there have been marches for women, science, the Dreamers—immigrants brought to the U.S. illegally as children—and most recently, gun control, a response to the school shooting in Parkland, Florida. In all those events, many voices—some more high-profile than others—have represented each cause.

Have America's protests changed so they rely more on the masses and less on one captivating leader?

The answer, some experts say, is yes, for two reasons: Progressive politics have moved in that direction—think Black Lives Matter, Occupy Wall Street—and social media has radically transformed activism. Decades ago, it could take weeks of planning, newspaper ads and a rousing speaker to organize a successful protest. Now a Facebook post or a series of tweets can fill the streets, jam a state capitol or block an expressway.

"With the rise of social media, it's definitely a lot easier for people to mobilize more quickly and you don't necessarily need to have one charismatic leader like Dr. King, who had almost some kind of magical quality," says Rachel Einwohner, a Purdue University sociology professor. "But you still do need some powerful message that really resonates with a lot of people."

Technology alone hasn't created the shift. Some progressives believe there's "something inherently wrong or problematic" about having a dynamic leader, says Fabio Rojas, an Indiana University sociology professor. "Modern progressive social movements see themselves as a very democratic form of politics," he says. "When they make decisions, they want a lot of consensus."

Black Lives Matter, which has been in the forefront of protests against police violence and fatal shootings of black men, is among the many movements that have adopted this approach.

"The model of the charismatic leader was not something that we were interested in, and in fact, many of us were trained to believe that the people themselves are going to set themselves free, not one person," says Patrisse Cullors, a co-founder of the group.

Cullors says her group is sometimes misunderstood.

"People assume because we hit the streets and protested that we don't believe in anything else ... and that because we don't have a single leader, we're aimless." Instead, she says, Black Lives Matter, which has 40 chapters in the U.S., Canada and England, has a clear strategy, including participating in electoral politics.

Another leaderless movement, Occupy Wall Street, rocked the heart of New York's financial district in 2011 with its encampment in a park and its rallying cry—"We are the 99 Percent"—that condemned the concentration of wealth in the U.S.

Many credit Occupy with putting economic inequality on the national radar, but Micah White, the group's co-founder, says the real goal—to end the influence of money on democracy—was "a constructive failure.... The main lesson is that street protests do not translate into political change because elected representatives are not required to listen to the majority."

While this democratic approach is effective, experts also say there are benefits to having a leader.

"A lot of people out there today feel there's something really wrong and broken with the country, with the world," says Karthik Ganapathy, rapid response director at MoveOn.org, a public policy advocacy group. "The value of having a centralized leader is there's someone saying, 'Here's what you can do about it.'" Yet now, he says, there's no one who "can really claim that mantle the way that King did."

But even in King's day, movements couldn't be reduced to a single face.

Whether it was the bus boycott in Montgomery, Alabama, the Vietnam War protest at the Lincoln Memorial or the farm workers' strike in California, each history-making event depended on hundreds or thousands of foot soldiers who organized, raised money and engaged in other grass-roots work.

And many leaders were backed by formidable organizations: For King, it was the Southern Christian Leadership Conference; for anti-war activist Tom Hayden, the Students for a Democratic Society; for feminist Betty Friedan, the National Organization for Women. ▶

Hasan Jeffries, an associate professor at Ohio State University and expert on African-American history, says the civil rights movement was always decentralized, but the media, looking for someone quotable, would zero in on one person—often, King.

These days, "activists are now able to push back, mainly through social media, and provide channels for multiple voices in ways that simply were unavailable on a large scale 50 years earlier," he says.

Einwohner, the Purdue sociologist, says when history books are written, they will include groups such as Black Lives Matter and the Dreamers.

"I can't think of a name or a face that necessarily is going to be remembered 50 years from now," she says. "But will these movements be remembered? Absolutely."

1. What purpose do you believe the author intends to achieve with this text?
2. What audience is the author addressing? How does she attempt to connect with that audience, and how successful do you think she is in doing so?
3. What kind of tone does the author use? Do you think her tone supports her purpose and helps her connect with the audience? Why or why not?
4. What typical features of news articles do you recognize in this text? What are your thoughts on how effectively that genre helps the author achieve her purpose and connect with the audience?
5. What context appears to have prompted the author to write this text? In what context was the text published?

2.3 Understand the rhetorical situation

We've asked you to think about rhetoric as a message that includes a purpose, an audience, an appropriate tone and genre, and that occurs within a social context. In this section, we want to dig a little deeper into what this context means for messages you want to convey.

Defining the rhetorical situation

All forms of communication take place in a context, a specific situation or combination of factors that influences how we present a message and how our readers or listeners receive that message. This context is called the *rhetorical situation*. It includes *all the factors* that affect how you present a message and how an audience interprets your message, including the following:

- **Audience needs, interests, and inclinations.** Effective writers consider the audience's frame of mind to determine how readers are likely to respond to the message. When we write an informative piece, for example, we need to be aware of how much our audience already knows about our topic. Writing something that repeats what our reader already knows isn't necessarily interesting. In other cases, audiences may be predisposed to agree with us (as when we are talking to a group of like-minded citizens working for the same political candidate). When an audience is likely to disagree, however, you can strengthen your case by appealing to what you *know* the audience values.

- **Connections to larger conversations.** If your message is connected to a larger issue being discussed in your local community or our culture at large, readers will likely find it engaging. Being mindful of those larger conversations will help you craft a more effective message.

- **The writer's credibility with the audience.** Your credibility is based on your audience's perception of your experience, knowledge, and trustworthiness. In other words, who you are and how you have treated your audience (or others) in the past definitely matters. In your daily life, this credibility is part of your personal ethos. In your academic writing, it's part of your academic ethos.

- **Writing style, tone, and visual appearance.** Words that resonate with readers; a style that's appropriate for the occasion; a tone that engages rather than alienates readers; and a clear, appealing visual presentation all work together to make your message more effective.

Understanding the impact of misreading the rhetorical situation

You may have heard of politicians or celebrities responding to a situation in a "tone-deaf" way. For example, if a celebrity tweets a photo of herself in a bikini with the hashtag #cantbetooskinny! just after a high-profile case of someone dying of anorexia, people who are concerned that she is ignoring the emotional aftermath of the recent anorexia death may accuse her of being tone-deaf. Being tone-deaf in this context means that a writer or speaker hasn't fully considered the rhetorical situation and doesn't appreciate the damage his or her comments may cause given the current context.

Similarly, communities sometimes deal with tone-deaf comments after a mass shooting. A few years ago, using multiple guns and lots of ammunition, a man in his twenties attacked a Marine recruiting center and a Navy operations center. Our local community college, which is right beside the Navy operations center, went on lockdown for several hours. Five servicemen died in this ambush attack, and many more were wounded, including first responders who rushed in to subdue the gunman. The shooting was a traumatic experience for our community, to say the least. The incident received national media attention, and the US vice president at the time, Joe Biden, came to town to speak at a community memorial service for those who were killed.

A day after the gunman's attack, a community member posted on social media a photo of his vast gun collection with the caption "Aren't these gorgeous?! Looking forward to firing these beauties tomorrow!!!" His intention was to take his collection to a firing range the next day and celebrate his birthday with some target practice.

After his Facebook post appeared, he was overwhelmed with people criticizing him for celebrating his hobby without acknowledging the gun-related violence of the day before and the shock and sadness people in the community were feeling. His critics weren't necessarily upset with him for having a big gun collection or enjoying using his guns at a firing range. They were upset because his post seemed horribly tone-deaf given what had just happened. In other words, he had failed to fully consider the rhetorical situation.

> ### REFLECT
> ## Consider your past rhetorical situations
>
> Now that you've seen a rhetorical situation in action, think back to a time when one of your communications was received really well or, frustratingly, didn't go over well at all. Looking back, why do you think it was received well or poorly by your audience? Even if you weren't familiar with the rhetorical terms *purpose, audience, tone, genre,* and *context,* how

might you have been taking those into consideration—or not—when writing your message? This communication could have been a Facebook post or tweet, a text message to a friend or family member, a school project, or something else.

Write a paragraph or more in which you reflect on a time when something you wrote effectively accounted for the rhetorical situation or whether it missed the mark. Why do you think the audience responded the way they did? In your response, use the terms purpose, audience, tone, genre, and context to explain what happened.

UNDERSTAND

Examine the rhetorical situation in two scenarios

Let's take a look at how the rhetorical situation works. Consider the following two scenarios in which students write emails to their instructor requesting an extension for turning in a final project. As you read each one, think about how well the writers keep the rhetorical situation in mind.

Scenario 1: Michael

Rhetorical situation: Michael's attendance in his first-year composition class this semester has been spotty at best. When he does come to class, he talks loudly to the people sitting around him about the great band he saw the night before. When class starts, however, he sometimes puts his head down on his desk and sleeps through class. His writing is pretty good, but he's turned in work after the deadline a few times this semester. On the day the final portfolio is due, Michael writes the following email to his teacher:

> Hi, I know portfolios were due 2day but ive been sick. I need more time to finish it. I will bring it to your office when i'm thru.

Scenario 2: Alonzo

Rhetorical situation: Alonzo is also in Michael's class and has attended regularly this semester, missing only one class meeting for a school-sponsored event that he was required to attend. During class, he often volunteers to read aloud and works actively in small groups. He has met with his instructor frequently to discuss his revisions, and he has also visited the college's writing center for extra help. The day the final portfolios are due, Alonzo sends the following email to his teacher:

> Hi Prof. Sansing,
>
> I saw the doctor this morning for a really bad sinus infection. I'm almost done with my revisions, but I'm not sure I can finish them today because the medicine he gave me really knocks me out. Could I possibly have another day or two to turn it in? I can email you the doctor's note if you want to see it.
>
> Thank you.
>
> Alonzo

In both scenarios, the students are asking for the same thing: more time to work on their final portfolios. Which student do you think is more likely to get an extension? Most of us would say Alonzo, but why? Sometimes we can sense when a writer is not effectively communicating a message for a specific audience and purpose. We intuitively analyze the rhetorical situation to determine who is more persuasive. Now let's break down the components of each of these rhetorical situations to see how we arrived at our response.

Thinking about audience needs, interests, and inclinations.   Time is a major consideration for Michael and Alonzo's audience—their instructor. At the end of a semester or quarter, teachers often have enormous amounts of student writing to evaluate, and they have to read and grade all of it in time to meet school-imposed deadlines. Michael seems oblivious to *any* concerns or constraints his instructor may be facing, such as a need to have grades turned in to the records office by a given date. By failing to consider the needs of his audience, Michael hurts his own case.

Alonzo's request, which specifies exactly how much extra time he needs (one or two days), allows the instructor to consider whether she can accommodate his request given her own constraints. When we think about audience inclination, we're considering what an audience is likely to do. We can't know whether this teacher is likely to give extensions to students, but we can surmise from the information we already have that if she *is* so inclined to give extensions, she may be more receptive to Alonzo's appeal than to Michael's.

Making connections to larger conversations.   Almost all college instructors address how they deal with late work at the beginning of a course, usually in the syllabus. Michael and Alonzo could benefit by considering their needs in the context of this larger conversation. Perhaps Professor Sansing mentioned on day one that she allows every student one late submission. In that case, Alonzo could remind his teacher of that policy since he hasn't submitted any assignments late. Perhaps during the semester, Professor Sansing has assigned readings on the difficulty of adjusting to college. In that case, Michael might appeal to Professor Sansing's demonstrated concern for students who have trouble adjusting to college in their early semesters.

These two email scenarios demonstrate how a message always exists within its rhetorical situation, a network of factors that help determine its effectiveness. No matter how clear a message's purpose, the other factors that make up the rhetorical situation—including the tone and style of the language, the author's credibility, the audience's relationship to the issue, and the visual appeal of the message—work together to make or break it. The rhetorical situation is at work no matter how trivial or important the message—and in both private and very public arenas, as you will see in later sections.

Thinking about the writer's credibility with the audience.   While the text is something that exists in the present, determining an author's (or speaker's) credibility requires you also to look to the past. What prior knowledge do you have of this writer? What has he or she done in the past to make them a believable authority on the current issue? Do they seem trustworthy? How can you tell?

In the cases of Michael and Alonzo, the behaviors they exhibited in the past now play into the decision that the audience (the teacher) will make in response to their messages. Because Michael routinely turns work in late and participates poorly in class, he doesn't seem to be a serious student. On the other hand, Alonzo's strong record of class attendance and meeting deadlines suggests that he would not ask for an extension without a good reason for doing so. Further, Alonzo has offered to supply a doctor's note to corroborate his story, a move that increases his credibility by using the "testimony" of an expert.

Thinking about writing style, tone, and visual appearance.   Notice that Michael doesn't even ask for an extension; he simply asserts that he will take one. Although Michael has demonstrated strong writing skills in the past, his email is full of errors and spelling shortcuts. While email is a more casual medium than a formal essay, Michael should still observe conventions like including the professor's name in the greeting and ending his message with a closing and his own name. Ignoring these conventions and submitting an email with everything run together in three clipped sentences could suggest to his teacher that he did not put much thought or time into his request, perhaps because he didn't think of it as a very important message. Michael's writing doesn't meet his audience's expectations for the purpose and style of this exchange.

In contrast, Alonzo presents his request respectfully. His language isn't too formal for an email, but he does express himself in complete sentences without errors. He provides a complete explanation and offers evidence from the doctor for support. His message looks like a standard letter, with a friendly greeting and a "thank you" followed by his name at the end. His writing style definitely matches audience expectations in the genre of email.

APPLY

Write while considering the rhetorical situation

We've encouraged you to consider the following information when trying to determine a rhetorical situation:

- Audience needs, interests, and inclinations
- Connections to larger conversations
- The writer's credibility with the audience
- Writing style, tone, and visual appearance

Earlier in this section, you read emails from Michael and Alonzo asking for additional time to turn in their final portfolios. To practice your understanding of rhetorical situations, write an email to your instructor asking for an extension on an imaginary assignment. (You will not actually send the email but you will submit it for this assignment.) You should consider statements the instructor has in your syllabus about late work, your own performance in the course to date, and any other context that might influence your instructor's response.

After you've written your email, write a paragraph or more explaining how you interpreted the rhetorical situation to compose your email. For example, how did thinking about audience needs and inclinations, broader context, your credibility, and considerations of style, tone, and visual appearance help shape your writing?

Chapter 2 Project
Write an essay evaluating how well a text responds to a rhetorical situation

---

In this chapter, we introduced you to the term *rhetoric* and encouraged you to set aside any preconceived ideas about it as being limited to overheated nonsense thrown around by political opponents. Instead, we want you to think of rhetoric as the power to effectively communicate a message.

We also asked you to think about rhetoric as having five key components: purpose, audience, tone, genre, and context. Writers use these elements together to create texts that connect with their audiences in meaningful ways. In the Section 2.2 Apply activity, you spent some time answering questions about how Sharon Cohen may have considered these five components to write her article "Today's Protests Rely on the Masses."

Next, we introduced you to the concept of the *rhetorical situation*, a broader understanding of a text's context that includes the following:

- Audience needs, interests, and inclinations
- Connections to larger conversations
- The writer's credibility with the audience
- Writing style, tone, and visual appearance

For the Chapter 2 Project, start with your notes on Sharon Cohen's article "Today's Protests Rely on the Masses" and expand them by further considering the rhetorical situation of the article. To understand the Associated Press audience, do a little web research to learn more about the organization and the kinds of content it publishes. Who would be interested in reading it? Other light research could help place the 2018 article in a broader context and help you discover more about the author's background and credibility.

When you have gathered more information, write an essay in which you evaluate how well you believe the article responds to its rhetorical situation. Your essay should address how well the writer appears to have achieved her purpose, reached her audience, selected a genre that appealed to the audience, struck an appropriate tone, and considered the larger context.

3

Understanding Writing as a Recursive Process

Achieve *If your instructor has assigned them, you can watch the videos for this chapter, complete the Reflect and Apply activities, and work on the Chapter Project in Achieve.*

3.1 Write in loops to achieve your purpose

You may already understand that writing is a process that generally happens in a sequence of stages. When we want to write something important, we plan what we want to say, compose a draft, review it to see what we want to change, make those changes, then deliver it to our intended audience. When we think of the process in this way, it seems very straightforward, and indeed, this is the basic sequence of stages writers generally follow. But we want to introduce you to a way of thinking about the process that makes it more productive and flexible for you: a looping process that allows you to look backwards and forwards as you move toward a final draft. Writing in loops will help you create a more effective final draft.

Seeing writing as a recursive process

A *recursive* process refers to the way writers often loop back or revisit earlier work as we write. Say a writer has planned pretty carefully how a draft will be organized. Even with careful planning, once in the middle of that draft, she might realize that part of that plan isn't working out as she imagined. So she loops back for a moment to the planning stage and adjusts her plans. At other times, we may be working on a writing project and realize that we need to go back and gather additional information to make our argument more persuasive. Writers are constantly looping back, rereading, making adjustments, and then moving forward again with a draft. The looping process actually helps you communicate more effectively.

Watch Meg explain the recursive writing process

In this video, Meg explains how a looping, recursive writing process works for her. As you watch, consider how her process might work for you.

Video: Understanding the Recursive Writing Process

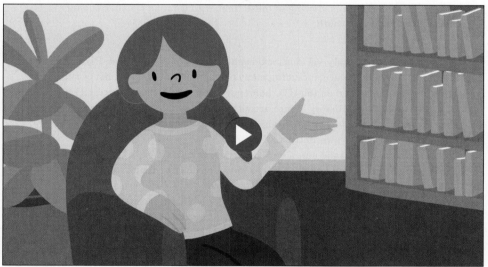

Getting started on a writing project by considering instructor guidelines

When you're writing for a college course, often your instructor will provide an assignment sheet that outlines the guidelines for the assignment. It's important to read these guidelines carefully to understand exactly what the instructor expects you to produce.

To understand how this works, take a look at the following assignment sheet for an assignment called "Black History Month Synthesis Project." Students in a first-year writing course have been reading and discussing *Between the World and Me* by Ta-Nehisi Coates, winner of the National Book Award for nonfiction in 2015. The assignment sheet features clearly labeled sections that outline the instructor's expectations.

Black History Month Synthesis Project

Context

In his book *Between the World and Me*, Ta-Nehisi Coates offers an intriguing perspective on Black History Month, recalling that as a youth, "it seemed that the month could not pass without a series of films dedicated to the glories of being beaten on camera" (page 32). Indeed, Coates seems to struggle reconciling at that time in his life what he is viewing in these films with what he is experiencing in his neighborhood as a youth.

Directions

As we enter into February, various local events commemorating Black History Month will be taking place, including many on-campus activities. (A list of such activities can be located on the UTC homepage.) Please choose and attend one UTC-sponsored Black History Month activity. (If unavoidable time constraints absolutely prohibit you from attending any of these events, please see me immediately to discuss alternatives.)

During the event, take notes, and, if appropriate, feel free to respectfully participate. As you listen and participate, consider how the issues under consideration at the event (Civil Rights Movement, African-American history, current events, etc.) are presented and in what light. Then, consider how Coates is viewing the same issue(s) in his text, noting in particular his thoughts on pages 32–39. Compare your observations from the event with Coates's perspective, noting the similarities as well as the differences. Then, in a **two-to-three-page essay**, *argue whether you ultimately agree or disagree with Coates's assessment of Black History Month*, as represented in his text, supporting your argument based upon your experiences attending a Black History Month event.

Specifications

Your essay should be typed, double-spaced, and written in 12-point Times New Roman font. Your essay should also include a proper heading and a clever title. You should follow MLA citation guidelines. No cover page is required. When citing direct information or quotations from the event you attend, please use proper citation and include a Works Cited page at the end of your essay. Please consult the Appendix: Understanding Academic Citation Styles for examples of proper citations.

Purpose

This activity will encourage you to attend and support a UTC-sponsored event during which you will hopefully participate in, or at least observe, an insightful engagement of ideas. Furthermore, this assignment will help sharpen both your synthesis and critical thinking/writing skills.

Audience

Your audience is a mix of college-aged students and college-educated individuals, both of whom have read *Between the World and Me*. In presenting your argument, you will, in a sense, be helping your classmates and those who are perhaps from an older generation, understand why you agree or disagree with Coates's assessment. As you craft your essay, consider a language and tone that will best suit this group of individuals.

Evaluation

This essay is ultimately a synthesized argument, which means you'll be graded primarily upon your ability to clearly, effectively, and convincingly argue your stated thesis, with appropriate evidence which you have synthesized with Coates's textual argument. Consideration will also be given to essay organization, style, source integration (if appropriate), grammar, mechanics, and formatting. Please consult the grading rubric for detailed information on grading guidelines for this assignment. Your final draft grade (portfolio) will be based primarily upon your ability to successfully revise your draft based upon the feedback given on your preliminary draft.

Due Dates

- A peer review of this draft will take place during class on **Tuesday, February 21**. To participate and earn credit, you must arrive to class with a typed, completed, hard-copy draft.

- The preliminary draft of this essay is due stapled and in a folder, along with the grading rubric, on **Thursday, February 23**, at the beginning of class.

- A final, polished (revised) draft of this essay will comprise a part of your course portfolio, due on **Wednesday, April 26**.

To get started on this assignment, you would need to consider what needs to happen first, in this case, making a plan to attend a Black History Month event on your campus. Once there, you'd need to take notes on what you observed and how you participated.

This assignment also gives specific guidelines about the audience students should address:

> Your audience is a mix of college-aged students and college-educated individuals, both of whom have read *Between the World and Me*. In presenting your argument, you will, in a sense, be helping your classmates and those who are perhaps from an older generation understand why you agree or disagree with Coates's assessment. As you craft your essay, consider a language and tone that will best suit this group of individuals.

As you planned your essay, you'd need to think about *how* to reach this mix of people—traditional college-aged students *and* college graduates from an older generation. For example, pop culture references you include in your essay would need to be framed in a way that would be appreciated by both groups in your audience.

Brainstorming ideas with friends and classmates can help you flesh out ideas. Once you have a few ideas about how to write this essay, you could start drafting passages and making an outline or other notes to organize your thoughts.

The assignment or project guidelines you receive in college courses—and later in your workplace—may not supply as many details as this assignment sheet does. But they provide important information to help you get started.

Considering five components of rhetoric during your recursive writing process

Writers are living, breathing producers of rhetoric, so it's important to keep in mind five essential components of rhetoric as you write. As we discussed in Section 2.2, your purpose, audience, tone, genre, and context work together like the parts of a completed puzzle to convey your message effectively.

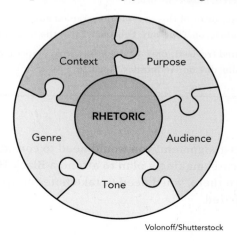

Volonoff/Shutterstock

As you begin planning a draft, ask yourself questions about each component:

- **Purpose.** What is my purpose for writing this text? What do I want it to accomplish? Will it persuade, inform, entertain, or fulfill some other kind of purpose?

- **Audience.** Who needs to receive this text? Why this audience? What do I need to include in my text to reach this audience? What information do they need?

- **Tone.** What kind of attitude do I need to convey in this text? What kinds of language and formatting choices can help me achieve that tone?

- **Genre.** What form should my message take to achieve my purpose and reach my audience? Does my text need to be multimodal?

- **Context.** What's going on in the world or my community in relation to what I'm writing about? How could this context affect the way my audience receives my text? Is the context likely to make my audience receptive to my message or hostile to it?

Keeping all these pieces of rhetoric in mind as you write will help you create a rhetorically effective text.

Making a recursive writing process work for you

We've said that using a recursive writing process is a more productive and natural way to achieve your intended purpose than marching straight through all the stages of writing without ever looking back. But all that looping back takes time and energy. You may be wondering if it's really worth investing in this process. We want to share four truths about why approaching writing this way can work for you as you continue to grow as a writer in your academic and everyday lives.

1. **Looping back actually prepares you to move forward.** Sometimes revisiting an earlier stage of writing allows you to see your text in a new way. When you loop back to an earlier stage, you metaphorically press a pause button. This gives you some time to figure out where you want to go.

2. **Looping back can get you "unstuck" when writing.** Even the most successful and accomplished writers find the whole process a little intimidating at times. That blinking cursor on an empty screen or completely blank piece of paper staring back at you can feel like a giant roadblock. In large part, what helps writers get past obstacles is knowing that the writing process is, in fact, recursive. We can move forward without the pressure of believing that the first drafts we compose have to be perfect because we

know that looping back is baked in to the process. Embracing a recursive writing process can give you that reassurance.

3. **Looping back makes the hard parts of writing easier.** One of the hardest things for writers is discarding words we worked hard to produce. Deleting a single sentence is one thing, but scratching a whole paragraph or a whole introduction? That's painful. Embracing a recursive writing process makes it easier. When we're willing to throw out words or ideas that aren't working, then loop back and figure out new choices that make more sense, the whole piece gets better. In this way, looping back also helps you gain confidence about your own rhetorical skills.

4. **Looping back buys you valuable time and puts you in control of your writing.** When you realize something isn't working in your writing and you allow yourself to "press pause," you're also giving yourself time to step away from your work and come back later with fresh eyes and new ideas. This practice allows you to take control over the quality of your writing.

Being strategic about looping back

We encourage you to loop back as often as necessary, but we want you to be strategic about it. Some writing decisions need immediate attention while others can be put on hold and addressed later. Effective writers learn to prioritize these decisions to keep the process moving forward as smoothly as possible.

The problem areas writers need to address fall into two categories: *higher-order concerns* (HOCs) and *lower-order concerns* (LOCs). HOCs generally need to be addressed as soon as you recognize them because they affect the viability and structure of the whole text. You can identify HOCs by asking yourself questions about how well you are achieving your purpose, reaching your audience, using effective organization, and supporting your ideas sufficiently. It's worth looping back and addressing these big issues as soon as you can because the success of your entire text is depending on it.

LOCs, on the other hand, can usually be ignored for the moment as you continue developing your text. LOCs are problem areas such as spelling, grammar, word choice, and punctuation issues that affect only an isolated part of your text. Effective writers usually wait until the very end of the process to deal with LOCs because doing so saves time. Why spend time reviewing and revising a paragraph before you're sure that it supports your purpose and will stay in the text? Addressing writing problems by treating HOCs before LOCs makes you a more efficient writer.

Higher-Order Concerns	Purpose
	Audience
	Organization
	Support for Ideas
Lower-Order Concerns	Spelling
	Grammar
	Word Choice
	Punctuation

REFLECT

Consider the impact of writing recursively

We've been making a case for approaching writing as a recursive process. While the basic process includes planning, drafting, reviewing, making changes, then delivering the text to the audience, along the way you should loop back strategically to address both higher-order and lower-order concerns in your emerging draft.

How will embracing a recursive writing process impact the way you currently go from start to finish in your own writing? Write a paragraph addressing the benefits and challenges you see a recursive writing process offering you.

UNDERSTAND

Watch Li write with a recursive process

Let's watch as Li uses the recursive writing process to write a paragraph about his first experiences at an American college. Pay special attention to how he loops back and forth between phases and how he addresses higher-order and lower-order concerns as he drafts the following paragraph.

Li's working draft

International students have experiences that are unique as they arrive in a new culture. During my first day on an American college campus, I experienced events that filled all five senses.

Video: Writing with a Recursive Process

First, I remember how vibrant the trees looked as I walked across campus, which was smaller than I expected. Then I smelled barbecue coming from the welcome cookout. When I tasted it, it was sweet like my favorite home dish, but smokier. I remember hearing students laughing as they tossed around a football. A new friend asked me to play Frisbee, and I was excited to start my first semester at my new school.

UNDERSTAND

Read a student's working draft of a literacy narrative

The following is the first draft of a literacy narrative written by our student Nia Hale. After she composed this draft, she stepped away from it for a bit, then reread it with fresh eyes. She made notes in the margin about how she wanted to loop back and improve her essay in the next draft.

The Girl Without an Imagination

I hated reading when I was a little kid. I would much

rather play on my GameCube or chat on AIM instant

messenger than pick up a book to read. When I tried to read,
I just couldn't picture what the words were describing like
everyone else. It felt as if my imagination was covered with
thick fog and nothing was clearing it. That's when I decided   *← Too harsh?*
that my imagination was broken.   *Add details about third grade, Mr. Owens's class*

    When I began fourth grade, I started at a new school.
After my first day, I realized that my worst nightmare
had come true: my new school had an entire class period
dedicated to reading. Not only was I now enrolled in a
private school, away from my public-school friends and with
kids I didn't know, but I had to sit through a class that was
focused solely on reading. I panicked at my table during the
first class period when my teacher, Ms. Sanders, explained
to the class that we would be reading five different
books throughout the course of the year. I knew that my
imagination didn't work and I was terrified that I would
make my first F in this class.   *Add transition. Maybe connect this paragraph to the one above?*

    I begged my mom to sign me up for a new school
because this one was not for me. I finally confessed to her
that my imagination was broken and that I needed to go to
an easier school because I would fail out of this one. Not only
did she ignore my request, she did something much worse:
she set up a parent-teacher conference.

    The next week, my mom met with Ms. Sanders to
discuss my dislike for reading and my broken imagination.
Not only was I at a new school, with new people and new
teachers, I now would be labeled as the crazy girl with no
imagination. The day after my mom's meeting, Ms. Sanders
asked me to come to her desk before class started. She   *Add dialogue to show what she told me about my broken imagination.*
walked over to the huge, red bookcase in the back of the
classroom. She studied the bookcase for a few moments,
and then grabbed a book and brought it over to me. It
was *The Magic Tree House.*   *Describe the book's cover — lots of color, knight riding a horse, castle*

I walked back to my desk and shoved the book in my desk. I didn't understand why she thought a book would cure me from my disease. I couldn't wait to get home. I knew my mom would let me switch schools after she found out that Ms. Sanders tried to cure my broken imagination by making me read another book.

For the next couple of days, I avoided reading my new book. My mom insisted that I give it a try but I was scared. I didn't know what I was more afraid of: finding out that this couldn't cure my broken imagination or telling my teacher that it didn't work. I dreaded going to reading class. Each day, before we started our short reading assignment, Ms. Sanders would ask me how Jack and Annie were. At first, I was confused, but she told me I needed to read the book.

One day, after a long day at school, I decided to give the book a chance. I don't know if my curiosity about Jack and Annie had gotten the best of me, or if Ms. Sanders's persistence had begun to annoy me, but I knew I couldn't keep putting it off. I was ready to finally prove to Ms. Sanders that my broken imagination was something that just couldn't be fixed. I opened the book and began to read. Before I knew it, an hour had passed. But not a normal hour. During this hour, I was whisked away to the Middle Ages with my new friends, Jack and Annie. We explored castles, fought off dragons, and ran into some trouble at the Great Feast in the Main Hall of the castle. I couldn't believe that I could actually picture what was going on in the places that Jack, Annie, and I visited. I was thrilled that my imagination had been restored! After that, I began to love reading.

Add a better conclusion that explains what happened once my imagination was "cured."

APPLY

Create a working draft of a literacy narrative

To practice writing using a recursive process, we invite you to start planning a *working draft* (writing that's still in progress and not yet finished) of your Chapter 3 Project: a three-to-four-page literacy narrative, a personal essay that explains and reflects on your experience as a writer or reader. You may focus on in-school or out-of-school literacy experiences. In fact, you are welcome to write about how you write or read social-media posts, create fan fiction, text with a loved one, protest with a sign you made, keep a personal journal, and so on. The ways you think about and describe your personal experience will be unique to you. So will your looped writing process!

As you plan, think about the five components of rhetoric and ask yourself questions about how you want to compose your text:

- **Purpose.** What is the purpose of my literacy narrative? What do I want people to understand about me after reading this text? What are some anecdotes I could describe from my past that would illustrate my experience?

- **Audience.** In this case, classmates and your instructor will certainly read your essay. Beyond that, who needs to hear your message? Is it people who have had similar experiences? Or perhaps you want to reach people who haven't shared these experiences to inform them.

- **Tone.** What tone do I need to adopt to be taken seriously? What kind of attitude should I project in my writing? What words or visuals should I use or avoid to maintain an effective tone?

- **Genre.** In this situation, your genre has been predetermined by your instructor. You're writing a literacy narrative, which is a type of personal essay. In other rhetorical situations, though, you may need to ask questions to help you determine an effective genre, questions such as what form my message needs to take and whether I should compose an email, formal letter, blog post, tweet, or other genre.

- **Context.** What context do I need to keep in mind? How might my literacy history be similar to and different from others? What specific circumstances might I need to explain in my literacy narrative?

3.2 Add recursive loops to improve your writing process

What kinds of moves would you make if you engaged in a looping writing process? In this section, we'll give you specific strategies to use to improve your working drafts.

Revisiting your draft to make it better

We've encouraged you to embrace a recursive writing process by considering higher-order and lower-order concerns as you repeatedly loop back through your working draft. What kinds of work might you do in these loops? Consider the following strategies as options.

- **Clarify your purpose.** Make sure everything in your draft points back to the purpose you want to achieve. This is a good time to reconsider whether the genre you're using is a good fit for your specific purpose and audience.

- **Imagine your audience's response.** As you reread your draft, keep your audience in mind. What kinds of questions might they have? What additional information will they need to fully understand your text? Have you fully considered the context surrounding your message?

- **Gather more information.** Most writers inadvertently leave important information out of early drafts. As you reread, consider what else your audience will need to find your message effective. Can you supply that information on your own, or do you need to consult other sources such as family members, friends, or former teachers?

- **Clarify your thinking.** Depending on the specifics of your text, you may need to reconsider your reasoning or imagine how others experienced the literacy experiences you recall. Perhaps this is a time for you to step away for a while and come back when you've had time to think through what you really want your text to achieve.

- **Review your organization.** Are you delivering information in an order that your audience can follow easily? Are stories and explanations that support your message structured in a way the audience can understand?

- **Delete ineffective parts.** This is the painful loop we mentioned earlier! If you find sections or words that don't really contribute to your purpose, now's the time to cut them.

- **Check the tone.** Think about the overall attitude you want to convey. Do any of your words seem to go in a different direction that doesn't support your intended tone?

- **Check for accuracy.** You want your message to be effective. Double-check your facts, dates, spelling, grammar, and punctuation.

> **REFLECT**
>
> ## Imagine how performing these loops might improve your draft
>
> As you think about the options for looping back that we've described, consider which ones might be most helpful as you revise your working draft. Write one or more paragraphs that discuss which looping strategies may be most productive for you at this stage. Why would trying these particular strategies be helpful and others less so?

UNDERSTAND

Watch Li loop back to create a stronger draft

In the following video, you'll see how Li strategically loops back into his draft paragraph to address problem areas. Working with Gabby, Li considers his audience's response, clarifies his thinking, and revises ineffective parts to produce this revised draft.

Li's revision

International students have experiences that are unique as they arrive in a new culture. During my first day on an American college campus, I experienced events that filled all five senses. First, I remember how vibrant the trees looked as I walked across campus, which ~~was~~ felt smaller than I expected and friendlier. Then I smelled barbecue coming from the welcome cookout. When I tasted it, it was sweet like my mom's sesame tofu, my favorite home dish, but smokier. I remember hearing students laughing as they tossed around a football. A new friend asked me to play Frisbee, and I was excited to start my first semester at my new school.

Video: Looping to Create a Stronger Draft

Read a student's revised draft of a literacy narrative

After reviewing her notes on her working draft, Nia wrote this revised draft. She used some of the revision strategies we've discussed, including imagining her audience's response and clarifying her purpose.

Hale 1

Nia Hale

Professor Ingraham

ENGL 1010

Revised Draft

The Girl Without an Imagination

Reading was never something that interested me as a child. Growing up in a world that was on the brink of many technological advancements, I would much rather play on my

Hale 2

GameCube or chat on AIM instant messenger than pick up a book to read. I would roll my eyes every time my teacher, Mr. Owens, reminded my third-grade class that we needed to read to obtain a sufficient amount points in the software system our school used to track our reading progress. Mr. Owens constantly lectured us on how reading a good book can be fun and can take you to another world. I didn't understand how a book with no pictures could take me to another world. I only read when it was required of me, and my constant sub-par grades on reading tests or book reports discouraged me even more. I grew increasingly frustrated with every book I read, desperately wanting to picture what the words were describing like everyone else. I longed to be normal but I just couldn't get past the sea of words on the page. I hated disappointing my teachers and myself with bad grades but I didn't know how to fix my problem. It felt as if my imagination was covered with thick fog and nothing was clearing it. That's when I decided that my imagination was broken.

> Nia provided more context for her readers by adding details about her reading experiences before she met Ms. Sanders.

When I began fourth grade, I started at a new school. After my first day, I realized that my worst nightmare had come true: my new school had an entire class period dedicated to reading. Not only was I now enrolled in a private school, away from my public-school friends and with kids I didn't know, but I had to sit through a class that was focused solely on reading. I panicked at my table during the first class period when my teacher, Ms. Sanders, explained to the class that we would be reading five different books throughout the course of the year. I knew that my imagination didn't work and I was terrified that I would make my first F in this class. When my mom picked me up from school that day, I begged her to sign me up for a new

Hale 3

school because this one was not for me. I finally confessed to her that my imagination was broken and that I needed to go to an easier school because I would fail out of this one. Not only did she ignore my request, she did something much worse: she set up a parent-teacher conference.

She added a transition to connect two paragraphs, helping readers follow the flow of her story.

The next week, my mom met with Ms. Sanders to discuss my dislike for reading and my broken imagination. Not only was I at a new school, with new people and new teachers, I now would be labeled as the crazy girl with no imagination. The day after my mom's meeting, Ms. Sanders asked me to come to her desk before class started.

"I hear that you suffer from a broken imagination," she said softly.

Nia decided to add dialogue, a typical feature of the narrative genre, to show her interaction with Ms. Sanders.

"Yes, ma'am. I'm afraid I can't participate in your class," I said.

"You know, my daughter suffered from the same thing as you. You know what cured her?" she asked.

Suddenly, I was intrigued. "What?"

Ms. Sanders got up from her desk and walked over to the huge, red bookcase in the back of the classroom. She studied the bookcase for a few moments, carefully reading the titles of the hundreds of books on the bookshelf and then grabbed a small chapter book and brought it over to me. I stared at the book for a moment and looked up at her.

"The Magic Treehouse?" I asked, looking back down at the book.

"Yes. I want you to go home tonight and read as much of this as you can. Even if it's only the first chapter. Just promise me that you will eventually finish it. When you do, come back to me and we will talk about your broken imagination."

Hale 4

I walked back to my desk and studied the cover of the
book. There were two kids on the cover. They were riding a
large, black, armored horse with a knight. They were in front of
a castle and the sky was a mix of blue and orange colors. I
shoved the book in my desk. *What does she not understand
about a broken imagination?* I wondered. I didn't understand
why she thought a book would cure me from my disease.
I couldn't wait to get home. I knew my mom would let me
switch schools after she found out that Ms. Sanders tried to
cure my broken imagination by making me read another book.

> Added descriptive details help readers picture what Nia saw.

For the next couple of days, I avoided reading my new
book. My mom insisted that I give it a try but I was scared.
I didn't know what I was more afraid of: finding out that
this couldn't cure my broken imagination or telling my
teacher that it didn't work. I dreaded going to reading class.
Each day, before we started our short reading assignment,
Ms. Sanders would ask me how Jack and Annie were. At first,
I was confused.

"Who are Jack and Annie?" I asked.

"I see you haven't read the book I gave you," she
answered. "You should give it a try. I think you will be good
friends with Jack and Annie."

One day, after a long day at school, I decided to give the
book a chance. I don't know if my curiosity about Jack and
Annie had gotten the best of me, or if Ms. Sanders's persistence
had begun to annoy me, but I knew I couldn't keep putting
it off. I was ready to finally prove to Ms. Sanders that my
broken imagination was something that just couldn't be fixed.
I opened the book and began to read. Before I knew it, an hour
had passed. But not a normal hour. During this hour, I was

Hale 5

whisked away to the Middle Ages with my new friends, Jack
and Annie. We explored castles, fought off dragons, and ran into
some trouble at the Great Feast in the Main Hall of the castle.
I couldn't believe that I could actually picture what was going
on in the places that Jack, Annie, and I visited. I would sit in my
bed for hours glued to the page, only leaving when it was time
for dinner. I was thrilled that my imagination had been restored!

For the next few weeks, all I wanted to do was read the
Magic Treehouse books. My mom was ecstatic about my
newfound love for reading and made many trips to our local
bookstore to get me more books in the series. By the time
Christmas came around, I had almost finished the entire series
and had moved on to other books such as the Junie B. Jones
series and *The Castle in the Attic*. I quickly became one of the top
readers in my class, accumulating many reading points and acing
tests. Once I got past my silly broken imagination self-diagnosis,
I began to love reading and asked for books from Santa and my
parents—and I owe it all to Jack, Annie, and Ms. Sanders.

> Nia's new concluding paragraph helps convey the significance of the moment and clarify her purpose for telling her story.

APPLY

Loop back through your working draft to get to a stronger draft

Now that you've seen how Li and Nia used looping processes to revisit
their working drafts, we invite you to take some loops through your
working draft of your Chapter 3 Project. Remember that you can use any
of the strategies discussed in this chapter as often as you need them, in

any order you find useful. And you might find that some of them aren't necessary for you at this point or with this working draft. It's OK not to use any you don't find helpful. Your looping writing process is individual and unique to you.

That said, we encourage you to focus as much as possible on higher-order concerns in this second draft (purpose, audience, organization). In your next draft, you'll have another opportunity to loop back to focus on lower-order concerns such as spelling and punctuation.

APPLY

Polish your revised draft

Now that you've revised your Chapter 3 Project draft with a focus on higher-order concerns, loop back through it one more time to focus on lower-order concerns such as spelling and punctuation. Create a polished draft you consider final for this project.

Chapter 3 Project
Write a literacy narrative

Working writers sometimes publish book-length memoirs about the life experiences—good and bad—that directly impacted the way they see themselves as writers. For this assignment, we're asking you to go small-scale and write a literacy narrative of three to four pages about your experience so far as a writer and reader. (For an example of a literacy narrative, refer back to student Nia Hale's essay, "The Girl Without an Imagination" in Section 3.2.)

How would you characterize yourself as a reader or writer? How have your experiences shaped the way you see yourself as a reader or writer? Use these questions to come up with a main idea you want to focus on for this essay. You may focus on meaningful experiences from both in-school and out-of-school settings. That is, you might choose to draw from school experiences that helped or hindered your development as a reader or writer. You are also welcome to write about how you write or read outside school, including how you post on social media, create fan fiction, text with a loved one, protest with a sign you made, write in the workplace, keep a personal journal, and the like. Most important, know that this narrative doesn't have to be a "happy story." You're welcome to write about struggles you've faced or challenges you haven't yet overcome.

In your literacy narrative, include these key features:

- **A well-told story focusing on a *specific moment* that illustrates a larger point.** Tell us a story of a moment in your life that illustrates how you see yourself now as a writer or reader. As with most narratives, those about literacy often set up some sort of situation that needs to be resolved. This need for resolution makes readers want to keep reading. The specific moment you focus on might include one that details...

  - any early memory about writing or reading that you recall vividly
  - someone who taught you to write or read
  - an in-school writing or reading experience that had a big impact on you
  - an out-of-school writing or reading experience that has shaped you

- **Vivid detail.** Include details that help us see, hear, smell, taste, or feel what you were experiencing during the moment you describe. The details you use when describing something can help readers picture places, people, and events; dialogue can help us hear what was being said in the moment.

- **Significance of the moment.** Your narrative needs to reveal why this moment matters to you as you continue to develop as a writer or reader. It's usually helpful if you include why or how you're still grappling with the same issues or experiencing the effects of that moment.

Your finished essay should be three to four pages, or about 1,000 words.

4

Improving Your Draft Using Feedback and Revision

≋ Achie√e *If your instructor has assigned them, you can watch the video for this chapter, complete the Reflect and Apply activities, and work on the Chapter Project in Achieve.*

4.1 Engage in peer review early in your writing process

As you work on peer review and revision in this section, follow your instructor's guidance on using one of your drafts from an earlier chapter or a new writing assignment.

Approaching feedback and revision like you're building a house

If you were building a house from scratch that you wanted to be sturdy and do its job well—providing shelter and comfort—you'd need to start with a firm foundation. You wouldn't apply your favorite paint color to flimsy walls or choose towels for your bathroom before you poured a concrete foundation and built a strong framework for the house. Writing works the same way. To end up with a strong and effective piece of writing, you have to make sure the foundation is in place before you worry too much about the surface issues.

One way to understand this process is to think about your writing project as a house you're building and the various elements you need to consider as the "bricks" in that house. You have to start at the bottom. The most important information—making sure the writing addresses its purpose and audience—has to be mortared in first. Once that level passes inspection, you're looking at the next step in the process: making sure your organization functions well to achieve your purpose and reach your audience. When you are satisfied with your organization, you're able to move to the next level: checking on things that act like the "glue" that holds your writing project together—transitions and a consistent tone, style, and voice. Finally, you're ready to make sure your "house's" décor is picture-perfect: edit out any errors in formatting, spelling, punctuation, or sentence structure.

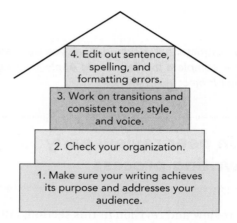

For now, let's focus on those lower "bricks"—working on purpose, audience, and organization.

Enlisting classmates to get feedback on your purpose, audience, and organization

All writers benefit from having other people read their work. Readers provide a perspective that's different from our own and can help us see places that are confusing or unconvincing. They also tell us what works! While writing the chapters of *The Writer's Loop*, we often turned to our peers—other writing instructors—to comment on our drafts, tell us what they liked best, and identify places that needed work.

In those early feedback sessions on *The Writer's Loop*, we asked our peer teachers to focus only on two areas that are foundational for a piece of writing to be effective:

1. achieving our purpose and reaching our audience, and

2. presenting the information in an order that makes sense

That's the same process we encourage you to try. When you're getting feedback on an early working draft, ask your peers to focus mostly on the *big picture*. Do all your paragraphs support the purpose you want to achieve? Do your words, overall argument, and genre work for the audience you're trying to reach? Have you presented the information in an organized way that helps your audience understand your point?

Providing important context to help your peers do their best work

To give the most helpful feedback, readers need some context. You need to let your readers know your thoughts on the current draft they're reading. We suggest that you introduce your draft by sharing the following information either orally or in writing.

- **Explain the purpose of the draft.** When reviewers understand what we *want* our draft to do, they're in a better position to tell us where the draft is working and where it's not. Sometimes we get feedback on an early draft that includes comments such as "I'm not sure what you're trying to do" or "this paragraph doesn't seem to fit in this paper." If this ever happens to you, you'll know that it's a good idea to review your draft to make sure your purpose is clear and that your paragraphs are working together to achieve your purpose overall.

- **Tell readers about your intended audience.** When your reviewers know your audience, they can help you flag some terms that need to be defined or note that you've ignored a counterclaim that might be persuasive to readers who don't already agree with you.

- **Explain the reasoning behind your organization.** Organizing writing requires you to take on a critical mindset that asks, "What do my readers need to know, and when do they need to know it?" Readers need contextual information in one paragraph that helps them make sense of new information in the next paragraph. If you hear from reviewers that they're not following what your draft is saying, and you find yourself replying, "Oh, I get to that on the next page," you have an organization problem.

Your readers are telling you that they need certain information to appear earlier in the paper in order to make sense of new information.

- **State what you think is going well and not so well with this draft so far.** Having this information helps reviewers understand how you're viewing the draft at this point. In their response, reviewers can confirm or challenge your perspective to help you see the strengths, weaknesses, and untapped potential of your current draft.

Providing helpful feedback to others

If you're asking your peers for their help with your draft, it's only fair that you offer to review some of your peers' writing. Some students worry that they aren't strong writers themselves, so they have no business telling others how to improve their writing. We don't believe that. We want to encourage you to see your role in this process as simply responding to what you see in your peer's draft. What do you see working? What doesn't make sense to you? To do that well, consider the strategies below.

- **Read through the draft once before making any comments.** Some people find it helpful to get a sense of the whole draft before trying to zero in on specific areas to address. It's kind of like knowing the final destination before you start strategizing about which route you want to take.

- **Consider any guidelines you've been given about what to focus on.** Your peer or your instructor may have asked you to provide general feedback, or they may have asked you to offer feedback on something specific such as support for the thesis or a clear pattern of organization. Feedback on a very early draft should focus on the central components—purpose, audience awareness, and organization—not on small details such as spelling and punctuation.

- **Give honest, tactful, detailed feedback.** It's OK to see things in a draft that aren't working and to point them out to the writer. In fact, that's the whole point of this process, right? But it's hard to receive this kind of information if it's delivered in a snarky or rude manner. When you see a problem area in a draft, say so in such a way that the writer will trust that you are invested in the process and want to help improve this draft. So rather than responding with "This is the worst paragraph I've ever read," try "I have questions about this paragraph because..." Explaining why you don't understand something can be really helpful to a writer.

- **Point out the positives and potential.** In addition to identifying areas that aren't working well, let the writer know what you like about the draft. Offer suggestions to make parts of it stronger.

Consider how to provide context for your peer review session

Read through your current draft of a project you are working on and consider what you think is working well and what is giving you trouble, as well as any questions you'd like to ask your reviewers about your draft. Make some notes about those questions and any information you'll need to share with reviewers about your purpose, audience, and intended organization.

Watch Li use peer feedback to improve an early draft

Watch as Li gets feedback on his working draft, an analysis of Twitter hashtags, from Jay, a student tutor in the writing center. Notice how Li provides some context for his draft and explains that right now he's mostly interested in feedback that helps him check for priorities we've been discussing in this section: purpose, audience, and effective organization.

Video: Getting Feedback on a Working Draft

APPLY

Write an introductory note asking for feedback from peers

Now's your chance to get some valuable feedback about your draft. Using your notes from the Reflect activity in Section 4.1, write an introductory note that you'll share with peer reviewers when you ask for feedback on your draft. Include any context they will need to give you useful feedback on the potential problems you're concerned about. Your instructor may ask you to bring hard copies of your introductory note and your draft to class.

4.2 Use peer feedback to help you revise your draft

So, what are you to do with the feedback you get from peers? First, we encourage you to read it all with an open mind. When you've worked hard on a draft, it can sting a little when it's critiqued. Just know that you can use this feedback to make your draft stronger. If you don't completely understand a peer's comment, follow up with a discussion to make sure you grasp the feedback.

Finally, remember that this is *your* project. You are not obligated to accept every comment or make every change suggested by your peers. The advice in this section will help you evaluate each comment thoughtfully and apply those that help you better achieve your purpose and reach your audience.

Considering your revision options

Using feedback from readers and your own thoughts about improving your early draft, it's important that you stay focused on addressing the most fundamental parts of your draft first: achieving your purpose, reaching your audience, and organizing your ideas rhetorically—that is, organizing so that you're delivering information in a way that makes sense to your readers.

When you revisit your working draft to consider purpose, audience, and organization, you have four basic options for revising the draft:

- **Add content.** What information is missing that readers need in order to make sense of your draft or understand your points more fully? You may need to add phrases or sentences here and there, and even whole paragraphs in other places.

- **Delete content.** In early drafts, we often have material that seemed to make sense at the time we wrote it, but after rereading we realize that it's really not connected or relevant. As much as it hurts, this stuff needs to go. If you're concerned you might change your mind and want to add it back later, just save it in a different file.

- **Change existing content.** Maybe you discover upon rereading (or feedback has let you know) that some of your material is not accurate or not presented in a way that will appeal to your audience. For example, you may have confused some dates or written something too informal for an academic argument. These are the kinds of things that can be changed when you're revising to address purpose and audience.

- **Rearrange existing content.** Some of the feedback you got may tell you that the order of your draft doesn't always make sense to readers. For example, you may have provided some historical context to shed light on current events, but your peer readers suggested that a more engaging organization may be diving into the current events first, then following up with the historical context for a "how'd we get here?" kind of approach. When you reshuffle parts of your existing draft, you may also have to update some of the language to make sure everything makes sense in its new position in your revised draft.

REFLECT

Make a plan to act on the feedback you receive

Now that you've learned about your revision options, consider the feedback you received on your draft in Section 4.1. Identify two or three substantial things you want to address as you revise your draft. For example, you might have concluded that you need to add content. If so, where and why? How do you hope this new content will improve your draft? Make some notes about what you intend to change and why.

UNDERSTAND

Consider how one student revised to address purpose, audience, and organization

Our student Mujtaba "MJ" Aljutel worked hard on his argument-driven research essay with the following thesis:

> Stigma for people with disabilities exists in the workplace because the general public is not aware of the full spectrum of disabilities or the nuances and complexities of living with those conditions. Until a certain amount of awareness is established, there will continue to be de facto discrimination against people with disabilities.

He learned through peer feedback that his draft was effective in many ways, but it still needed some revision and reorganization to better achieve its purpose and reach its academic audience.

First, read MJ's draft and see some of the feedback a classmate gave him.

MJ's draft with comments from a peer reviewer

Combating Social and Workplace Stigma:

An Argument for Awareness of Disabilities

This sounds kind of vague. Can you connect it to the specific issue you're writing about?

Do you mean with statistics? Maybe add some here to show readers what you mean.

The modern world is engaged in a constant negotiation for equality. In recent years, big gains have been made for women's rights, marriage equality, and the rights of many marginalized groups. Inequality remains, however, and this is true in all areas of life. In the workplace, for instance, inequalities can be clearly observed and are sometimes even quantifiable. People with disabilities live with challenges that are rarely considered by others, and these challenges can be both numerous and daunting. Stigma for people with disabilities exists in the workplace because the general public is not aware of the full spectrum of disabilities or the nuances and complexities of living with those conditions. Until a certain amount of awareness is established, there will continue to be de facto discrimination against people with disabilities.

Part of the problem surrounding workplace discrimination is that many people do not know what a disability is. Simply put, they do not know what constitutes a disability and what does not. Dyslexia, for example, is an unseen disability. It is not immediately noticeable on meeting a person, and because of this, people might discriminate against people with dyslexia without even knowing it. According to Nicola Brunswick, a professor at Middlesex University, "43% of dyslexic students are identified as being dyslexic only after they have started at university" (1). So, it is clear that access to higher education for some disabled adults is available, but what does that say about progression? How does a dyslexic adult perform in the workplace?

Seems like you should define "disability" in this paragraph.

There are many contributing factors to success and failure in the workplace for those who face disability. For many employees with disabilities, there is a stigma attached to them as soon as they inform their employer of their condition. This stigma is evidenced in a research study focused on the experience of those with dyslexia. In a book chapter entitled "Disclosing Dyslexia: An Exercise in Self-Advocacy," University of Buckingham professors Alan Martin and David McLoughlin describe a study that found that about a third of dyslexic workers felt that if they told their boss about their condition they would be discriminated against. The same study found that "over half of the sample (54.5%) reported that they had had more than three jobs, with one person reporting that they had had 13 jobs since leaving university" (129). It is clear, then, that even though dyslexic adults are able to get an education as well as employment, there is still not a sense of stability.

You focus a lot on dyslexia. Should you talk about other disabilities too?

Lucy Paterson, a clinical psychologist in the NHS Tayside Psychological Therapies Service in Scotland, comments on this instability in her doctoral thesis, "Stigma, Social Comparison and Physiological Distress in Adults with a Learning Disability." The mental health implications in Paterson's work are important to note when looking at the issue of stigma in the workplace as a whole. "Research has shown that for people with a learning disability, as well as for other stigmatized groups, such stigmatization can have a negative impact on their psychological wellbeing, lowering their self-esteem and affecting their mood," writes Paterson (1). She claims that much of this workplace shame is internal, and it actually has to do with how the current working society chooses to define learning disabilities. The current "definitions do not consider the way in which carrying this label is experienced by the individuals" (9). Paterson later notes that feeling intellectually inadequate is one of the most common and devastating sources of stigma for humans to face; this feeling of inadequacy within those with disabilities comes about through comparisons to others within a community. She explains, "[p]erception of stigma was shown to be related to psychological distress and social comparison, and social comparison was shown to be related to psychological distress" (68). In order to break down these social comparisons, greater awareness of the realities of living with disabilities needs to be established in the community as a whole.

Martha Ross, in her article "The Last Stigma: Mental Illness and the Workplace," gives many examples of when the law does not do justice for those with mental health and disability issues. "Employers simply may choose not to consider an applicant they suspect has a mental illness," writes Ross, "and workers are hesitant to ask for time off

This part about the law seems to come out of the blue. Can you be clearer about how it's connected to the rest of your paper?

or other accommodations for their illness." She goes on to add that "this is especially true for people who work in any field—from law enforcement to high tech—where depression or anxiety could be viewed as 'a weakness.'" The problem with this dynamic is that it discourages employees from being honest with their employers because the employers see certain mental disabilities with a degree of permanence that does not take into account the medical options available to those with mental health and disability issues.

In a workplace mental health promotion campaign, the Canadian Mental Health Association claims that "mental health literacy in the workplace is critical to combating stigma" (21). If a higher priority were placed on mental health literacy, many of the issues surrounding stigma for workers with disabilities would be abolished from the outset. In a book chapter entitled "Stigma, Discrimination, and Employment Outcomes among Persons with Mental Health Disabilities," scholars Marjorie Baldwin and Steven Marcus report that "depression-related disorders will be the single leading cause of global disease burden by the year 2020" (53). So, since the growth of the problem is inevitable, effective solutions, techniques and strategies for the problem need to be in place as soon as possible. If this does not happen, then the trends of underemployment of those with disability will continue, creating a shameful shadow in every industry and field of business.

In addition to greater mental health literacy, there needs to be a change in attitude and perception around all those who face a wide spectrum of disabilities. In a study conducted by *Scope.org*, 30 percent of people with disabilities reported that they "would most like to see a change in the general public's attitudes, which underlines just how prevalent negative attitudes are"

(Aiden and McCarthy 12). After that, nearly a quarter of study participants suggested a change in government and authority attitudes is needed, and then nearly another quarter reported that a change in attitude is needed from health and social staff (Aiden and McCarthy 12). These statistics are startling. The social and workplace stigma surrounding disabilities is so strong that people with disabilities feel it even from the health professionals charged with helping them.

There are many reasons for businesses to hire, reward, and respect employees with disabilities. These employees are not weak links in the chain of command. In fact, in a *Forbes* article entitled "The Benefits of Disability in the Workplace," contributor Judy Owen reports that "providing accommodations result[s] [for employers] in such benefits as retaining valuable employees, improving productivity and morale, reducing workers' compensation and training costs, and improving company diversity." Accommodations can be as simple as allowing for a flexible work schedule or an expansion of dress code rules. They are low cost and often high reward.

Some accommodations are simple, but others aren't. Can you say more about how employers feel about that?

None of this is about angling for special treatment or special consideration. It is actually about having a chance to feel normal. In an article entitled "Mental Illness and Employment Discrimination," Heather Stuart explains that "for people with a serious mental disorder, employment is an important stepping-stone to recovery" (522). It is important for people with disabilities to work because it "is a normalizing factor that provides daily structure and routine, meaningful goals, improves self-esteem and self-image, increases finances, alleviates poverty, provides opportunities to make friendships and obtain social support, enriches quality of life and decreases disability" (522). And so, the complexities of living with a disability are too often and unjustly made simple. What people with disabilities really want and value are the exact things people without disability take for granted, and in order for this script to be flipped a general acceptance of disability must occur.

This is a powerful statement!!

Social pressure is usually required before meaningful legislation is put in place to ensure legal equality. In a book chapter entitled "The Stigma of Disabilities and the Americans with Disabilities Act," Michael Selmi raises some concerns about the original drafting of the act. For instance, the very defining of someone as disabled causes problems for Selmi. Who wants to admit they are disabled, just so they can enjoy the privileges offered to everyone else? "With greater social pressure or attention," Selmi argues, "Congress may have drafted more specific legislation, or at least addressed some of the imminent issues more clearly" (141). Selmi understands that without a certain amount of awareness and social pressure, the solutions offered by law will continue to fall short. In a democratic government, citizens get what they demand, and since workplace equality is in everyone's best interest, citizens must demand that equality for workers with disabilities.

Disabilities can be confusing and frustrating, for both the disabled and those trying to understand the disabled. The problems and challenges of fighting the stigma surrounding disabilities are complicated and vast. However, there is hope in fighting it. Simple awareness and an ethic of listening would allow employers to better understand their employees with disabilities. Social pressure from the broader community would allow those with invisible disabilities to get the legislation they need passed into law. Change will come with acceptance, and greater acceptance can be fostered within the workplace. The world is in a constant negotiation for equality, but in order to achieve it, we must realize that equality is in everyone's best interest—it is not something to negotiate.

Overall, I like what you're trying to do here! Try checking your overall organization and think about whether you focus too much on dyslexia early in the paper. Good luck!

Works Cited

Aiden, Hardeep, and Andrea McCarthy. "Current Attitudes towards Disabled People." *Scope,* May 2014, www.scope.org.uk/Scope/media/Images/Publication%20Directory/Current-attitudes-towards-disabled-people.pdf.

Baldwin, Marjorie L., and Steven C. Marcus. "Stigma, Discrimination, and Employment Outcomes among Persons with Mental Health Disabilities." *Work Accommodation and Retention in Mental Health*, edited by Izabela Z. Schultz and E. Sally Rogers, Springer, 2011, pp. 53-69.

Brunswick, Nicola, editor. *Supporting Dyslexic Adults in Higher Education and the Workplace*. Wiley, 2012.

Canadian Mental Health Association, Ontario. *Workplace Mental Health Promotion: A How-To Guide*. 2015, toronto.cmha.ca/wp-content/uploads/2017/03/WorkplaceMentalHealthPromotionGuide.pdf.

Centers for Disease Control and Prevention. "Disability Overview." *Centers for Disease Control and Prevention*, 1 Aug. 2017, www.cdc.gov/ncbddd/disabilityandhealth/disability.html.

Martin, Alan, and David McLoughlin. "Disclosing Dyslexia: An Exercise in Self-Advocacy." *Supporting Dyslexic Adults in Higher Education and the Workplace*, edited by Nicola Brunswick, Wiley, 2012, pp. 125-35.

Owen, Judy. "The Benefits of Disability in the Workplace." *Forbes*, 12 May 2012, www.forbes.com/sites/judyowen/2012/05/12/a-cost-benefit-analysis-of-disability-in-the-workplace/#117f12c13501.

Paterson, Lucy. "Stigma, Social Comparison and Physiological Distress in Adults with a Learning Disability." Dissertation, University of Edinburgh, 2007. *Edinburgh Research Archive*, www.era.lib.ed.ac.uk/handle/1842/2630.

Ross, Martha. "The Last Stigma: Mental Illness and the Workplace." *Mercury News*, 5 Mar. 2014, www.mercurynews.com/2014/03/05/the-last-stigma-mental-illness-and-the-workplace/.

Selmi, Michael. "The Stigma of Disabilities and the Americans with Disabilities Act." *Disability and Aging Discrimination: Perspectives in Law and Psychology*, edited by Richard L. Wiener and Steven L. Willborn, Springer, 2011, pp. 123-43.

Stuart, Heather. "Mental Illness and Employment Discrimination." *Current Opinion in Psychiatry*, vol. 19, no. 5, 2006, pp. 522-26.

After he got his paper back with his classmate's feedback, MJ made some notes to himself about how he needed to revise the draft. His notes helped him make a plan for finding additional content.

MJ's revision notes

- Find a good *inclusive* definition of "disability" (seen and unseen).

- Make sure I'm focusing on all disabilities, but use different ones as examples. That could help with the issue of talking so much about dyslexia in the first part. That makes it seem like the paper is more focused on it than on disabilities in general.

- Clear up the part about the law. I forgot to explain the ADA!

- Add more details on how health professionals contribute to stigmatization. Find at least one source.

- Add info on how employers feel about accommodations.

After taking time to consider his peer's feedback, MJ went back to his draft to fill in some holes and make existing passages clearer to his audience. Take a look at how MJ revised to address problem areas related to purpose, audience, and organization. Passages in bold represent text he changed to address those problem areas.

MJ's revised draft

Aljutel 1

Mujtaba "MJ" Aljutel

Professor Ingraham

ENGL 1010

27 November 2018

Combating Social and Workplace Stigma:

An Argument for Awareness of Disabilities

The modern world is engaged in a constant negotiation for equality. In recent years, big gains have been made for women's rights, marriage equality, and the rights of many

Aljutel 2

marginalized groups. Inequality remains, however, and **it is especially apparent in the treatment of individuals with real or perceived disabilities**. In the workplace, for instance, inequalities can be clearly observed. **For example, although people with disabilities are just as ambitious as others, 57 percent report feeling held back compared to 44 percent of those without disabilities (Layne).** People with disabilities live with challenges that are rarely considered by others, and these challenges can be both numerous and daunting. Stigma for people with disabilities exists in the workplace because the general public is not aware of the full spectrum of disabilities or the nuances and complexities of living with those conditions. Until a certain amount of awareness is established, there will continue to be de facto discrimination against people with disabilities.

Part of the problem surrounding workplace discrimination is that many people do not know what a disability is. **The Centers for Disease Control defines disability as "any condition of the body or mind (impairment) that makes it more difficult for the person with the condition to do certain activities (activity limitation) and interact with the world around them (participation restrictions)." Simply put, people can easily recognize that a person using a wheelchair has a disability, but the same people often overlook less visible disabilities.** Hearing loss, for example, is an unseen disability. It is not immediately noticeable on meeting a person, and because of this, hearing people might discriminate against people with hearing loss without even knowing it. **Similarly, learning disabilities, mental health disorders, and certain**

[Margin annotations:]

Revised vague language to be more specific.

Added statistics to support his point that inequalities can be quantified.

Defines important terms for readers.

Added more examples of invisible disabilities.

Aljutel 3

chronic physical conditions are not always recognized by the general public as disabilities.

There are many contributing factors to success and failure in the workplace for those who face disability. For many employees with disabilities, there is a stigma attached to them as soon as they inform their employer of their condition. This stigma is evidenced in a research study focused on the experience of those with dyslexia. In a book chapter entitled "Disclosing Dyslexia: An Exercise in Self-Advocacy," University of Buckingham professors Alan Martin and David McLoughlin describe a study that found that about a third of dyslexic workers felt that if they told their boss about their condition they would be discriminated against. The same study found that "over half of the sample (54.5%) reported that they had had more than three jobs, with one person reporting that they had had 13 jobs since leaving university" (129). It is clear, then, that even though **adults with disabilities** are able to get an education as well as employment, there is still not a sense of stability.

Lucy Paterson, a clinical psychologist in the NHS Tayside Psychological Therapies Service in Scotland, comments on this instability in her doctoral thesis, a "Stigma, Social Comparison and Physiological Distress in Adults with a Learning Disability." The mental health implications in Paterson's work are important to note when looking at the issue of stigma in the workplace as a whole. "Research has shown that for people with a learning disability, as well as for other stigmatized groups, such stigmatization can have a negative impact on their psychological wellbeing, lowering their self-esteem and affecting their mood," writes Paterson (1). She claims that

> Readers will now see this discussion of dyslexia as just one example among many types of disabilities.

> Connects the specific example to his argument.

Aljutel 4

much of this workplace shame is internal, and it actually has to do with how the current working society chooses to define learning disabilities. The current "definitions do not consider the way in which carrying this label is experienced by the individuals" (9). Paterson later notes that feeling intellectually inadequate is one of the most common and devastating sources of stigma for humans to face; this feeling of inadequacy within those with disabilities comes about through comparisons to others within a community. She explains, "[p]erception of stigma was shown to be related to psychological distress and social comparison, and social comparison was shown to be related to psychological distress" (68). In order to break down these social comparisons, greater awareness of the realities of living with disabilities needs to be established in the community as a whole.

In the United States, the Americans With Disabilities Act—passed into law in 1990—is thought to protect people with disabilities from discrimination. However, Martha Ross, in her article "The Last Stigma: Mental Illness and the Workplace," gives many examples of when the law does not do justice for those with mental health and disability issues. "Employers simply may choose not to consider an applicant they suspect has a mental illness," writes Ross, "and workers are hesitant to ask for time off or other accommodations for their illness." She goes on to add that "this is especially true for people who work in any field—from law enforcement to high tech—where depression or anxiety could be viewed as 'a weakness.'" The problem with this dynamic is that it discourages employees from being honest with their employers

A brief explanation of the law helps readers understand the relevance of this paragraph.

Aljutel 5

because the employers see certain mental disabilities with a degree of permanence that does not take into account the medical options available to those with mental health and disability issues.

In a workplace mental health promotion campaign, the Canadian Mental Health Association claims that "mental health literacy in the workplace is critical to combating stigma" (21). If a higher priority were placed on mental health literacy, many of the issues surrounding stigma for workers with mental health issues would be abolished from the outset. In a book chapter entitled "Stigma, Discrimination, and Employment Outcomes among Persons with Mental Health Disabilities," scholars Marjorie Baldwin and Steven Marcus report that "depression-related disorders will be the single leading cause of global disease burden by the year 2020" (53). So, since the growth of the problem is inevitable, effective solutions, techniques, and strategies for the problem need to be in place as soon as possible. If this does not happen, then the trends of underemployment of those with disability will continue, creating a shameful shadow in every industry and field of business.

In addition to greater mental health literacy, there needs to be a change in attitude and perception around all those who face a wide spectrum of disabilities. In a study conducted by *Scope.org*, 30 percent of people with disabilities reported that they "would most like to see a change in the general public's attitudes, which underlines just how prevalent negative attitudes are" (Aiden and McCarthy 12). After that, nearly a quarter of the study participants suggested a change

Aljutel 6

in government and authority attitudes is needed, and then nearly another quarter reported that a change in attitude is needed from health and social staff (Aiden and McCarthy 12). These statistics are startling. The social and workplace stigma surrounding disabilities is so strong that people with disabilities feel it even from the health professionals charged with helping them.

There are many reasons for businesses to hire, reward, and respect employees with disabilities. These employees are not weak links in the chain of command. In fact, in a *Forbes* article entitled "The Benefits of Disability in the Workplace," contributor Judy Owen reports that "providing accommodations result[s] [for employers] in such benefits as retaining valuable employees, improving productivity and morale, reducing workers' compensation and training costs, and improving company diversity." Accommodations can be as simple as allowing for a flexible work schedule or an expansion of dress code rules. They are low cost and often high reward.

Added a paragraph to fill out his argument.

Employers often don't know how to deal with people who ask for accommodations, especially when those employees do not have an obvious physical disability. Legal expert Joyce Smithey says that some employers respond to request for accommodations with "We don't do that as a policy" (qtd. in Gingold). Companies do not understand that it is in the interest of both parties to offer certain accommodations, but the fact that they do not, Smithey argues, is a problem "because that person is not asking to partake of a benefit that's offered in a policy; that person is asking for an accommodation they're entitled to under the law" (qtd. in Gingold). These

Aljutel 7

situations make it apparent that real people suffer from workplace stigma. The issue again goes back to simple and basic awareness, for "when a disability isn't immediately obvious, others...sometimes doubt it exists and accuse those who suffer from invisible conditions of simply angling for special treatment" (Gingold).

Added new source to the Works Cited list.

None of this is about angling for special treatment or special consideration. It is actually about having a chance to feel normal. In an article entitled "Mental Illness and Employment Discrimination," Heather Stuart explains that "for people with a serious mental disorder, employment is an important stepping-stone to recovery" (522). It is important for people with disabilities to work because it "is a normalizing factor that provides daily structure and routine, meaningful goals, improves self-esteem and self-image, increases finances, alleviates poverty, provides opportunities to make friendships and obtain social support, enriches quality of life and decreases disability" (522). And so, the complexities of living with a disability are too often and unjustly made simple. What people with disabilities really want and value are the exact things people without disability take for granted, and in order for this script to be flipped a general acceptance of disability must occur.

Kept a passage that his peer reviewer found valuable.

Social pressure is usually required before meaningful legislation is put in place to ensure legal equality. In a book chapter entitled "The Stigma of Disabilities and the Americans with Disabilities Act," Michael Selmi raises some concerns about the original drafting of the act. For instance, the very defining of someone as disabled causes problems for Selmi. Who wants to admit they are disabled, just so they can enjoy the privileges offered to everyone else? "With greater social pressure or attention," Selmi argues, "Congress may have drafted more specific legislation, or at least addressed some of the imminent issues more clearly" (141). Selmi understands that without a certain amount of awareness and social pressure, the solutions offered by law will continue to fall short. In a democratic government, citizens get what they demand, and since workplace equality is in everyone's best interest, citizens must demand that equality for workers with disabilities.

Disabilities can be confusing and frustrating, for both the disabled and those trying to understand the disabled. The problems and challenges of fighting the stigma surrounding disabilities are complicated and vast. However, there is hope in fighting it. Simple awareness and an ethic of listening would allow employers to better understand their employees with disabilities. Social pressure from the broader community would allow those with invisible disabilities to get the legislation they need passed into law. Change will come with acceptance, and greater acceptance can be fostered within the workplace. The world is in a constant negotiation for equality, but in order to achieve it, we must realize that equality is in everyone's best interest—it is not something to negotiate.

Aljutel 9

Works Cited

Aiden, Hardeep, and Andrea McCarthy. "Current Attitudes towards Disabled People." *Scope,* May 2014, www.scope .org.uk/Scope/media/Images/Publication%20Directory/ Current-attitudes-towards-disabled-people.pdf.

Baldwin, Marjorie L., and Steven C. Marcus. "Stigma, Discrimination, and Employment Outcomes among Persons with Mental Health Disabilities." *Work Accommodation and Retention in Mental Health*, edited by Izabela Z. Schultz and E. Sally Rogers, Springer, 2011, pp. 53-69.

Canadian Mental Health Association, Ontario. *Workplace Mental Health Promotion: A How-To Guide.* 2015, https://toronto.cmha.ca/wp-content/uploads/2017/03/ WorkplaceMentalHealthPromotionGuide.pdf.

Centers for Disease Control and Prevention. "Disability Overview." *Centers for Disease Control and Prevention*, 1 Aug. 2017, www .cdc.gov/ncbddd/disabilityandhealth/disability.html.

Gingold, Naomi. "People with 'Invisible Disabilities' Fight for Understanding." *NPR*, 8 Mar. 2015, www.npr.org/2015/03/ 08/391517412/people-with-invisible-disabilities-fight -for-understanding.

Layne, Rachel. "The Hidden Cost of Disability Discrimination." *CBS News*, 16 Oct. 2017, www.cbsnews.com/news/ the-hidden-cost-of-disability-discrimination/.

Martin, Alan, and David McLoughlin. "Disclosing Dyslexia: An Exercise in Self-Advocacy." *Supporting Dyslexic Adults in Higher Education and the Workplace*, edited by Nicola Brunswick, Wiley, 2012, pp. 125-35.

Owen, Judy. "The Benefits of Disability in the Workplace." *Forbes*, 12 May 2012, www.forbes.com/sites/judyowen/ 2012/05/12/a-cost-benefit-analysis-of-disability-in-the -workplace/#117f12c13501.

Deleted entry for a source he decided not to use.

Added entries for new sources quoted in the paper.

Aljutel 10

Paterson, Lucy. "Stigma, Social Comparison and Physiological Distress in Adults with a Learning Disability." Dissertation, University of Edinburgh, 2007. *Edinburgh Research Archive*, www.era.lib.ed.ac.uk/handle/1842/2630.

Ross, Martha. "The Last Stigma: Mental Illness and the Workplace." *Mercury News*, 5 Mar. 2014, www.mercurynews.com/2014/03/05/the-last-stigma-mental-illness-and-the-workplace/.

Selmi, Michael. "The Stigma of Disabilities and the Americans with Disabilities Act." *Disability and Aging Discrimination: Perspectives in Law and Psychology*, edited by Richard L. Wiener and Steven L. Willborn, Springer, 2011, pp. 123-43.

Stuart, Heather. "Mental Illness and Employment Discrimination." *Current Opinion in Psychiatry*, vol. 19, no. 5, 2006, pp. 522-26.

APPLY

Revise your draft to improve purpose, audience, and organization

You've read an example of how MJ carefully considered the feedback he got from peers, made some notes about what to revise, and then revised his paper to improve the ways it achieves its purpose, addresses its audience, and uses an organization that makes sense. Now it's your turn.

Using the notes you made in the Reflect activity in Section 4.2, revise your draft to improve the way it addresses purpose and audience. If any of your sentences or paragraphs seemed out of sequence, revise parts of the organization as well.

4.3　Revise to polish your draft

In Section 4.2, we encouraged you to think about composing a writing project as if you were building a house: build a strong foundation first by focusing on purpose, audience, and organization, then work on the finer details to create the finished look you want. In that section, we focused on the bottom two "bricks" in the house. Now it's time to focus on the top two bricks: the details that will make your final draft shine!

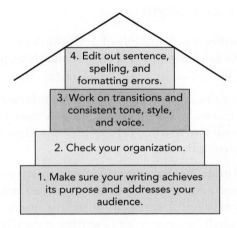

In this section, we'll guide you through ways to consider issues such as creating effective transitions between paragraphs and sentences, adjusting the formality of your style, making sure your sentences are grammatically correct, and proofreading your draft for spelling errors.

Using effective transitions

Transitions are words and phrases that help your draft have better coherence. In other words, they act like direction signals to help readers follow along with your thoughts more easily. What did the transition "in other words" in the previous sentence signal to you? Transitions typically help writers indicate the following moves in a piece of writing:

- **Introduce an example:** *for example, for instance, specifically, in this case*
- **Compare things:** *also, likewise, similarly*

- **Contrast things:** *but, however, on the other hand*
- **Indicate relationship in time:** *before, after, then, now, later, meanwhile, subsequently*
- **Show cause or effect:** *as a result, because, therefore, consequently*
- **Indicate place in a sequence:** *first, second, next, last*

In these ways, transitions serve as important hints at what's coming next for readers. When you see the phrase "in other words," for example, you know that what's coming next will be a restating of something you just read that you may not have understood completely.

Adjusting tone and style

Once you've put together a well-organized draft that's full of smart ideas, you want to make sure those ideas are expressed as clearly as possible. That's where style and tone come in.

Style refers to the *way* the piece is written. A more informal style is very casual or personal and freely uses a conversational tone. A more formal style, which you need for most academic writing, is reasoned and objective without becoming stuffy and overly complicated.

Tone refers to the attitude you have toward what you are writing about. Depending on the purpose and audience, as well as the subject matter, a writer might choose a tone that is respectful, sarcastic, objective, angry, or any number of other attitudes. Research-based academic writing typically calls for an objective or measured tone, but your specific purpose and audience might lead you to strike a somewhat different tone in all or part of your writing.

Style and tone can be tricky to manage because they don't rely on hard-and-fast rules. One way to stay on top of your style and tone is through *diction*—the words and phrases you choose to use. If you've ever had someone write on your papers "word choice" or "awk," a problem with diction was probably at work. As you write and revise, consider how the following seven guidelines can help you improve your writing.

1. **Consider connotation.** Words have definitions, but they also have connotations—the emotions or associations the words evoke in a reader. If you were trying to convey the low cost of an item, you could call it "cheap" (which often has a negative connotation) or "inexpensive" (which usually has a more positive connotation). Carefully consider your audience, and try to avoid choosing words that will have a negative connotation for them.

2. **Avoid clichés.** These are overused sayings such as "avoid it like the plague" and "like a kid in a candy store." Instead of using a cliché, ask yourself what you really mean and use precise language to express it.

3. **Eliminate wordiness.** We'll let you in on a little secret. Teachers are partly to blame when students use more words than necessary to express an idea. We often focus too much on required word counts for writing assignments instead of the content. Saying "due to the fact that" instead of "because" is great for boosting your word count, but not so great when it comes to streamlining your sentences. Consider the following longer phrases and their more efficient substitutes as you revise.

Wordy Phrase		Better Choice
despite the fact that	→	even though
in the event that	→	if
with the exception of	→	except

4. **Avoid pretentious language.** When we feel insecure about the language we're using, we often try to make ourselves sound "smarter" by using what our grandmothers would have called a "highfalutin" word instead of a more precise word that suits our context, style, and tone. This often happens when we search a thesaurus for a replacement word and select one without really understanding what it means. For instance, if I wrote the sentence "The church ladies had a spread of homemade food on the tables," and I wanted to replace "spread," online thesaurus tools might suggest the word "diaspora," a word that sounds interesting but doesn't at all convey what I meant in my original sentence.

5. **Use contractions carefully.** Contractions are those mashup words we use to combine two words into one using an apostrophe: "I'm" for "I am" and "don't" for "do not" are examples. Formal writing often frowns on using contractions. Unless you've gotten the OK from your instructor to use them, it's probably best to avoid them.

6. **Use active verbs.** Verbs convey the action in a sentence. Try to construct your sentences and clauses with the person or thing doing the action at the front, followed by a verb that expresses the action. Active verbs allow you to write "Wide receiver Thompson sprinted to the end zone for a touchdown" instead of the more boring (and wordier) "The ball was carried by wide receiver Thompson to the end zone for a touchdown."

7. **Avoid weak verbs.** Because we just advised you to use active verbs, it may sound like overkill to now advise you to avoid weak verbs. But we mean "weak verbs" in a very particular sense: "be" verbs. "Be" verbs are variations of the verb "to be," so they include *am, is, are, was,* and *were.* Because verbs convey the action in a sentence, "be" verbs are really low-energy performers. They don't actually do anything in a sentence. You'll be much better off if you substitute a boring "be" verb with one that more precisely indicates action.

Addressing common sentence-level errors

Errors in sentences make it harder for readers to understand your intended meaning. Even when an error doesn't completely obscure your idea, it can still distract your reader and, in some cases, undermine your credibility. Making your writing as free of errors as you can shows respect for your readers and helps you get your point across. But even the most experienced writers can have a hard time identifying sentence-level errors in their own writing. Below are two bits of advice that can help with this process.

Check that your modifiers are placed correctly.   Modifiers are words, phrases, or clauses that describe, expand, or limit the noun they modify. In your mind, the idea you want to convey in your sentence makes perfect sense even if the modifier placement is off. For readers, though, out-of-place modifiers are confusing. Consider this example:

> Because its claws hadn't been trimmed in months, the wood floor showed scratches from the family dog.

Clearly the writer meant to communicate that the dog's claws were so long that they were scratching the floor, but as written, the sentence implies that the wood floor has claws that haven't been trimmed. To make the sentence clearer, start by moving the modifier so that it logically refers to the noun it modifies (dog):

> The wood floor showed scratches from the family dog because its claws hadn't been trimmed in months.

This version is better, but the pronoun "its" may still cause confusion for readers. Does it refer to the wood floor or the dog? Editing the sentence further can clear up any confusion:

> The wood floor showed scratches from the family dog, ~~because its~~ ^whose^ claws hadn't been trimmed in months.

Check that pronouns agree with the words they stand in for.   Singular pronouns have to refer to singular nouns, and plural pronouns have to refer to plural nouns. Consider the following sentence.

> Though the term "millennial" can evoke images of helicopter parents and sheltered children, they are also known to be very team-oriented and sociable.

The plural pronoun "they" doesn't agree with the singular subject phrase "the term 'millennial.'" The person who wrote this sentence likely made the error because she was thinking about the plural nouns "helicopter parents and sheltered children" that follow the subject. Correcting the sentence, however, requires more than simply making the pronoun and verb singular as depicted below.

> Though the term "millennial" can evoke images of helicopter parents
> and sheltered children, ~~they are~~ *it is* also known to be very team-oriented
> and sociable.

Changing the pronoun and verb doesn't improve the sentence enough because the end of the sentence doesn't make sense after the change. In this case, the writer would need to edit the entire sentence so that it works as a unit.

> Though the term "millennial" can evoke *negative* images of helicopter parents
> and sheltered children, ~~they are~~ *people in this generation are* also known to be very team-oriented
> and sociable.

Because you already know what you want to say, you might not notice sentence-level problems that could distract or confuse your readers. As you review your draft to check sentence mechanics, consider various resources available to you. Your instructor may have assigned a handbook or directed you to online resources. And as you know, we're big fans of our campus writing centers. You may also want to work with a writing center consultant at your school to get another perspective on your writing.

Correcting spelling, typing, and punctuation errors

When we write, we all sometimes have clumsy fingers that spell or type our words wrong. To catch some of those mistakes, try reading your draft out loud to hear the errors as you read. You might also have someone else read it out loud while you follow along on the page. Often, the person reading it out loud will automatically correct it, but if you're reading along on the page (or screen), the disconnect between what you see and what you hear can help you find those little mistakes that need to be fixed before you submit a final draft.

REFLECT

Proofread backwards—one sentence at a time

This sounds like a huge irony, but one of the biggest obstacles to proofreading well is getting our brains out of the way. It's true! When we read over our drafts, our brains often automatically supply the "correct" version in our minds from the context that appears earlier in the draft and ignore errors that are actually on the page or screen. That's because we're reading our drafts from beginning to end and our brains are programmed to make sense of things—even when the words in front of us don't actually make complete sense. One really good strategy for proofreading involves limiting the brain's "autocorrect" impulse.

So, here's your challenge. Open a copy of your most recent version of the draft you're working on. Instead of reading it from start to finish looking for sentence problems, start at the last sentence and read it sentence by sentence from end to beginning. Make some notes as you're "proofreading backwards" about the sentence errors and typos you found. Then, write a paragraph reflecting on your experience of proofreading backwards. What kinds of sentence mistakes did you find? How was it similar to or different from your current proofreading practice?

UNDERSTAND

Compare drafts to see improvement in style, tone, and mechanics

In Section 4.2, we focused on revising to ensure that your draft is generally fulfilling your purpose and reaching your audience in an organized manner. Now, let's look at how revising that focuses on improving style, tone, and mechanics is also an important part of our writing processes. Following are two paragraphs—one unrevised and one revised—that demonstrate how addressing style, tone, and sentence level problems can help improve your writing.

As you read the unrevised paragraph, notice the words a peer has identified and numbered as potential problem areas that we've discussed.

Unrevised paragraph

When students come to college, a lot of us have anxiety that
could be helped [1] if we could bring our beloved pets with us to school or
adopt a mutt [2] or a cat once we're [3] moved in. Some people say that pets
in dorms are [4] messy, stinky, and possibly dangerous, but they haven't
kept an open mind about how a pet-friendly policy could actually work.
Due to the fact that [5] having pets on campus could improve the lives of
students, we should consider ways to allow pets in some cases.

1 *Passive verb:* The verb *could be helped* is not active. As written, it makes *anxiety* the star of the sentence instead of *students* who have anxiety.

2 *Connotation:* For some people, *mutt* has a bad connotation. They associate the word with dangerous—maybe even rabid—dogs roaming the streets ready to attack people.

3 *Contraction:* This contraction may work perfectly well, but it's worth noticing and considering if it's appropriate in this context.

4 *Weak verb:* *Are* is one of the *be* verbs that don't convey much energy in the sentence. It's not grammatically wrong, but consider whether a stronger, more active verb would improve the sentence.

5 *Wordiness:* The phrase *due to the fact that* is a really wordy way to say *because.*

After considering this feedback, the student revised the paragraph.

Revised paragraph

When anxious students come to college, we would benefit [1] if we
could bring our beloved pets with us to school or adopt a rescue dog [2]
or cat once we're [3] moved in. Some people say that pets in dorms
create huge messes, stink up the rooms, and threaten the safety of [4]
human and pet residents, but these people haven't kept an open mind
about how a pet-friendly policy could actually work. Because having [5]

pets on campus could potentially improve the lives of students, we should consider ways to allow pets in some cases.

1. **Active verb:** The writer revised the first sentence to make students, not anxiety, the focus. Moving the reference to anxiety earlier in the sentence allows students ("we") to be the subject and use a more active verb, *would benefit*.

2. **Connotation:** The term *rescue dog* has a more positive connotation than *mutt*.

3. **Contraction:** The writer considered changing *we're* to *we are* but decided that the contraction works in this context. It's OK not to make changes sometimes as long as you at least think about whether something is working well in the draft.

4. **Strong verb:** To avoid the boring verb *are*, the student rewrote the sentence to use the active verbs *create*, *stink*, and *threaten*.

5. **Wordiness:** The student eliminated the wordy phrase *due to the fact that* with a more concise single word that conveys the same meaning: *because*.

As you can see, taking the time to consider your word choices—your diction—when revising is an important step in making your draft more effective.

APPLY

Revise your draft to improve sentence-level issues

Using the advice in Section 4.3 and the notes you made in the Reflect activity about proofreading backwards, revise your draft to correct minor errors and improve your sentences overall.

Chapter 4 Project
Reflect on your experience of working with feedback

In Chapter 4, you've had opportunities to get feedback from others to help you make sure that your draft is rhetorically effective. First, you considered "big picture" issues: achieving the draft's purpose and reaching its intended audience in a well-organized way. Then, you looked at more detailed parts of your draft that contribute to style and tone, including transitions, word choice, and sentence mechanics.

Write a thoughtful reflection (one to two pages) on your experience of peer review and, if applicable, responding to feedback from your instructor. In your reflection, consider how you'll use peer review and instructor feedback in the future to help you improve your writing.

5

Reading Actively and Critically to Create Meaning

☆ Achieve *If your instructor has assigned them, you can watch the videos for this chapter, complete the Reflect and Apply activities, and work on the Chapter Project in Achieve.*

5.1 Develop active and critical reading strategies

You may remember learning about active or critical reading in high school. The terms *active* and *critical* describe the thought processes we use when we read to create meaning from a text. What do we actually mean when we talk about "active reading" or "critical reading"? How is this kind of reading different from casual reading?

When we read casually, we read for our own entertainment or simply to find information or facts that we assume are accurate. For example, when we check our Fandango app to find a movie time, we assume that if the app says the movie we want to see is scheduled to start at 7:05 p.m. at our local theatre, then it's going to start at 7:05 p.m. We don't need to think critically about the words on the screen because we assume they're correct.

When we read actively, however, we work to understand the details of what an author is trying to say. And when we read critically, we go even further, evaluating the evidence or reasoning an author uses to support main points or arguments, and then forming our own ideas about the text based on our analysis. Many of the texts you will encounter in college invite a deeper kind of interaction between reader and text, one that encourages readers to take an active and critical perspective.

In this section, we'll introduce you to some practices that will help improve your active and critical reading.

Annotating to mark important points and record your thoughts

Annotating simply means making notes on something you're reading to help you process it as you're reading it, then later recall what you read.

Annotating creates a record of your active and critical reading. When you read something that you want to engage with, it helps to make notes on the text. We suggest the following strategies:

- Underline passages you want to remember.
- Circle terms you need to define.
- Use the margins to make comments or ask questions.
- Draw on the text if it helps you remember a concept or make connections to another important idea or text. For example, arrows pointing to other passages or stars drawn to indicate that something is important can help you recall that a passage is important.

Questioning the text before, during, and after reading

Reading actively will help you connect your own experiences to what you're reading. You can then use that connection to help you understand and evaluate the reading. The key to reading actively and critically is to question the text and your understanding of it as thoroughly as you can. This questioning happens at all stages of your reading, but the kinds of questions can be broken into three different phases:

- Phase 1: Questions to ask *before* you read
- Phase 2: Questions to ask *as* you read
- Phase 3: Questions to ask *after* you read

Phase 1: Questioning the text *before* you read.   To read a text actively and critically, start with a questioning mind by "previewing" the text. Any time you encounter a text for the first time, even before you read the whole text, ask yourself some questions and annotate as you look it over:

- **What do I already know about this topic?** Typically, a text's title and first few lines will give you some clue about what the topic is. Always look for an abstract of the text—a brief summary provided by the author—as well, since you will find key ideas from the article located there. Think about what you already know about the topic. What have you read about this topic before? What personal experience have you had with it? What have you heard from friends about it? What have you heard about it in the news lately? Recalling what you already know about a topic can help you respond to the ideas you find in a text.

- **What visual clues are available to help me understand the text?** Skim the whole text, looking for headings—subtitles that introduce sections of the text, often in bold or larger font, different from the body text. Likewise, look for phrases or words that are meant to stand out because they are underlined, bolded, or appear in italics. These are keywords that will help you sharpen your understanding of the text.

- **Where and when was the text published?** Understanding the type of text you're seeing and where it was published can give you a heads up about the text. For example, if you know that the text is an article published on a local television station's website, chances are that the content will deal mostly with issues important to the local community, not a worldwide audience. Likewise, knowing the date of a text's publication can also provide insight. Consider what was going on in the world or in your community when the piece was published. How would the timing affect readers' responses to the piece? How does it affect your perspective?

- **Who published the text?** All publications have agendas, but some are more apparent than others. For example, we expect newsletters published by a religious institution or business to explicitly promote the values and interests of their organizations. Even publications often assumed to be objective, such as news magazines and newspapers, are not neutral. Each has an editorial board that shapes both the published content and the angle from which topics are explored. For example, the *Wall Street Journal* is typically thought to be politically conservative or to the right of the political center, while the *Washington Post* is characterized as left of the political center, or more liberal. Thinking about the writer's background and the publication's editorial perspective helps you understand the text on a deeper level.

Phase 2: Questioning the text *as* you read. Sometimes, if we are tired or simply not interested in something we are asked to read, we "read" the text just by moving our eyes over the words without really thinking about what those words say or how the text makes its point. Active and critical reading won't allow us to read so passively. Instead, we have to respond to what we are reading and ask questions as we go. The questions you ask will vary with each piece you encounter, but some typical questions that readers often ask themselves to connect with a text and uncover its meaning include the following:

- What is the text trying to say? What's its main point?
- How do I know that's the main point?
- In what ways do I agree or disagree with the writer's ideas?
- To whom is the text speaking?
- What kinds of support or evidence does the text rely on? Possibilities include facts, careful reasoning, the author's informed opinions, personal experience, and emotion.
- Is the support credible? For example, if the information is largely based on the writer's opinion, is it an *informed* opinion—does the author have credible expertise? If the information includes facts, do the facts come from reliable sources?
- Is there enough evidence to support the main ideas?
- Have I looked up the definitions of words I don't understand to make sure I fully comprehend the text?
- How does the text use photographs or other visuals?
- What questions does this text implicitly raise but not explicitly state or answer?
- Do I think the text's conclusions are valid?

Phase 3: Questioning the text *after* you read. After you read a text, you want to extend your understanding of it and create meanings for yourself. The idea here is to keep thinking about the text and what it means after you finish reading it. But to understand a text thoroughly, most of us have to read it more than once. And, to some extent, we have to read as skeptics. Do you really believe what it says? Is the message consistent? How do you know you can trust the information?

As you reread and skim your notes, continue to ask the kinds of questions you asked yourself when you read the piece the first time but add specific questions to your personal, informed stance:

- What questions do I still have after reading about this topic?
- What surprised me about what I read?
- What was confusing?
- What connections can I make between this text and others I've read?
- How does my understanding of the text now compare to what I expected to find when I first looked it over?
- What potentially contradictory explanations or arguments are left out of this text?

When you've actively and critically read a text, you can do everything from summarizing it in your own words to evaluating the text using your own informed voice.

REFLECT

Consider your reading practices

In Section 5.1, we've asked you to think about actively and critically reading texts by approaching them in three phases. Like most readers, you're busy, and you might sometimes feel like this careful reading takes too much time. The truth is that reading actively and critically is a skill; the more you practice it, the better you get. And the more careful reading you do, the easier it will be for you to apply the three phases we discussed. Many readers get to the point where this practice becomes automatic. You'll get there too!

Take a few minutes to reflect on your practice of active reading by answering the following questions.

1. Describe some strategies you already use when you read a text carefully. For example, do you jot down questions in the margin? Look up vocabulary words? Read through more than once? Check for an abstract? Write about your process.

2. What specific advice about reading do you think you could use to approach texts in the future? List some active reading strategies you want to try out.

See Jay's three-phase active reading process

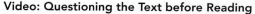

We want to show you what it might look like for a student to read—and understand—a challenging text using the strategies of annotating and questioning the text in three phases. In the two videos and annotated text that follow, you'll see how Jay reads an article called "Death: The End We All Have to Face(book)" by Christine Martorana.

Phase 1: Jay previews the text.   In this video, Jay previews the article by looking at the title, headings, and first paragraph. He asks himself questions about where the text was published and what experience he already has with the topic.

Video: Questioning the Text before Reading

Phase 2: Jay annotates and questions the text while reading.   As Jay reads the article, he annotates it by circling or underlining important parts and making notes in the margins. As you read through the article he's annotated on the following pages, notice how he identifies the main points and supporting evidence, defines unfamiliar words, and asks questions to follow up on later, perhaps in a class discussion of the article.

Death: The End We All Have to Face(book)

CHRISTINE MARTORANA

> *Christine Martorana was a graduate student at Florida State University when she wrote this essay. In 2015, a longer version of it was published in the digital magazine* Harlot, *which is "dedicated to exploring rhetoric in everyday life." In this piece, Martorana explores the phenomenon of people posting messages to Facebook pages of deceased friends or family.*

When my friend Aaron unexpectedly died several years ago, I gained firsthand experience with a growing online phenomenon: mourners turning to online spaces following the death of a loved one. In what follows, I present details from Aaron's Facebook page in order to illustrate two specific observations: (1) Digital technologies are reconfiguring the permanence of death, inviting the living to recreate the deceased as a heavenly intermediary, and (2) this continued virtual existence of the deceased alongside the constant accessibility of digital technologies is opening a space for death-related egocentrism.

main points

link or mediator

Aaron has 616 Facebook friends. His profile picture is a close-up of his face, eyebrows slightly furrowed, sunglasses resting atop his head. A quick scroll through his Facebook photos reveals his active social life and love for the outdoors. His Facebook wall contains countless posts from friends and family featuring messages, photos, and videos. Aaron's Facebook page appears typical; however, a closer look reveals that although Aaron's friends continue to post messages to him, Aaron has not responded to these messages in more than five years. This is because Aaron unexpectedly passed away in 2008—and yet, his Facebook page remains active.[1]

Aaron's Facebook page is an example of a growing phenomenon: mourners turning to online spaces following the death of a loved one.[2] In the face of death, everything from blogs to YouTube series, Instagram feeds, and Tumblr pages are emerging, "bringing the conversation about bereavement and the deceased into a very public forum. [Users] seem eager for spaces to express not just the good stuff that litters everyone's Facebook newsfeed, but also the painful" (Seligson). After Aaron's passing, I became one of these online users.

Dying in a Digital Age

Digital technologies have seeped into practically every aspect of our lives: eating, sleeping, exercising, driving, shopping, dating, entertainment—and now, dying. As *USA Today* writer Laura Petrecca notes, we are living in the age of "Mourning 2.0," where digital technology is inseparable from grieving, forever changing the ways in which we cope with lost loved ones. Grieving, which used to be "private and personal" (Farber 6), now regularly occurs online. Aaron's Facebook page provides evidence that this is indeed true: "Mourning 2.0" is in full swing.

His page not only demonstrates our "ability to instantly congregate, at least virtually, and commiserate" (Brondou), it also supports two valuable claims regarding this age of digital mourning. First, digital technologies are reconfiguring the permanence of death, inviting the living to recreate the deceased as a heavenly intermediary—a being with access to both our physical world and a heavenly world beyond. Second, this continued virtual existence of the deceased alongside the constant accessibility of digital technologies is opening a space for death-related egocentrism—a self-serving attitude that shifts responses to death from mourning loss to requesting help.

Not Physically Here, but Still Present

The vast majority of us—73% according to Pew Internet Research—lead both physical and virtual lives. This impacts not only how we live from day to day but also our experiences with death. For although we might stand graveside and bid farewell to a loved one, we can later stand with our digital technologies and access that person's social media profile. From this perspective, death is a force with the power to remove our physical bodies yet unable to eliminate our virtual ones.

My experiences with Aaron and his Facebook page testify to this. Although I have not seen Aaron's physical body in more than five years, I see his face on a regular basis. With just a few keystrokes, I can pull up his profile picture, the same picture that has been there since the day he passed away. This photo, with its static, fixed quality, seems to freeze time, maintaining a visual representation of Aaron as he was while physically alive. When I look at his Facebook page, I see the same teenage boy I remember; as he looks back at me from the computer screen, it is as if he continues to exist virtually despite his physical passing.

The deceased remain frozen in online spaces; the presence of their virtual profiles, pictures, and status updates belie their physical absence.

My Digital Guardian Angel

The digital platform also impacts our grieving process. According to Dr. April Hames, there are six stages of healthy grief: acknowledgment of loss, reaction to loss, recollection of the departed, relinquishing attachments, readjusting, and reinvesting (qtd. in King). My observations of Aaron's page suggest that the fourth stage, relinquishing attachments, is complicated by Facebook. That is, since we can often access Facebook pages even after Facebook users have passed away, this digital platform offers a new method of grieving, one that does not require relinquishment.

marriage & family therapist = credible source

true? not sure

Specifically, the Facebook users I observed, rather than relinquishing attachments to Aaron, have evolved their attachments to Aaron so that they come to view him as an intercessor between this physical world and another cosmic, divine space. This is evidenced in posts like these:

- "I GOT INTO MICHIGAN YESTERDAY! omg Im still soo excited.. tell God I said thanks for getting me in cuz I know he had his hand in that."

- "so it was snowing this mornign and i definately think it had something to do with you becuase you would have been BOUNCING off teh walls at the first snow. haha. so it made me smile. ps. you think you could work out a snow day sometime soon??"

- "please watch over us all during this holiday season & maybe you talk the Big man into some snow? because this rain simply will not do."

- "Lots of people need prayers and watching over…I know you're the invisible hero in action…the angel of our prayers…thanks."

friends are still "talking" to him on FB page = not relinquished

Through these posts, we can see how Aaron's virtual presence continues as well as how living Facebook users communicate directly with Aaron in the same way they might offer a prayer to a divine being. That is, instead of *letting go of their attachments* to Aaron, they have *evolved these attachments* so that Aaron moves from a lost loved one to an available intermediary, one who can communicate with God, control the weather, and hear prayers.

?? People do this in real life, too. Grandma still talks to Uncle Frank...but that's private, not public.

I am not the first to consider the impact of the digital on grieving. Robert Dobler offers a related discussion of grief as it manifests on the social networking site MySpace. According to Dobler's analysis of MySpace pages of the departed, MySpace users post "personal expressions of grief [in an] attempt to mitigate the permanence of the loss by keeping up a direct correspondence with the departed" (176). I have found similar practices on Facebook; both social media sites offer a space in which users can construct new relationships with the deceased, evolving their attachments instead of relinquishing them.

Is MySpace still around??

However, whereas Dobler's analysis leads him to characterize the deceased as a "ghost" (185), my observations suggest otherwise. A ghost implies a haunting, restless spirit; however, the posts on Aaron's wall do not cast Aaron as either haunting or restless. Rather, a more appropriate image might be that of a guardian angel, what one of Aaron's friends calls "the invisible hero in action" —a comforting intercessor watching over the living, providing services and guidance as needed and requested.

Aaron = guardian angel to his friends

It's All about Me

Recognizing the ways in which Facebook reconfigures the permanence of death brings us to my second observation regarding this age of digital mourning: death-related egocentrism. That is, instead of explicitly mourning—or even mentioning—Aaron's death, Facebook users view his continued virtual existence as an outlet for them to share concerns and needs *about their own lives*, positing Aaron as an ever-available heavenly intermediary. The posts I have observed express candid requests for help from Aaron, explicitly describing the ways in which he can positively intervene in the lives of the living:

- "please help me finish up my last year of school. give me the strength to get through this so i can finally be a RVT!"

- "thanks for getting me through my surgery well. now please help my dad get through his!"

- "Thank you for helping me out with my Mirco exam on thursday means alot....Plz help me out this week for finals!! Miss you"

what Aaron's friends leave on his FB page now

As evidenced by the above posts, the living Facebook users seem to view Aaron as a heavenly intermediary through an egocentric focus, casting Aaron as an intercessor present and available to *meet their needs*.

The constant accessibility of digital technologies undoubtedly feeds into this online egocentrism. We spend countless hours uploading pictures, videos, and details about ourselves to multiple social media platforms. Why? Because we can.

More specifically, we can no matter where we are: work, school, the grocery store, the bathroom. The omnipresence of social media, the fact that we can post from anywhere at any time, promotes an attitude of "individualism [and] self-gratification" (Taylor). Every thought, no matter how inconsequential or fleeting, can be and often is digitally documented, uploaded, and shared.

In the context of Aaron's Facebook page, then, we can consider the ways in which our ability to access Facebook via any number of digital devices invites these egocentric posts. Not only do we have constant access to Aaron's page, but also we have constant access to a page where the Facebook user is physically unable to participate. The only activity on Aaron's page, therefore, is what living users post, turning his page into a breeding ground for egocentricity, a space that gradually becomes all about the living users. A quick look at some numbers illustrates this point:

Months since Aaron's Passing	% of Posts That Are Egocentric
2	1%
6	30%
24	77%

Today, more than five years after his death, an egocentric focus dominates, suggesting that the longer Aaron is physically absent, the more likely living Facebook users are to conceptualize his continued virtual existence from a self-serving perspective.

Death and iCulture

Most teenagers today (at least in mainstream contexts) cannot recall a time without the Internet. Constituting what has been called the "iCulture" generation, teens occupy a narcissistic sphere dominated by "'ME'-centered profiles [and] the rise of technologies like cell phones that allow individuals to continually wonder, 'Who's called Me? Or texted Me?'" ("The Rise of iCulture"). Perhaps it should not be surprising, then, that egocentrism characterizes the majority of the posts on Aaron's wall. Aaron was, after all, a teenager when he died as were the majority of his friends. Just as many of us today cannot imagine relationships without the existence of Facebook and other social media venues, will we also soon be unable to imagine death without such platforms?

We are already experiencing what might be considered the next move of "Mourning 2.0" in such things as "Living Headstones"—which have, interestingly, been described as "similar to a personal Facebook page" (*Living Headstones*)—and funeral webcasting, the live-streaming and digital recording of funeral services. It seems that the patterns and behaviors I have observed on Aaron's Facebook page are just one part of a larger shift in the mourning and memorialization practices of this iCulture generation.

Sounds a little creepy

Shaping Our Post-Death Identities

As Aaron's page reveals, the virtual choices we make today, although perhaps seemingly inconsequential in the present moment, have the potential for indefinite impact. These choices include …

- *The profile pictures we post:* When Aaron posted his current profile picture, he was unknowingly posting his final profile picture, the one that would greet me each time I access his page, forever positing this image as the face of his post-death virtual identity.

what will be on FB after we die

- *The messages we type:* The messages Aaron posted to his own wall prior to his death, the information he shared in his "About Me" section, and his list of favorite quotes are permanently and publicly displayed on his Facebook page, indefinitely connected to his post-death virtual identity.

- *The Facebook friends we accept:* Throughout my observation of Aaron's page, I discovered that only those users who were Facebook friends with Aaron *before* he died can interact with his page *after* his death. This means that, in selecting his Facebook friends, Aaron was unknowingly and simultaneously selecting who would help construct his post-death virtual identity.

Ultimately, my hope is that this discussion of Aaron's page adds to our understanding of online spaces such as Facebook and will lead to more conscious and thoughtful interactions with others, both those who are still physically with us and those who are not.

NOTES

1. Aaron is not the individual's actual name. I have changed his name to respect his privacy and that of his friends and family. For the same reason, I purposefully feature Facebook posts throughout this discussion that do not include identifying information about Aaron or other Facebook users. Additionally, based on the visual heuristic of research variables provided in *The Ethics of Internet Research* (McKee and Porter 88), I decided informed consent was not necessary for this discussion.

2. This phenomenon is occurring so regularly that both Google and Facebook are responding: In April of 2013, Google piloted an "Inactive Account Manager" that offers Facebook users the opportunity to suspend their account after a designated period of inactivity. This feature is "targeted at people who want to create an automated digital will" (Gates). Additionally, Facebook offers the option to memorialize a Facebook user's page. While the Facebook page remains active after it is memorialized, no new friend requests can be accepted and no one can log into the memorialized account.   *Interesting info buried in the notes. I need to look up what happened to this pilot.*

WORKS CITED

Brondou, Colleen. "Grieving 2.0: As Students Turn to Facebook to Mourn, How Should Parents, Teachers and Counselors React?" *Finding Dulcinea*, 28 Sept. 2010, www.findingdulcinea .com/news/education/2010/march/Grieving-2-0--As-Students-Turn-to-Facebook-to-Mourn --How-Should-Parents--Teachers-and-Counselors-React-.html.

Dobler, Robert. "Ghosts in the Machine: Mourning the MySpace Dead." *Folklore and the Internet: Vernacular Expression in a Digital World*, edited by Trevor Blank, Utah State UP, 2009, pp. 175-93.

Farber, Lauren. "American Vernacular Memorial Art: The Politics of Mourning and Remembrance." Major Research Project, London Institute, Camberwell College of Arts, 2003.

Gates, Sara. "Google 'Inactive Account Manager': New Feature Helps Users Plan for Death." *Huffington Post*, 11 Apr. 2013, www.huffingtonpost.com/2013/04/11/google-inactive-account-manager-plan-death_n_3063577.html?.

King, Mary. "Breaking the Silence: Social Media's Impact on the Way We Grieve." *WISTV.com*, 8 May 2013, www.wistv.com/story/22192051/breaking-the-silence-social-medias-impact-on-the-way-we-grieve.

"Living Headstones." *Quiring Monuments*, 2013, www.monuments.com/living-headstones.

Petrecca, Laura. "Mourning Becomes Electric: Tech Changes the Way We Grieve." *USA Today*, 30 May 2012, usatoday30.usatoday.com/money/industries/technology/story/2012-05-07/digital-mourning/55268806/1.

Pew Research Center. "Social Media Update 2013." *Pew Research Center*, 30 Dec. 2013, www.pewinternet.org/2013/12/30/social-media-update-2013/.

Seligson, Hannah. "An Online Generation Redefines Mourning." *New York Times*, 21 Mar. 2014, https://nyti.ms/NAS9GI.

Taylor, Jim. "Narcissism: On the Rise in America?" *Huffington Post*, 28 May 2011, www.huffingtonpost.com/dr-jim-taylor/narcissism-america_b_861887.html.

"The Rise of iCulture." *New York Times*, 24 Sept. 2007, essay.blogs.nytimes.com/2007/09/24/the-rise-of-iculture/.

The World Wide Cemetery. 2014, cemetery.org.

Phase 3: Jay questions the text after reading.   This video shows how, after reading the article, Jay questions some of the author's points and his own initial reactions to create meaning from the text.

Video: Questioning the Text after Reading

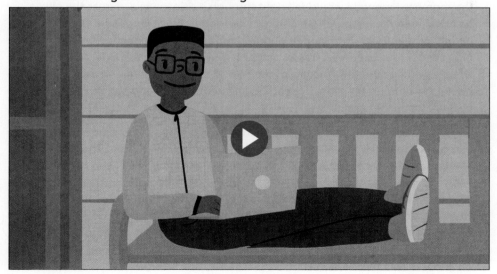

Practice active and critical reading

You've seen one student's process for actively and critically reading the article "Death: The End We All Have to Face(book)." Now we want you practice careful reading by applying the three-phase reading model we've discussed to a related text, "The Space between Mourning and Grief." As you move through the three phases, consider what new insights you can offer at each phase. Annotate the text three times: before, during, and after your thorough reading. Use the questions that follow the text to help you.

The Space between Mourning and Grief

CLAIRE WILMOT

Claire Wilmot is a writer from Toronto. This piece was originally published in the Atlantic *in June 2016.*

The morning after my sister Lauren died was cold and quiet, a mid-March prairie dawn, lit by gray half-light. For several hours I tried to figure out how to get out of bed. The most routine tasks are extraordinarily difficult in the early days of grief—Lauren's death had torn a hole in my universe, and I knew the moment I moved I would fall right through it. Meanwhile, across the city, a former classmate of Lauren's learned of her death. I'm still not sure how—she hadn't kept in touch with Lauren during the three years since they graduated high school. But bad news travels astonishingly fast. The classmate selected what is perhaps the only picture of the two of them together, and decided to post it on Lauren's timeline. Beneath it, she wrote "RIP" and something about heaven gaining an angel.

This Facebook post is how many of Lauren's close friends learned that she had died. We—her family—hadn't yet been able to call people. The first post sparked a cascade of statuses and pictures, many from people who barely knew her. It was as though an online community felt the need to claim a stake in her death, through syrupy posts that profoundly misrepresented who she was and sanitized what had happened to her. Lauren was an intensely private person, not one to identify with her diagnosis—a rare form of neurological cancer. And she would have had little patience for the mawkish kind of tributes on social media that followed.

The way people mourn online has been the subject of much cultural comment recently, particularly in the wake of mass tragedies and high-profile celebrity deaths, such as those of David Bowie and Prince. Some argue that the likes of Facebook and Twitter have opened up public space for displays of grief that had been restricted to private spheres of secular culture. But rather than reconstructing an outlet for public grief, social media often reproduces the worst cultural failings surrounding death, namely platitudes that help those on the periphery of a tragedy rationalize what has happened, but obscure the uncomfortable, messy reality of loss.

Social media has increased the speed and ease of communication to an unprecedented degree, and yet sites like Facebook and Twitter are poorly suited to grief's strangeness. By design, social media demands tidy conclusions, and dilutes tragedy so that it's comprehensible even to those only distantly aware of what has happened. The majority of Facebook posts mourning Lauren's death were full of "silver linings" comments that were so far removed from the horror of the reality that I found them isolating and offensive. Implicit in claims that Lauren was no longer suffering, or that "everything happens for a reason" are redemptive clauses—ones that have a silencing effect on those who find no value in their pain.

It makes sense that those who knew Lauren sought some kind of meaning in her death in an attempt to re-order a universe disrupted. My sister was a smart, kind, athletic business student and a social entrepreneur—and she had an incredibly rare form of brain cancer that ended up killing her. It's naively assumed that good, healthy people deserve good, healthy lives. When they're robbed of what cosmic justice is owed to them, the laws that many believe govern human lives become suddenly suspect, or are revealed as illusory.

So if the impulse to ascribe meaning to senseless tragedy can be misguided, it's also deeply human. The notion that suffering brings meaning and growth is common to many religious traditions, and lies at the heart of countless great stories. Scholars of tragedy and horror fiction have long argued that people seek out symbolic encounters with death as a way to confront their own mortality, albeit from a safe distance. From this vantage point, suffering and death take on an aesthetic quality that's all but invisible to those enduring grief.

In her 2003 book, *Regarding the Pain of Others*, Susan Sontag described how civilians respond to pictures of wartime dead, writing, "We truly can't imagine what it is like." Anyone who's spent time under fire, she says, knows this intuitively. Those who've experienced the final weeks of a loved one's life need no reminder of the loneliness of that time. The novelist Aleksandar Hemon ▶

compared the sense of separateness he felt when caring for his daughter, who was dying of a brain tumor, to living inside an aquarium. Those on the outside could see in, to a degree, but those inside the glass led a completely alien existence.

The cultural anthropologist Renato Rosaldo thoughtfully addressed the subject of accessing the experiences of others in his essay "Grief and a Headhunter's Rage." He reflects on the years he spent studying how the Ilongot people in the Northern Philippines coped with loss: via the now-defunct practice of cutting off human heads. Although he documented life in Ilongot communities for most of his career, it wasn't until his wife Michelle Rosaldo (a celebrated anthropologist in her own right) died suddenly that Rosaldo finally understood the kind of pain, born out of traumatic grief, that could manifest as headhunting. He writes that before Michelle's death, he equated grief with sadness, adding that "certainly no personal experience allowed me to imagine the powerful rage Illongots claimed to find in bereavement."

Grief responses in the secular West can seem equally strange to the outsider—but they tend to take place behind closed doors, in the early hours after another sleepless night, or hidden away in the minds of bodies that appear, for the most part, to be doing well, considering. The inner world of a grieving person is essentially other.

Anyone who's experienced the loss of a loved one understands that most people are profoundly uncomfortable addressing death in physical interactions with the bereaved, which is where social media can come in. In response to the online mourning of David Bowie, *The Atlantic*'s Megan Garber argued that social media has allowed people to express their sadness and support the bereaved—a welcome return to an earlier era where social norms to help people cope with death were well established. A growing number of researchers agree—the media psychologist Jocelyn DeGroot posits that social networks can help people make sense of death, and maintain a relationship with the deceased. However, there's an important distinction between mourning, a behavior, and grief, an internal emotional experience. Social media may have opened space for public mourning, but etiquette for ensuring that outpouring supports the bereaved (or at the very least doesn't make their situation more painful) has yet to develop.

Certainly, there are people who welcome social media as an effective medium for working through their grief—but nothing could be further from my own experience. The problem with trying to definitively evaluate tools for grief management is that the feeling itself is so poorly understood. Even Elisabeth Kübler-Ross, the champion of grief's "five stages," realized on her deathbed that it was futile to try and break up or categorize grief into distinct components. Perhaps more so than any other emotional response, grief reacts with individual personalities in alchemical ways.

As for me, I have gained nothing through Lauren's death, and she gained nothing from four years of arduous treatment. We have only lost. She lost her life, and I lost the person I love most in the world. And she didn't "pass away," as her online eulogizers wrote. She died choking on fluid that could no longer be cleared from her lungs because of a tumor pressing on her midbrain. And she died loudly, in my arms, as I tried to help her breathe. In spite of the grace with which she coped, her struggle was not an enriching experience for her; it made life more difficult. I am not stronger because of this experience; I am weaker, my life emptier than it was with her in it.

In light of grief's complexity, it's easy to see the appeal of platitudes. But because these narratives are so palatable, they become not only the dominant narratives of tragedy, but also, seemingly, the only acceptable ones. When I requested the removal of some of the most offensive posts, I was met not with understanding, but hostility. "My intention was to celebrate Lauren," one wrote, defensively, as if good intentions were all that mattered. At my most cynical, I wondered if posts about other people's deaths are used no differently than other content on social media—as a means of identity assertion in a busy online environment. It seemed that space had been created for certain interpretations of Lauren's death, but it was a space inaccessible to me. There are some things that cannot be represented without cheapening the message; I think loss like this is one of them.

To be clear, I am not trying to tell anyone how to grieve. But rather than defending the rise of a new space for public morning as unambiguously good, perhaps the online community is in even greater need of a critical discussion—about what it means to make room for your own sadness while being sensitive to those closest to a loss. My proposal is simple: Wait. If the deceased is not a close family member, do not take it upon yourself to announce their death online. Consider where you fall in the geography of a loss, and tailor your behavior in response to the lead of those at the center. Listen. Rather than assuming the bereaved are ready for (or comfortable with) Facebook or Twitter tributes, send a private message, or even better, pick up the phone and call.

▶

If you don't feel comfortable expressing your condolences to the deceased's friends and family, perhaps it isn't your place to publicly eulogize. The simple acknowledgment that you may not understand what it's like to grieve is itself a powerful act of empathy. The really important kind of empathy—the only kind worth practicing—asks us to imagine ourselves in the lives of others, and also, critically, to imagine our limits.

1. **Phase 1: Question the text *before* you read.** What does this text seem to be? What can you learn from its visual clues? What is the topic of the text? What do you already know about the topic? What predictions can you make about the text?

2. **Phase 2: Question the text *as* you read.** What does the main point seem to be? What kinds of support are offered, and are they credible? How did you deal with unfamiliar words? Do the author's conclusions seem valid?

3. **Phase 3: Question the text *after* you read.** What lingering questions do you have? What surprised you in the text? What parts are still confusing? Does any information seem to be missing?

5.2 Apply active and critical reading strategies to multimodal texts

So far, we've been looking at how readers of printed texts can use the strategies of annotating and questioning a text in three phases. In this section, we'll consider how to adapt those strategies to understand texts that include visual and other elements in addition to written words.

Reading, viewing, and listening to multimodal texts

You may think you're not familiar with multimodal texts, but you encounter them every day. A *multimodal text* creates meaning using two or more modes such as written words, visuals, audio, movement, and expressions. The following figure elaborates on what those modes might include.

Types of Modes in Multimodal Texts

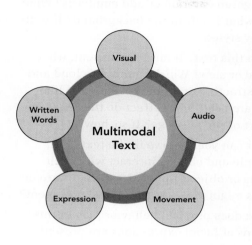

Written Words	Paragraphs, sentences, individual words, titles, captions, and footnotes
Visual Elements	Images, illustrations, color, design, layout, and spacing
Audio Elements	Spoken language, sound effects, music, volume of sound, and silence
Movement	Speed of movement, lack of movement, and interaction between people and objects
Expressions and Gestures	Physical behavior, facial expressions, and emotions conveyed through gestures

Multimodal texts, then, are things like videos, magazine ads, billboards, memes, films, podcasts, TV commercials and shows, and websites—texts that you view and listen to on a regular basis.

We've suggested that actively and critically reading a text means asking questions about the text before, during, and after your reading so that you might create your own informed meaning of the text. When engaging with multimodal texts, the key is to consider carefully how each mode of communication contributes to the overall meaning of the text.

Considering various parts of a multimodal text

Carefully interpreting a multimodal text requires you to unpack its various modes and consider how each one contributes to the text's overall meaning. Before, during, and after you encounter a multimodal text, ask yourself questions about each of the following modes separately. Once you recognize how the individual modes work in the text, you'll be in a strong position to understand how they work together to form the message of the entire text. Remember that multimodal texts aren't required to include *all* the modes we explain here, but they will include some combination of written words, visual effects, audio effects, movement, and expressions.

- **Written words.** Does the text include any written words? If so, what do they say? What kinds of emotions do they evoke? Are all the words in one location, or do they appear in various places in the text?

- **Visual elements.** What do I see in the text? What images seem most important? How is color used to heighten emotion or add emphasis? What seems to be in the foreground, and what is left in the background? If written words are included, how are they styled?

- **Audio elements.** What sounds are in this text? If music is present, what mood does it convey? Is it fast-paced or slow? Which sounds are loud and which are softer? Are the sounds distracting or do they seem more like background noise? If sound effects are used, what effect do they have on the audience? Is silence used as part of the message? If so, how?

- **Movement.** What kind of movement can you observe in the text (fast, slow, halting, or none)? How do people and objects interact with each other? Within the text, do characters or objects appear to move toward or away from others? What conclusions might you draw from this movement?

- **Expressions and gestures.** What role does physical behavior play in this text? Especially in videos, what kinds of facial expressions are present? In what way does the position of people's bodies suggest how audiences might interpret the text's meaning?

> **REFLECT**
>
> ## Explore individual elements of a multimodal text
>
> The following ad was created by the Centers for Disease Control (CDC), a US government organization dedicated to preventing the spread of disease in our communities. As you study this ad, consider which modes it relies on most and how various elements work in this multimodal text. Make some notes about how each mode functions (or doesn't) in this text, using the following questions to help you.
>
> 1. **Written words.** What written words are part of this text? What is the significance of the single sentence to the left of the baby's face? How do the words in the ad support the mission of the CDC? How do the words in different areas of the ad relate to each other?
>
> 2. **Visual elements.** What do you actually see in this text? How would you describe the scene in the ad? What colors are used and what do they suggest? How are the written words designed?
>
> 3. **Audio elements.** Though this ad is a still image, it suggests sounds you might hear if the sound were suddenly switched "on." What voices or background noises might you hear? How loud or quiet would the scene be?

4. **Movement.** As a static image, this ad doesn't actually move like a video would, but movement is implied. If the baby was suddenly "unfrozen," what kind of movements would she most likely make?

5. **Expressions and gestures.** How would you describe the baby's facial expression? What about her posture and the position of her torso and face?

REFLECT

Consider multiple elements of a multimodal text

Now that you've made some notes about the ways individual modes work in the CDC's ad, write a paragraph or two in response to the text. How well do you think the various modes work together to communicate an effective pro-vaccination message?

Watch Meg read a multimodal text

Meg practiced actively reading a different multimodal ad from the CDC. You can see the poster she viewed below. In the video that follows, you'll see Meg's process of actively reading the CDC poster. Notice the ways Meg comments on how various elements—written words, visuals, audio, movement, and expressions—work to make meaning in the ad.

CDC Poster

CDC

Video: Reading a Multimodal Text

APPLY

Practice actively reading a multimodal text

You've seen Meg's process for actively viewing the CDC's ad that encourages patients to work with health care providers to ensure healthy travel. Now we want you to try reading a multimodal text yourself. Using YouTube or other platforms, find an interesting brief video to analyze. As you watch the video, consider how written words, visuals, audio, movement, and expressions contribute to the meaning of the video.

As you analyze your chosen video, consider the following questions:

1. What's the text's main message?

2. How do written words support the text's message?

3. How do visual elements contribute to this text's message?

4. How do audio elements play a role in this text's message?

5. How does movement in the video (or the suggestion of it) help the text's message?

6. How do expressions or gestures contribute to the video's message?

5.3 Understand logos, pathos, and ethos

In Section 2.2, we introduced you to five essential components of effective writing—purpose, audience, genre, tone, and context—and asked you to analyze a variety of texts to see how authors address these concepts in their messages. In that section, we considered the "what" of effective writing. In this section, we discuss *how* writers craft texts to make big impacts on their audiences.

Understanding the purpose of rhetorical appeals

How do authors make elements of rhetoric work together to make a text effective? *How* does an author reach her audience to achieve a specific writing purpose, all the while maintaining a specific tone, following the conventions of a particular genre, and remaining aware of the social context in which the message occurs?

One key strategy is to use *rhetorical appeals*—specific kinds of persuasion chosen by the writer because of the effect they are likely to have on the audience. We suggest you think of these appeals in three categories, which we'll discuss throughout this section:

- **Logical appeals**, often called *logos*
- **Emotional appeals**, often called *pathos*
- **Ethical appeals**, often called *ethos*

Defining logos, pathos, and ethos

Way back in the fourth century BCE, the ancient Greek philosopher Aristotle wrote about methods of persuasion. He explained that people are persuaded by an author's reasonable argument, use of emotion to reach an audience, and the personal credibility of the speaker or writer. The Greek terms he used to explain these persuasive methods are *logos*, *pathos*, and *ethos*. We're several centuries past Aristotle, but his terms still help us explain how writers today create persuasive messages.

- **Logos** is the use of facts, numbers, statistics, reasoning based on evidence, and other forms of "objective" information to support a claim. Logical appeals are often considered the most important kinds of support to use in serious arguments, academic or otherwise, because those arguments make their case by relying on reasoning and strong evidence rather than emotions or the likeability of the speaker or writer.

- **Pathos** draws on readers' emotional responses and deeply held values to make an argument stronger or more memorable. All forms of communication can draw on pathos to increase their effectiveness. Both positive and negative emotional responses are part of pathos. In all types of messages, certain words tend to make readers feel happy or sad, angry or defiant, proud or ashamed. When these words are used, the emotions they evoke prompt an audience to align with or distance themselves from the message to some extent. Visual messages such as photos, videos, memes, GIFs, or image-rich texts like infographics often rely on emotional appeals because the use of color, the posing of characters, or the choice of images prompt emotional, gut responses from the audience. While emotional appeals are often very effective, relying too heavily on them may create the impression that the author is using sensationalism and not "real" evidence to prove a point.

- **Ethos** reflects the writer's credibility. A writer builds a strong *ethos* by showing readers that she is knowledgeable, trustworthy, and fair. Writers may cite research and informed opinions of experts in a subject, refer to their own personal experiences that give them insight into the message being conveyed, and take care to present the ideas of others with tact, fairness, and goodwill. Messages that successfully combine logical and emotional appeals can be made even more effective when the author's ethos is strong.

The table "Comparing Types of Appeals" examines the reasons for and limits of each appeal's effectiveness. While you are still learning about different kinds of support, it's convenient to think of the three appeals separately as if a single message relies on *only* one kind of support. In reality, though, most messages use a blend of these appeals, even if they rely more heavily on one type than the others. Even in the classical era, Aristotle claimed that the most persuasive arguments were those that employed a balance of the three appeals.

Comparing Types of Appeals

Type of Appeal	Why the Appeal Works	Limits of This Appeal
Logical Appeal	People like logical appeals because we value the concepts these appeals use: clear reasoning, facts, and scientific evidence. Messages based on logical appeals benefit from an assumption that anything presented as fact must be true.	Messages that rely too heavily on facts or statistics or that work hard to remain completely objective are sometimes so dry and boring that they fail to hold readers' interest. ▶

Type of Appeal	Why the Appeal Works	Limits of This Appeal
Emotional Appeal	Messages based on emotional appeals create powerful emotional responses such as sympathy, fear, joy, pride, pity, and anger. Effective emotional appeals use techniques like jokes or humor to bond with their audience, scorn or mockery to encourage an audience to dislike a bad idea, and detailed storytelling to create sympathy for another person's misfortune.	Emotional appeals such as the appeal to sympathy or fear-mongering are sometimes used to gloss over weak evidence. An argument that relies only on emotional appeals risks being dismissed as sensationalism.
Ethical Appeal	Readers tend to believe a claim more readily when they also trust that the speaker is knowledgeable, fair, trustworthy, and sensitive to the audience's needs and interests.	Relying exclusively on one's ethos to build a case is a risky move. A *critical* audience will not accept a claim *only* because the speaker encourages them to do so.

REFLECT

Think about when each appeal may work best

You've been thinking about three different types of appeals to an audience—logos, pathos, and ethos. The success of these appeals depends on using them effectively with specific audiences and for specific purposes. Think back to some times when you've tried to argue a point—face to face, online, or in a school assignment. Consider how you've used the three types of appeals at various times, then describe the situations and how successful your appeals were at the time.

1. Describe a situation in which you attempted to use logos (logical appeals). How successful were you?

2. Describe a situation in which you attempted to use pathos (emotional appeals). How successful were you?

3. Describe a situation in which you attempted to use ethos (ethical appeals). How successful were you?

UNDERSTAND

Watch Gabby and Meg read for logos, pathos, and ethos

To see how a text uses a blend of logos, pathos, and ethos to achieve its purpose, let's consider the website of Heifer International, a nonprofit organization that provides needy families with farm animals that can be both a source of food and income when they sell the animal's products—such as milk, eggs, or honey. For example, Heifer might provide a family with an ox that can plow fields or a goat that can produce milk for the family to sell or trade.

In this video, Gabby and Meg talk about how the Heifer International site uses all three appeals—logos, pathos, and ethos—to encourage people to support its cause.

Video: Recognizing Logos, Pathos, and Ethos

APPLY

Identify logos, pathos, and ethos on your own

You've seen how one humanitarian organization, Heifer International, relies on logos, pathos, and ethos to reach its audiences. Now spend some time exploring the websites of other charitable relief organizations　▶

to consider how they include logos, pathos, and ethos on their sites. Use your favorite search engine to find the websites for the following organizations:

Doctors Without Borders

Relief International

International Rescue Committee

Save the Children

Care International

Choose one of the websites to write about for this activity. In your response, address the following questions.

1. Which organization's website are you writing about?

2. Write three to four sentences that provide at least two examples of how the website relies on **logos**. Explain how these examples help or don't help the website reach its audience.

3. Write three to four sentences that provide at least two examples of how the website relies on **pathos**. Explain how these examples help or don't help the website reach its audience.

4. Write three to four sentences that provide at least two examples of how the website relies on **ethos**. Explain how these examples help or don't help the website reach its audience.

5.4 Recognize rhetorical fallacies

Credible writers use logos, pathos, and ethos with the best of intentions. When used successfully, they help us achieve our writing purpose and reach our audience. Sometimes, however, writers use these appeals in misleading ways—often simply by mistake and at other times as a way of intentionally deceiving or distracting the audience. Using a rhetorical appeal in a flawed way results in a fallacy, which the Merriam-Webster Dictionary defines as a "false or mistaken idea." In this section, you'll learn how and why rhetorical fallacies happen and how to identify them in print and multimodal texts.

Understanding flawed thinking that creates fallacies

Rhetorical fallacies typically fall into three categories based on the type of flawed appeal that is being used:

- **Logical fallacies** occur when the evidence provided does not support the claim. In short, the logic doesn't work.

Example	Why the Example Is a Fallacy
"Senior citizens shouldn't be allowed to drive. An 80-year-old woman rear-ended my car yesterday!"	An incident involving one person isn't enough to justify a broad claim about a whole category of people.

- **Emotional fallacies** occur when an author tries to manipulate the audience by evoking unwarranted or inconsistent emotions from them. Effective messages often rely on emotion-based evidence; however, deliberately trying to sway an audience by misdirecting emotion or by appealing only to a sense of peer pressure or "everyone's doing it" creates a fallacy.

Example	Why the Example Is a Fallacy
"Officer, I don't deserve this speeding ticket. Everyone drives fast on this road, and I'm really late for work."	The driver is trying to get out of a speeding ticket, even though he was speeding. By telling the officer that everyone speeds on this road, he is trying to minimize his own behavior. He further tries to manipulate the officer by both implicitly appealing to the officer's compassion with the excuse of being "late for work" and further implying that the officer should be ashamed of ticketing a hardworking citizen who's just trying to get to his job.

- **Ethical fallacies** occur when false or misleading statements are made or implied about the people involved in the message. For example, the speaker might stretch the truth to make himself look better or suggest something unsavory about the people he is talking about.

Example	Why the Example Is a Fallacy
Advertisers often claim their product is worthwhile because "it's the one more Americans prefer."	The suggestion of a product's popularity, even if true, doesn't necessarily mean it will benefit you personally.

Understanding fallacies in multimodal texts

In popular culture, fallacies are used routinely. For example, in advertising, fallacies are used to claim that using a particular product will automatically result in phenomenal success. In political ads, making outrageous or exaggerated claims about a political opponent has become the norm. And many memes are funny precisely because of the fallacies they employ. Take a look at the memes below to see how they use fallacies.

Logical Fallacy

This meme violates logical reasoning because it's extremely unlikely that attending class so rarely would result in an A.

Emotional Fallacy

This meme works by using images that suggest American patriotism rather than making an argument about why it's important to be patriotic.

Ethical Fallacy

When posted by college students, this meme attacks the maturity of all college students by showing this single cartoon student choosing to drink away his problems instead of facing them responsibly.

REFLECT

Consider the intent of fallacies

Some fallacies are so outrageously inaccurate that we might wonder what motivates a person to use them. And yet, people do use them—consciously or not—because they expect their statements will be persuasive to a specific audience. Below are some fallacies we've observed in posts on social media. For each statement, explain why the reasoning is flawed and what may have motivated the writer to use the flawed reasoning.

1. "I'd think twice about hiring Barbara to do your taxes. Her neighbor used to work for that accountant who went to prison for tax evasion."

    What makes the reasoning flawed? What may have motivated the writer to use this flawed reasoning?

2. "The test scores for Mountaintop High School dropped three percent from their scores last year. Kids today are just plain lazy."

    What makes the reasoning flawed? What may have motivated the writer to use this flawed reasoning?

3. "We can't change the start time for first period! It's *always* started at 8:00!"

    What makes the reasoning flawed? What may have motivated the writer to use this flawed reasoning?

UNDERSTAND

Recognize specific rhetorical fallacies

So far, we've been discussing rhetorical fallacies in three broad categories: logical, emotional, and ethical. Within each of those categories, however, are several specific types of fallacies. The table "Rhetorical Fallacies" identifies and explains commonly used fallacies and provides an example of each one. As you examine the table, think about how each fallacy can be used innocently by writers trying to make a point or used purposefully by skillful persuaders trying to divert their audience's attention. For convenience's sake, this table breaks down fallacies into three categories (logical, emotional, and ethical); however, fallacies frequently blur these strict divisions.

Rhetorical Fallacies

Kind of Fallacy	What is it?	Example	Why is this example a fallacy?
Logical Fallacies			
Hasty Generalization/ Sweeping Generalization	A statement that jumps to a conclusion without sufficient evidence.	"Senior citizens shouldn't be allowed to drive. An 80-year-old woman rear-ended my car yesterday!"	An incident involving one person isn't enough to justify a broad claim about a category of people.
Non Sequitur	An argument whose conclusions do not follow from the original premise or whose evidence is irrelevant to the claim.	"I always placed in the top three at swim meets, so I should make an A in your College Algebra course, Professor Houghton."	The fact that a person performed well in one context has no bearing on how he or she will perform in a different context.
Begging the Question (Circular Reasoning)	Restating the claim as the evidence to support the claim.	"I deserve an A because I am an A student."	The support (because I am an A student) simply restates the claim (I deserve an A) rather than providing evidence (high-quality course work) to support the claim.
Stacking the Deck (Telling a Half-Truth)	Exaggerating and leaving out relevant information or tampering with the facts.	"We should support the proposal to widen Asbury Lane because eighty-eight percent of the people polled support doing so."	If the only people polled were those most likely to support the proposal, such as merchants on Asbury Lane who favor widening the road to create more parking, it's a fallacy.

Kind of Fallacy	What is it?	Example	Why is this example a fallacy?
Faulty Cause or Effect	Assumes that because one event preceded another, the first event caused the second to happen *or* because an event occurred at the same time as another, the two events are related.	"Because the economy was strong during a president's administration, the president's policies were directly responsible for the strong economy."	Such a statement ignores other potential causes unrelated to the president's policies.
Slippery Slope	Assumes that a single, apparently harmless step in a perilous direction will doom us to slide out of control toward a dangerous end.	"If we vote to legalize marijuana, it won't be long until heroin and crack cocaine are on sale at your local drugstore."	While this fallacy results from flaws in logic, it also appeals to people's fear of the unknown and thus blurs into the category of emotional fallacies.
False Dilemma/ Either-Or Choice	This fallacy oversimplifies a situation, creating only two options, one of which is not tolerable. The goal is to get the audience to quickly accept only the choice favored by the person making the argument.	Bumper sticker that reads "America: Love it or Leave It!"	The either-or choice on the sticker implies that Americans should support the majority opinion in the country at any given time or literally get out of the country. In reality, few situations, including this one, offer only two choices. Working to solve a specific problem in our society would be a more productive alternative than leaving the country or bowing to majority opinion. ▶

Kind of Fallacy	What is it?	Example	Why is this example a fallacy?
Red Herring	A new and unrelated topic is introduced as a way to draw attention away from an unpopular or uncomfortable issue at hand.	Politicians sometimes use red herrings to respond to reporters' questions: "I'm glad you asked me about my record on child welfare legislation. Have I shown you a picture of my cute grandson?"	The speaker's "evidence" does not address the claim at all.
Appeal to Accepted Practices	A claim that something is good (or bad) or right (or wrong) based on what is traditional, popular, or an accepted practice.	It was OK for me to copy my daughter's birthday party invitations on the office photocopier because everyone else uses it for personal copying.	These fallacies assume that the original accepted practice is right, which may not be true.
Emotional Fallacies			
Appeal to Tradition	An argument based on a pattern of past behavior, not evidence related to the claim.	We have to go to Grandma's for Easter because that's what we always do.	The claim ignores other possibilities in favor of only what is known or comfortable.
Appeal to Provincialism (the known is always better than the unknown)	An argument that encourages the status quo by appealing to people's comfort with their surroundings and their fears of the unknown.	"Those Apple computers are hard to operate. I've always used a PC!"	The claim ignores other possibilities in favor of only what is known or comfortable.

Kind of Fallacy	What is it?	Example	Why is this example a fallacy?
Appeal to Stirring Symbols	An argument that refuses to provide supporting evidence and instead deliberately gets its persuasive power from a symbol or idea that evokes strong emotion.	A restaurant marquee in wartime that reads "Support Our Troops … Best Breakfast in Town!"	The quality of the breakfast served has nothing to do with the restaurant's attitude toward the military. The restaurant is appealing to people's overwhelming sense of patriotism to entice them into the restaurant.
Ethical Fallacies			
Personal Attack/Ad Hominem Argument	A claim that ignores an opponent's ideas and instead attacks that person's character. Irrelevant or erroneous details of the person's personality or life, rather than the issues of the argument, take center stage.	Book title: *Rush Limbaugh Is a Big, Fat Idiot.*	*Ad hominem* arguments ignore the actual issues being discussed and take the focus off real support for an argument.
Bandwagon Appeal/Ad Populum ("to the people")	Arguing that a position is right or worthwhile only because most people agree with it.	Advertisers often claim their products are worthwhile because "it's the one more Americans prefer."	The suggestion of a product's popularity, even if true, doesn't address its benefits to you.

▶

Kind of Fallacy	What is it?	Example	Why is this example a fallacy?
Moral Equivalence	To equate a heinous crime with a much lesser offense is to commit a fallacy of moral equivalence.	Comparing anything to the practices of Hitler or the Nazi party during World War II. Using the term "feminazi" to refer to feminists.	Few actions, even serious wrongdoings, compare with the atrocities committed by Hitler and his Nazi followers.
False Authority	When writers offer only themselves as sufficient reason to believe a claim, or when they appeal to "authorities" that are not recognized by the audience.	An argument that relies heavily on principles from a sacred text such as the Koran or the Bible but tries to reach an audience outside that faith community. "Eating pork is wrong because the Bible says so."	Sometimes the author isn't an "expert" and can't speak authoritatively on the subject. In other cases, the audience may not see a cited expert as authoritative, thus weakening the argument.
Glory or Guilt by Association	Attempts to bolster or doom an idea simply by connecting it to someone or some idea that the intended audience either respects or dislikes. Marketers have used this tactic with great success to pitch products using endorsements from various celebrities.	Glory: "Eat Wheaties, the Breakfast of Champions!" Guilt: "Don't re-elect Councilman Jones. He once belonged to a union!"	Glory: This slogan suggests that anyone who eats Wheaties will also be a champion. Guilt: The statement does not argue against Jones' re-election on the basis of his record or ideas. The claim is based solely on an association.

U N D E R S T A N D

See one student's rhetorical analysis essay

Chapter 5 has focused on reading actively and critically by asking you to think about how texts work to achieve their purposes. We've encouraged you to ask questions and make notes as you read. And we have introduced you to the rhetorical appeals of logos, pathos, and ethos, as well as the fallacies that occur when those appeals are used misleadingly or inaccurately. Once you've done that careful reading, how could you present your thoughts on the text you read? One way is to write a rhetorical analysis essay, which is the Chapter 5 Project. In a rhetorical analysis, the writer focuses on a particular text (or group of texts) and examines what makes the text largely effective or ineffective. To do this work, it's important to consider the text in the larger rhetorical situation, as we discussed in Section 2.3.

In the following rhetorical analysis essay, take a look at how our student Jared Glidden analyzed the Nike ad "Dream Crazy." As you work on your rhetorical analysis for the Chapter 5 Project, consider reviewing this essay to use as a model.

Glidden 1

Jared Glidden

Professor Ingraham

ENGL 1010

27 November 2018

Just Dream It: A Rhetorical Analysis of Nike's

"Dream Crazy" Ad

In 2016, NFL quarterback Colin Kaepernick made headlines by choosing to kneel instead of stand during the national anthem before each of his football games to protest racial injustice and police brutality. This situation was quickly politicized as many fans saw Kaepernick bravely using his platform for good, while others viewed his actions as disrespectful toward military service members and the U.S. flag. Democrats generally supported Kaepernick, while many

> Jared combines Nike's signature tagline "Just do it" with the ad's name ("Dream Crazy") to create a catchy pun for his title.

> The first paragraph presents background context to set up the rhetorical situation.

Glidden 2

Republicans, including President Donald Trump, believed that Kaepernick should be punished for unpatriotic actions. After this controversial season, Kaepernick decided not to renew his contract with the San Francisco 49ers, and when no other team would hire him, he later sued the NFL for collusion. Roughly two years later, Nike made the controversial decision to create and release a new ad starring Kaepernick. Because of the controversy surrounding him, the Kaepernick ad was met with strong reactions from viewers across the political spectrum. Those who were happy with the ad shared it widely, but those who opposed it went as far as destroying their Nike apparel to express their displeasure with Nike's decision. Despite all of the controversy, I believe that Nike took a calculated risk that resulted in a successful ad.

The message of the ad, which was released by Nike in September 2018, is that you can achieve your wildest dreams, despite what everyone will tell you. The ad features images of athletes who might be considered "crazy" for trying to reach their dreams: a wrestler with a disability and a group of refugee children playing soccer, among others. The offscreen narrator encourages viewers to interpret being told your dream is "crazy" not as an insult but as a compliment. At the moment the narrator says "Believe in something, even if it means sacrificing everything," the camera focuses on Kaepernick, revealing him to be the narrator of the ad. By the end, he tells viewers, "So don't ask if your dreams are crazy, ask if they're crazy enough." With these words, the ad encourages the audience not just to strive for physical greatness, but to find something more important to believe in.

The thesis appears at the end of the first paragraph and contains a judgment about the ad's effectiveness.

A summary of the ad helps provide important context for essay readers who may be unfamiliar with the ad.

Glidden 3

This ad was clearly designed with young athletes in mind, not only because of the people it features and the message it conveys, but also because of the way it was published. This ad originally aired on many different TV channels but can also be found online in several different ways, such as on Nike's YouTube channel. Airing such a controversial ad might seem like a foolish decision, but Nike likely did extensive research to determine how their audience would respond to it. Because of the pressure put on them by stockholders to keep sales up, they could not afford to put out an ad that would not be profitable for the company. They must have been fairly sure that, based on their audience demographics, the profits gained from those who approved of the ad would be enough to counteract their losses from those who didn't. I believe that even the negative reactions to the ad benefitted Nike in a way. People who saw Nike products being burned by conservatives were probably more enticed to buy Nike products as a way to oppose those attitudes than they would have been otherwise. Overall, I believe that Nike made the right decisions when it came to how to communicate their message in a way that would maximize profits.

> This paragraph considers Nike's motivations and likely demographic research to support the company's "calculated risk" mentioned in the thesis.

Most pieces of media use logos, pathos, and ethos to effectively persuade their audiences. This ad in particular puts more focus on pathos by emotionally appealing to its audience. The narrative of overcoming obstacles and striving to achieve your dreams is something that many young people can relate to. By inspiring their audience to work hard to improve their performance, Nike has effectively associated its brand with athletic success, meaning that young athletes will be influenced to purchase Nike products. Logos is almost entirely

> This essay avoids trying to devote separate paragraphs to logos, pathos, and ethos. Instead it focuses on the appeals used most effectively in the ad.

Glidden 4

absent from this ad, as no facts or statistics about the products themselves are included. Nike also banked on the emotional reactions that viewers would have to seeing Kaepernick starring in this ad. As discussed above, they had likely determined that the positive reactions would be valuable enough to offset the negative reactions. Through the years, Nike has established itself as a trustworthy brand that makes quality products. This ad further increases its ethos as a company that inspires people to reach their highest potential.

Pointing to specific evidence from the ad helps supports the thesis.

This ad uses a variety of methods to persuade the audience. Throughout the whole video, Kaepernick's voice encourages athletes to surpass the goals they have set for themselves. Soft, joyful piano music accompanies the voiceover, further adding to the inspirational feeling that it evokes. Finally, as the ad concludes, the words "Just Do It" flash across the screen. This has been Nike's slogan for years and it is easy to see why. This call to action can be an extremely powerful motivator. I feel that this ad is incredibly successful in using these elements to inspire people who view it.

Addressing the ad's fallacies offers a measured and reasoned view of the ad's success.

While this ad is effective in many ways, it does commit a few fallacies. Showing many different successful athletes clothed exclusively in Nike products creates an emotional fallacy because it relies on the viewer feeling that they do not belong unless they are also wearing Nike products. It also creates an ethical fallacy because it implies that a product's popularity somehow ensures that you, specifically, will benefit from purchasing it.

The conclusion reinforces the thesis by suggesting that the ad is successful on two fronts.

While this ad does have a few problems, I believe that it ultimately accomplishes its goal of inspiring young athletes to pursue their dreams, while also ensuring that Nike is one of the brands most associated with improving their performance. Largely, this success rests on its emotional appeal. It is difficult

Glidden 5

to watch something like this and not feel inspired to work hard just like the athletes that are featured in the videos. This ad is successful for Nike because it inspires young athletes and calls more attention to its brand.

Glidden 6

Work Cited

Nike. "Dream Crazy." *YouTube*, 5 Sept. 2018, www.youtube .com/watch?v=Fq2CvmgoO7I. Advertisement.

APPLY

Practice correcting fallacies

Below are some sentences from first-year college essays that contain fallacies. After reading each statement, first, explain why it contains a fallacy. Then, rewrite the statement using solid reasoning. You can invent any reasonable details to help explain why the statement is a fallacy or correct the fallacy.

> I asked some students in my psychology class if they are happy with our college mascot, and they are. This shows that there is no reason to change the mascot.

1. What's the flawed reasoning?
2. Rewrite the sentences to eliminate the flawed reasoning.

> We should keep club sports meetings on Tuesday nights because that's when we've always had them.

3. What's the flawed reasoning?
4. Rewrite the sentence to eliminate the flawed reasoning. ▶

> Marijuana should not be legalized because parents who smoke on occasion will neglect their children.
>
> 5.   What's the flawed reasoning?
> 6.   Rewrite the sentence to eliminate the flawed reasoning.

Chapter 5 Project
Write a rhetorical analysis

In Chapter 5, you've been learning strategies for actively and critically reading texts. You've learned to use a three-phase model to question the text before, during, and after reading. You've also learned to consider how a variety of elements—written words, visuals, audio, movement, and expressions—work together to communicate meaning in multimodal texts. Finally, you were introduced to the rhetorical appeals logos, pathos, and ethos and learned how fallacies occur when appeals are misused. Using these strategies, you can determine how effectively a text conveys its message to its intended audience.

For the Chapter 5 Project, write an essay in which you analyze how effectively Claire Wilmot achieves her rhetorical purpose in the article you read earlier, "The Space between Mourning and Grief" (your instructor may opt to have you write about a different text). In 500–750 words, analyze the rhetorical effectiveness of the text. Your essay should address the following questions in some way:

- What is the title of the text and who is the author?
- What is the purpose (central message or argument) of the text?
- How would you describe the intended audience of the text? Consider where the text was published to help you determine the audience.
- How does the author use logos, pathos, and ethos to achieve her purpose?
- What are the limitations of this text? Does it contain any fallacies?
- Overall, would you say this text is generally effective or not and why? Your response to this question should be the thesis of your essay.

Before you begin, you may wish to review the five key components of rhetoric in Section 2.2. If you're writing about the Wilmot article, be sure to consult the notes you wrote in your three-stage reading of the text in Section 5.1 as you begin to plan your project. You might also look at the sample rhetorical analysis by Jared Glidden, "Just Dream It," in Section 5.4.

6

Writing Academic Arguments

≋ Achie√e *If your instructor has assigned them, you can watch the video for this chapter, complete the Reflect and Apply activities, and work on the Chapter Project in Achieve.*

6.1 Use academic essay structure to present a persuasive argument

In this section, you'll learn how different parts of academic arguments work together to communicate your position to your audience. Throughout the section, we'll discuss this process using our student Kristjan Grimson's essay "Bloodshed Cinema: Dehumanization in the Opening Scene of *Saving Private Ryan*." If you haven't seen the film *Saving Private Ryan*, we encourage you to check it out. It was released in 1998 and is now considered a classic because of its striking cinematography and the revolutionary way it depicts the harsh realities of war.

Understanding how academic argument differs from other kinds of arguments

These days, it feels like people are arguing all the time. Our social media feeds are full of stories about how people are calling each other out for having a different opinion on an issue. Cable news invites people from different perspectives to appear on shows and encourages them to yell their perspectives at each other and tell the other guest that their position is 100 percent wrong. This is completely the opposite of how academic argument works.

In academic argument, the goal isn't to vanquish your opponents at all costs. It's simply inviting others to consider your perspective and start a conversation with you. An academic argument offers its audience a position and some evidence and reasoning, then it expects the conversation to continue.

Considering what your audience needs to know and when they need to know it

In writing an argument, you have to think about how to convey your message meaningfully and persuasively. If your audience is likely to be familiar with and lean favorably toward your position on the topic, you might dive right in by mentioning important events or concepts without a lot of explanatory background information. If they're probably not as familiar with your topic and your position on it, help them find a connection using comparisons to other more familiar topics and offering additional background information.

These decisions about how much information to include and where to put it in relation to your main thesis have to be made for multiple levels of the argument: within the entire text, within each paragraph, and within each sentence. As you progress through Chapter 6, you'll find advice for effective sequencing at every stage.

Following expected academic conventions to connect with readers

Most buildings have a structural layout that stays pretty much the same across different individual locations. Think about movie theater multiplexes. If you've been to see movies in a multiplex in your town, you could show up at one in another city and navigate it without too much difficulty. While the details may be different—maybe the carpet is a different color, or the posters advertise different movies that are "coming soon"—you still instinctively know the order in which you'll encounter different parts of the multiplex. You'll get in a ticket line, buy a ticket or show a clerk that you've bought one online, pass the concession stand (they really want you to buy that pricey popcorn!), pass another ticket-taker who directs you to your theater, take a few turns to find that theater, then choose your perfect seat to enjoy the movie.

Like these multiplexes, academic arguments unfold in fairly predictable ways, so readers have come to expect to find various components of the argument in specific places within it. In this way, academic arguments are similar to the academic essays we discussed in Section 1.3, with a few key differences. Readers expect a *title* that not only announces your subject matter but also reveals your take on it. Then they anticipate an *introduction* that will engage and guide them into your argument and lead them to your thesis. In Section 1.2, we explained that a thesis in academic writing states the main point or central idea of your essay. In an academic argument, however, the thesis is called a *claim* because it advocates for a specific, debatable position. It literally claims a position in the argument—pro, con, or often somewhere in between—and may preview the evidence or reasoning the essay will present to support the claim.

Once readers understand your claim, they know to look for multiple *support paragraphs* that contain the evidence and reasoning you'll use to support your claim. As readers get near the end of your argument, they expect a *conclusion* that brings it to a close. If your argument includes outside sources, they also expect to see *in-text citations* and a reference page or *bibliography* at the end of the argument. Because this is the organization that readers expect, arranging your academic argument using this typical sequence helps you connect with readers and persuade them to accept your argument.

The introduction prepares readers to accept your claim. Introductions in academic arguments usually have three jobs. One job is to engage the audience sufficiently so that they'll read the whole text. A second job is to provide background information that the audience needs to be able to fairly consider the claim and its supporting paragraphs. A third job is to forecast the argument and evidence that will be presented in the whole text.

To understand what this looks like, consider the introduction of Kristjan's academic argument "Bloodshed Cinema: Dehumanization in the Opening Scene of *Saving Private Ryan*."

> When Steven Spielberg's *Saving Private Ryan* (1998) was released, it shocked viewers with its impeccably accurate depiction of World War II. The opening scene of the movie, which shows the battle at Omaha Beach in grisly detail, truly captures the heartless violence of the war. The scene focuses mainly on the American viewpoint of the battle; Captain Miller (Tom Hanks) and Sergeant Horvath (Tom Sizemore) lead the American troops onto the beaches of Normandy while under constant deadly fire from the Germans positioned on bluffs high above them. In this opening scene, Spielberg uses several filming techniques to show that the brutality of World War II dehumanized the soldiers who fought it.

In this introduction, you can see Kristjan's attempt to engage the audience by saying the movie "shocked viewers." The introduction also provides important background information by including a brief overview of the opening scene and presenting major characters (Captain Miller and Sergeant Horvath). By the end of the paragraph, we learn the writer's claim: "In this opening scene, Spielberg uses several filming techniques to show that the brutality of World War II dehumanized the soldiers who fought it."

The thesis states your claim.   As you learned in Section 1.2, the thesis represents the main point you are making in the text, so it's a really big deal. In academic arguments, the thesis presents the central position — or claim — you want to argue. Just as in other academic writing, it tends to come at or near the end of the first paragraph. In Kristjan's essay on *Saving Private Ryan*, the claim appears as the last sentence of the introduction.

> **Claim:** In this opening scene, Spielberg uses several filming techniques to show that the brutality of World War II dehumanized the soldiers who fought it.

From this claim, we learn some important things about the argument Kristjan is about to make:

1. He's writing about the opening scene only, not the whole movie.

2. He will discuss various filming techniques to support his argument.

3. He will argue that the scene's brutality was important to show its effects on the soldiers who fought in that war.

4. He will have to present a definition of *dehumanized* to support his argument.

With this information, we're prepared to engage with Kristjan's argument throughout the essay and decide how effective we think it is.

Additional paragraphs provide evidence to support the claim. Supporting paragraphs provide the evidence and background information that will persuade readers that your claim is valid. If the point of your project is to make an argument about a text, the supporting paragraphs you write will dig into the text you're discussing and pull words and images from it to support the argument that you're making in your claim. Sometimes these supporting paragraphs provide additional background context that supports your claim. They might also pull in outside sources that lend credibility to your argument. Let's take a look at Kristjan's supporting paragraphs one by one to see how they each support his claim in different ways.

… In this opening scene, Spielberg uses several filming techniques to show that the brutality of World War II dehumanized the soldiers who fought it.

Claim

The way Spielberg directs the opening scene creates the illusion that it contains actual footage of the soldiers sailing toward and landing on Omaha Beach in 1944. Early on, a long shot of numerous landing crafts full of American soldiers is shaky and seems to be recorded on a handheld camera, making the action very realistic. In some shots, the viewpoint

Support paragraph 1
This paragraph explains how specific filming techniques effectively capture the brutality of the war.

seems to be that of other soldiers on another boat also approaching the beach. The extreme goriness of the opening minutes — soldiers are mowed down by German machine guns, they drown, they lose limbs and spurt blood, some even catch fire — is enough to make most people cringe. This gore adds to the intensity and realism of the battle in which there is a constant sound of explosions, bullets clinking off metal, and men screaming in pain. In his article "Hollywood's D-Day from the Perspective of the 1960s and 1990s," R. B. Toplin argues that "through abundant use of the shaky handheld camera, numerous loud and distant noises, occasional silences, and shocking imagery, Spielberg gave his movie the appearance of a documentary film shot at the scene of military action by combat cameramen" (27). This documentary-type filming style in the opening scene is crucial to depicting the brutality of the battle.

Support paragraph 2
Kristjan introduces a different filming technique and explains how it contributes to depicting the brutality the soldiers experienced.

Along with the documentary style of filming, the opening scene captures the soldiers' point of view. From the start of the movie, the viewer sees what the U.S. soldiers see. The camera puts us on the landing craft with Captain Miller, Sargent Horvath, and the rest of the soldiers. Then the camera focuses on numerous men on the boat to reveal their nervousness, fear, and bravery. As soon as the first landing craft's doors open, massive numbers of American soldiers are killed by German artillery. The camera films this shocking event from the back of the boat as if viewers are there on the boat with them. During the heat of the battle, Captain Miller becomes consumed by the reality of his surroundings and simply sits and observes for a few moments. During this time, we are put directly into his point of view. For a few seconds, we get to see exactly what the Captain is seeing. Soldiers are blown to pieces by German forces, some cling to their brothers in arms, and one man is seen searching through rubble trying to find his arm that has been dismembered.

Because the scene often uses the American soldiers' point of view, viewers get to see how they see the German fighters. The Germans are shown in an elevated tower where they are not vulnerable to any gunfire. The viewer sees the German soldiers gunning down the Americans without the slightest hesitation. They and their mounted machine guns are shown as silhouettes to keep the audience from forming a bond with them. Their faces are never shown, a filming technique that dehumanizes them by depicting them as anonymous, heartless creatures instead of fellow human beings (even though they are doing awful things). The German soldiers are further dehumanized by the way the American soldiers speak about them. For example, Sergeant Horvath refers to a group of five Germans as a "juicy opportunity" and a "waste of ammo."

Support paragraph 3
This paragraph shows how the filming techniques help characterize the German fighters as "heartless" and faceless, introducing readers to Kristjan's dehumanization angle.

While the German soldiers are dehumanized mostly through how they appear on camera, the American soldiers are dehumanized through extreme violence. Unlike the German troops, the American forces lose their human significance when they are violently killed in shocking numbers. As soon as the landing craft doors opened and the shooting began, the American bloodshed does not stop until the scene ends. The sheer number of American soldiers who die in the scene becomes overwhelming to the viewer. There is no sense of nobility in their deaths either; as more and more soldiers are gunned down, their bodies float out to sea to be forgotten or lie lifeless on the beach like trash. When Captain Miller makes his

Support paragraph 4
Kristjan moves the focus from German to American soldiers and uses pathos—strong emotion—to help his audience feel outraged by the soldiers' dehumanization.

way from the landing craft to the beach, he is shown walking slowly through the water while tripping and stumbling over his fallen brothers. Not only have they been killed, but they are now merely stepping stones for other men.

The conclusion emphasizes your claim.   The last part of an academic argument is the conclusion. This section gives you a chance to wrap up your argument by recapping important points, highlighting your strongest support, and inviting readers to consider the broader significance of your argument. Depending on how long your argument is, the conclusion could be a single paragraph, a few paragraphs, or a whole section that's introduced with its own heading. Kristjan was writing a short essay, so his conclusion is relatively short as well.

Through his masterful filming, Spielberg captures the essence of D-Day and the suffering endured by soldiers there. Unlike most war movies made before it that glorify war, the opening scene of *Saving Private Ryan* exposes the harsh reality of war. When countless American soldiers are mowed down by German gunners who are shown not to be worth human life, both groups of soldiers no longer abide by common humanistic characteristics. They now abide by an unwritten set of rules that are built around the sole goal of killing their opposition. They have been degraded to nothing more than expendable instruments of war.

In this conclusion, Kristjan points to the significance of *Saving Private Ryan*'s opening scene: unlike many previous war films, it showcases the real brutality of war. Kristjan recaps his claim and characterizes dehumanized soldiers as "nothing more than expendable instruments of war."

Sources are cited to support the argument.   When academic writers cite outside sources as part of an essay or other project, they include indicators within their text to show which ideas or words are not their own and from which source those ideas or words came from. These indicators are called *in-text citations*. In a sentence, an academic writer might name the author of an outside source or the title of that source, but not necessarily both. Then the sentence might continue with a quote from the source. At the end of the sentence, academic writers include parentheses that include the page number—if available—and sometimes additional information about the source. In-text citations are sometimes called "parenthetical citations" because the citation usually happens inside parentheses. When readers see an in-text citation, they know that the full source information will be on the bibliography page at the end of the project.

Kristjan's first support paragraph contains a good example of an in-text citation:

> In his article "Hollywood's D-Day from the Perspective of the 1960s and 1990s," R. B. Toplin argues that "through abundant use of the shaky handheld camera, numerous loud and distant noises, occasional silences, and shocking imagery, Spielberg gave his movie the appearance of a documentary film shot at the scene of military action by combat cameramen" (27).

Source title and author

Quotation

Page number

Kristjan tells readers the source's title and author before quoting from the source. In parentheses, he gives the page number where the quote appears in the source.

If an academic argument includes in-text citations, readers know to expect a bibliography at the end. Different subject areas use a variety of formats and styles for these pages, but they all share a common goal: to provide readers with a complete list of all sources mentioned in the body of the text. In Kristjan's case, his instructor asked students to use MLA style, a style often used in first-year writing courses. In MLA style, the bibliography page is titled "Works Cited," as in "these are all the works I cited in my essay." Let's have a look at Kristjan's Works Cited page. Note that the entries on the Works Cited page provide complete information about Kristjan's sources so that readers can find the film he discussed and the article he quoted from.

Works Cited

Spielberg, Steven, director. *Saving Private Ryan*. Paramount
   Productions, 1998.

Toplin, Robert Brent. "Hollywood's D-Day from the Perspective
   of the 1960s and the 1990s: *The Longest Day* and *Saving
   Private Ryan*." *Film & History: An Interdisciplinary Journal
   of Film and Television Studies*, vol. 36, no. 2, Spring 2006,
   pp. 25-29.

The title presents the main argument.   As we discussed in Section 1.3, while the title *appears first* in a polished academic text, it doesn't have to be the first thing you write when you start working on a piece of academic writing. Many academic writers come up with the title well after they start composing the text. For some people, it's the last thing they work on before the text is finished. Whether you write the title last, first, or somewhere in the middle of your process, always keep in mind the important ways it communicates with your readers.

Your title helps you connect with your audience and capture their attention right away. Just as news headlines try to capture audiences, academic writers try to reach audiences through their titles. To do that, academic arguments often have a two-part title. The first part is an intriguing or catchy phrase that resembles a popular culture reference. It's followed by a colon. Then, after the colon, the writer expresses the main argument or theme of the text. This is the approach Kristjan used in his argument. Take a look at his title:

> Bloodshed Cinema: Dehumanization in the Opening Scene of *Saving Private Ryan*

Some of the words that most likely stand out to you are *bloodshed* and *dehumanization.* They serve an important rhetorical purpose: to catch an audience's attention.

In this example, Kristjan uses pathos to interest readers with the first part of his title, "Bloodshed Cinema." These highly charged words might elicit alarm or dismay from readers who then want to continue reading to learn what "bloodshed cinema" could possibly be. After the colon, he presents the theme he will explore in his paper. Sometimes the title presents or hints at the thesis, but often it simply sticks to the theme the academic argument will address.

> **REFLECT**
>
> ## Consider your experience with academic argument
>
> You've been reading about the ways academic arguments should be written to connect with their readers. You've learned that you should:
>
> - write an introduction that draws readers in, provides important background information, and ends with a strong claim that presents your argument
> - use supporting paragraphs to support the claim made in the thesis
> - close with a conclusion paragraph that recaps your most important evidence and invites readers to consider the larger significance of your argument
> - include in-text citations and a bibliography page if your text includes outside sources
> - compose a title that engages readers and conveys the position your argument takes
>
> While the idea of writing an academic argument to connect with your audience might be new to you, you've probably had some experience writing academic texts or papers. Here, we invite you to reflect on the part of writing an academic *argument* that you find most challenging.
>
> Maybe you've had trouble finding an argument that's worthy of your efforts to persuade others. It's OK to write about that. If you do have a claim in mind, perhaps you're unsure about how to present sufficient evidence to get others to agree with it. You might also be worried ahead ▶

of time that you don't know how to format the outside sources you'll need to support your argument. Everything's fair game at this point.

Choose one element of writing academic arguments that seems most challenging to you and write a paragraph that reflects on your experience with it. Has anything you've encountered in this section helped you reconsider your approach to that component?

U N D E R S T A N D

Consider logos, pathos, and ethos as you organize your argument

As you're developing an argument, you need to think about how to place your appeals to logos, pathos, and ethos. We explained how each of these appeals work in Section 5.3, so feel free to review that section. Briefly, recall that *logos* refers to support for an argument that consists of logical reasoning, facts, and statistics. *Pathos* refers to support that appeals to emotion, and *ethos* refers to support that lends credibility or trustworthiness to the argument. It might seem like building an effective argument means writing separate paragraphs that individually focus on logos, pathos, and ethos-based appeals. But that's not how most effective arguments work. Effective writers take a more holistic approach and often interweave support based on logos, pathos, and ethos throughout the argument.

As you're building your argument, be careful to avoid using fallacies—misrepresentations of evidence to skew it toward your position (see Section 5.4 for a review). If you make a claim, you must back it up with evidence to support it. Further, choosing only evidence that supports your claims without acknowledging other counterclaims undermines your audience's faith in you and decreases your ethos as a writer.

To see how one writer developed an academic argument that incorporates logos-, pathos-, and ethos-based support at various points in the argument, consider the following essay written by student Kathryn Johnson about a speech by the poet and activist Audre Lorde. We've annotated the essay to show how Kathryn uses logos, pathos, and ethos throughout her argument. As you read, you'll see that she integrates logos and ethos quite often and uses pathos in a more limited but critical way.

Kathryn Johnson

Dr. Bohannon

English 1011

2 October 2018

Audre Lorde's "I Am Your Sister": An Effective Model for
Arguments for Intersectional Feminism

The Women's March on Washington in January 2017 helped bring the term *intersectional feminism* to many people's awareness for the first time. The march's original organizers, mainly white women, were criticized for not doing enough to include women of color and oppressed and marginalized groups (Tolentino). When the organizers tried to correct this problem by issuing a diversity statement, some white women then criticized them for allowing issues of race to become part of their protest about women's rights (Tolentino). What those critics did not understand is that minority women do not have the same option white women have of leaving their race out of the conversation about their rights as women. As Audre Lorde put it, "I recognize that my power as well as my primary oppressions come as a result of my Blackness as well as my womanness, and therefore my struggles on both these fronts are inseparable" (20). Intersectional feminism is a way of thinking that acknowledges this inseparability of race and gender (as well as other aspects of identity such as sexuality and disability). It affirms that "different kinds of prejudice can be amplified in different ways when put together" (International Women's Development Agency). This means that not all women face the same amounts of prejudice or discrimination. For example, the prejudices that a black lesbian woman faces are far greater than the prejudices that a white straight woman faces, even though both face discrimination as women.

Ethos
The introduction (which is two paragraphs long) provides context and background information.

Johnson 2

The debate over the 2017 Women's March on Washington shows that not all feminists support the idea of intersectional feminism, similar to the way not all black women activists supported black members of the LGBT community when Audre Lorde delivered her speech "I Am Your Sister: Black Women Organizing across Sexualities" at Medgar Evers College in 1985. In this speech, Lorde creates an effective argument for inclusion of the LGBT community in black activism by acknowledging the potential resistance of her audience, being clear and specific, using a variety of examples to support her argument, and suggesting a course of action. Activists who want to make the feminist movement more inclusive should look to Lorde's speech as an effective model for how to persuade those who are resistant to intersectional feminism.

Thesis
The main claim is given in two sentences at the end of paragraph 2.

Lorde knows that she faces an audience who might be resistant to her message, so she begins by building a sense of goodwill. In her opening paragraphs, she refers to her audience as family and says that speaking at the college "feels like coming home" (19). She acknowledges that families don't have to agree on everything by saying "unity does not require that we be identical to each other" (19). Statements like this put her audience at ease and give them permission to disagree with parts of her message, making them more open to parts they might agree with. She acknowledges that the audience might find her message difficult but points out that she also faces difficulty in speaking with them, knowing that they might reject her message. Lorde refers to the effort required on both sides as "mutual stretching" (20). By showing she is willing to do some of this "stretching" herself, she inspires her audience to work to find common ground with her.

Logos
Specific quotations from the text support the writer's analysis.

Johnson 3

Next, Lorde defines the obstacle she sees in connecting with her audience: "heterosexism and homophobia, two grave barriers to organizing among Black women" (20). She shares specific definitions of the terms *heterosexism* and *homophobia* so that she and her audience will "have a common language" (20). She explains what she means when she says she is a *black feminist* and a *black lesbian*, and she offers personal examples of some of the hurtful and discriminatory comments she has heard from fellow black feminists. By being clear and specific about how she defines all of these terms and by offering personal examples, she ensures that her audience understands her message and can feel how damaging heterosexism and homophobia can be. She also encourages her audience to think about how overcoming those barriers might bring them more unity and amplify their voices as black women. In other words, she is careful to show her audience the potential benefits of changing their attitudes and behaviors.

Lorde builds her argument through a variety of evidence. Although she appeals to her audience's emotions and sense of what is right, she is also careful to use logic to support her points. She offers numerous examples of how members of the black LGBT community have always been involved in activism, even if they were not recognized. Some of these examples are drawn from her own accomplishments, as when she says, "when I fought institutionalized racism in the New York City schools, I was a Black Lesbian" (23). Others are drawn from the accomplishments of well-known gay and lesbian writers such as Langston Hughes, Angelina Weld Grimké, and Lorraine Hansberry. Lorde also points out numerous gay and lesbian organizations that are "committed to and engaged in antiracist

Logos
The writer uses reasoning to interpret Lorde's argument and draw conclusions from it.

Johnson 4

activity" (24). These examples help her audience see that LGBT people are already members of their activist community.

Much as some of Lorde's audience was resistant to her message about inclusiveness for gay and lesbian activists, some feminists are resistant to the idea of focusing on the needs of minority groups through intersectional feminism. Brittney Cooper, Assistant Professor of Women's and Gender Studies and Africana Studies at Rutgers University, explains the resistance this way: "No one wants to feel like a bad person. Finding out that you might be harming people simply because you have been oblivious to them and their needs is a hard truth to confront" (qtd. in Desmond-Harris). Lorde's method of trying to help her audience find common ground with her and making it easier for them to accept her way of thinking is a useful model for those who want to counter this kind of resistance in the feminist movement.

Some feminists might criticize Lorde's methods as going too easy on her audience. Many women who identify with minority groups have given up on intersectional feminism out of frustration with people who aren't willing to confront their own prejudices. Tamela J. Gordon, the creator of the women's empowerment group Sisters with Aspiration, explained in a 2018 essay why she was "breaking up" with intersectional feminism. In her essay, Gordon illustrates why she believes that intersectional feminism "doesn't care about me" and states, "Intersectional feminism doesn't mean anything if white women still struggle to support those whose identities cross intersections that are foreign to theirs." Women like Gordon may feel justifiably angry about being forced to do all the work

Ethos
Quoting an expert and citing sources in the text enhance credibility.

Ethos
Presenting a counterclaim shows willingness to consider other perspectives fairly.

Pathos
The words *justifiably angry* invite readers to sympathize with this emotion.

Johnson 5

to overcome other people's prejudice and may therefore feel that Lorde's speech is too easy on her audience.

However, Lorde also makes some hard demands of her audience. She tells them, "[I]t is necessary for you to stop oppressing me through false judgment. I do not want you to ignore my identity, nor do I want you to make it an insurmountable barrier between our sharing of strengths" (20). She asks her audience to take action when she says, "How do we organize around our difference, neither denying them nor blowing them up out of proportion? The first step is an effort of will on your part" (25). She also offers her audience a specific plan of action by saying, "Even if you *do* believe any of these stereotypes about Black Lesbians, begin to practice *acting* like you don't believe them…. [T]hose stereotypes are yours to solve, not mine, and they are a terrible and wasteful barrier to our working together" (25-26). Lorde makes it clear that she expects effort from her audience and that she expects them to do their own work to overcome the stereotypes they believe.

Activists who want to make the feminist movement more inclusive should also ask their audience to do the difficult work involved, and modeling their arguments after Lorde's speech could make their audiences more receptive to that demand. By acknowledging the audience's resistance and creating a sense of goodwill, Lorde effectively prepares listeners to be open to her message. She then explains clearly and specifically how the audience's willingness to overcome their own prejudice will help the whole community. She uses a variety of evidence to appeal to their emotions, their sense of what is right, and their desire to reach shared goals.

Logos
The writer rebuts the counterclaim by providing specific examples to support her own interpretation.

Johnson 6

Finally, she suggests a course of action for her audience to take. Her method of persuasion could be used just as effectively to explain what intersectional feminism means and to convince people of its benefits.

Johnson 7

Works Cited

Desmond-Harris, Jenée. "To Understand the Women's March on Washington, You Need to Understand Intersectional Feminism." *Vox*, 21 Jan. 2017, www.vox.com/identities/ 2017/1/17/14267766/womens-march-on-washington -inauguration-trump-feminism-intersectionaltiy-race-class.

Gordon, Tamela J. "Breaking Up with Intersectional Feminism." *Medium*, 26 Apr. 2018, medium.com/@shewritestolive/ breaking-up-with-intersectional-feminism-689cfab82b7e.

International Women's Development Agency. "What Does Intersectional Feminism Actually Mean?" *IWDA*, 11 May 2018, iwda.org.au/what-does-intersectional -feminism-actually-mean/.

Lorde, Audre. "I Am Your Sister: Black Women Organizing across Sexualities." *A Burst of Light: Essays by Audre Lorde,* Firebrand Books, 1988, pp. 19-26.

Tolentino, Jia. "The Somehow Controversial Women's March on Washington." *New Yorker*, 18 Jan. 2017, www.newyorker .com/culture/jia-tolentino/the-somehow-controversial -womens-march-on-washington.

Ethos
Source citations follow the conventions of MLA Style.

Begin planning an academic argument

Now that you've studied the parts of an academic argument and how each one plays an important role in making the argument persuasive, consider the Chapter 6 Project assignment and begin making some notes toward a plan for tackling that argument assignment. In your notes, you might consider responding to the following questions:

- What topics interest me that fit with this assignment?
- What informed opinions do I have that could potentially become a claim?
- What kinds of support or evidence would I need to back up my opinions/working thesis?

6.2   Introduce your main claim

In this section, we'll walk you through a process of developing your introduction for an academic argument. While we're discussing this paragraph first, remember that lots of writers prefer to delay writing the introduction until after they have some of their body paragraphs drafted. As long as you have a clear sense of your claim, you can draft content to begin making your argument. As you loop back to check your thinking during your writing process, you'll have plenty of opportunities to move content around, develop new material, and cut passages that don't fit with your overall argument.

Writing a persuasive introduction

The first paragraph of an academic argument introduces readers to your general topic. While the content of an opening paragraph varies depending upon the type of argument you're writing, it typically has three common features that appear in order: a hook, background/context, and the claim.

- **Hook.** The opening sentences should grab the reader's attention with an interesting or intriguing rhetorical question, fact, quote, or brief anecdote. The hook "pulls in" the audience by inviting them into the conversation presented in the text.

- **Background/context.** The sentences following the hook continue to draw readers in by providing information they need to be able to consider your claim. This information could be historical context, relevant statistics, or personal experience. You're not trying to build your entire argument in the opening paragraph, but it's OK to mention ideas that you'll explore in more depth in the supporting paragraphs that follow.

- **Claim.** In academic arguments, the claim often appears as the last sentence in the opening paragraph. It presents your informed position and may briefly describe how you plan to support it in the body of your work. The claim serves as a kind of map to help readers know where you're going to take them in your text.

Take a closer look at Kristjan's introduction to his argument "Bloodshed Cinema: Dehumanization in the Opening Scene of *Saving Private Ryan*" to see how this works.

(1) When Steven Spielberg's *Saving Private Ryan* (1998) was released, it shocked viewers with its impeccably accurate depiction of World **(2)** War II. The opening scene of the movie, which shows the battle at Omaha Beach in grisly detail, truly captures the heartless violence of the war. The scene focuses mainly on the American viewpoint of the battle; Captain Miller (Tom Hanks) and Sergeant Horvath (Tom Sizemore) lead the American troops onto the beaches of Normandy while under constant deadly fire from the Germans positioned **(3)** on bluffs high above them. In this opening scene, Spielberg uses several filming techniques to show that the brutality of World War II dehumanized the soldiers who fought it.

(1) *Hook.* Revealing that viewers were "shocked" when they saw the opening scene of this movie is a way to invite readers into the argument by making them wonder what was so shocking about the opening scene.

(2) *Background/context.* Kristjan introduces the setting of the opening scene (the battle on Omaha Beach), prepares readers for the fact that the scene is "grisly" and difficult to watch, and introduces some characters and actors who play them who'll be central to later discussion in his argument.

3 *Claim.* Kristjan's thesis suggests that he'll discuss "several filming techniques" in the body of his argument to make the case that the opening scene was indeed revolutionary in the way it depicted war's horrors.

Avoiding common pitfalls in your introduction

Even writers who know what's supposed to happen in well-written introductory paragraphs sometimes hit trouble spots. The following guidelines will help you avoid some common problems.

- **Provide appropriate and specific context.** Writers who know the importance of providing context in the opening paragraphs sometimes go too far back in time or provide more context than readers need. If you find yourself referring to enormous concepts such as "the entire world" or "for all of time," consider narrowing your focus. Perhaps a smaller group or timeframe is what you need to help readers understand your specific position.

- **Use language that invites, not alienates, readers.** Sometimes, when trying to generate interest in the hook, writers inadvertently push readers away. Consider how readers might react to the following provocative opening sentence: "Meat eaters are bloodthirsty murderers." That sentence is going to generate attention, but not the kind of attention you want. The meat eaters in that writer's audience have just been labeled killers and are unlikely to want to read further.

A helpful practice is to share your draft introduction with others and ask them to tell you whether it makes them interested in what you'll say in the whole text or is off-putting or ineffective as an appeal to your audience, and what makes it so.

REFLECT

Consider your process for writing introductory paragraphs

Writers have different processes for writing introductions. Some people dive right in and write a draft of the introduction first. Others put it off until the rest of the text is written and come back to it near the end of ▶

the writing process. Here, we invite you to reflect on your experience with writing introductory paragraphs for arguments. What assumptions have you made in the past about how they should be written? Do you have a go-to method or structure for opening paragraphs? What parts of writing an introduction for an academic argument are challenging for you? Write a paragraph or more that reflects on your process for writing introductory paragraphs for an academic argument.

UNDERSTAND

Explore one student's introduction to an academic argument

To better understand how the parts of an introduction work in an academic argument, consider the example below. The paragraph, written by our student Rebekah Jones, illustrates the parts of an opening paragraph in her argument essay.

①How many visual images do you see in a 24-hour period? Hundreds? ②Thousands? In twenty-first-century America, we are bombarded by visual images including screen images, movies, TV, and video games. ③Every day we encounter ideas and personal agendas in visual form that try to convince us to think a certain way or buy a product or service. ④One way that this is done is through advertising. ⑤Another much more respected and refined way is through art. ⑥While art can be admired for its beauty or represent the artist's perspective, the purpose of its creation usually runs much deeper. ⑦Artists want people to dissect a piece of art in their own way to glean meaning from it. ⑧To do this, artists use rhetoric as a tool to convey deeper messages and establish a certain point of view that they want the viewer to understand.

1   *Hook.* This hook directly engages readers (using "you") and invites them to consider an interesting question that affects our daily lives.

2   *Background/context.* After the hook, Sentence 2 limits the scope of the context ("In twenty-first-century America") and introduces examples of visual images that readers will relate to.

3   Sentence 3 uses a common experience to connect with readers and introduce various purposes for visual images.

4   Sentence 4 acknowledges what readers may think is the most common format for visual images that attempt to have a rhetorical effect on us: advertising.

5   Sentence 5 pushes beyond reader expectations by adding art to options for visual forms of persuasion. It also lays the groundwork for introducing the writer's position in the thesis.

6   Sentence 6 extends the assertion in Sentence 5 that art is a form of visual persuasion.

7   Sentence 7 brings the viewers of art into the conversation and prepares readers for the thesis that will say that artists use rhetoric when creating art. The writer—Rebekah—is reminding her audience that rhetoric requires a relationship between the rhetor and the audience.

8   *Claim.* The last sentence states Rebekah's informed position ("artists use rhetoric as a tool") and forecasts two areas of support that later paragraphs will develop ("to convey deeper messages" and "establish a certain point of view that they want the viewer to understand").

In the supporting paragraphs that would follow Rebekah's claim, we could expect that the text would tackle these two points in the order they appear in the thesis. However, Rebekah might need more than one paragraph to fully support each piece of her argument. Two areas of support don't necessarily default to only two body paragraphs.

> **APPLY**
>
> ## Draft an introductory paragraph for an academic argument
>
> In Section 6.1, you started making notes about options for writing the Chapter 6 Project. Here, we invite you to look back at those notes to write a working draft of your introductory paragraph for that argument. To do ▶

this, you'll need to settle on the working claim you want to support in the argument. You may also need to do a little research to begin thinking about the background context your first paragraph needs to provide your audience. And you'll need to consider what kind of story, interesting fact, or other information could serve as a hook to draw in your audience at the start of your paragraph.

6.3 Write persuasive paragraphs to support your claim

In this section, we'll help you understand a variety of ways to make your argument more persuasive for your audience. We'll show you how the paragraphs you include in your academic arguments work together to build your argument for the Chapter 6 Project.

Considering multiple ways to support your claim

We've said that academic writing relies heavily on evidence to support a thesis. But what might this evidence look like? Evidence can appear in a variety of forms, generally falling into four overarching categories of logical reasoning, outside source material, visuals, and personal experience.

- **Logical reasoning.** Start with a broad claim and present a series of statements that clearly show readers why your claim is true. The pattern of reasoning can be based on your own thoughts alone, or it can also use outside source material as part of your reasoning. Generally, we call this type of support logos.

- **Outside source material.** Quoting or paraphrasing outside source material can bolster your argument by providing informed opinions to support your claims. Bringing in these additional voices that have expertise related to your topic increases your academic ethos as well.

- **Visuals.** Charts, illustrations, photographs, and other types of visuals often enhance an academic argument by giving readers an additional way to process the evidence you present. For example, rather than presenting several statistics as written words, you might consider using a table or chart to present that information. Visuals also help break up long passages of text and provide readers a place to pause and further process your argument.

- **Personal experience.** Sharing brief stories that recount your experience with something related to your argument often captures readers' attention and deepens your ethos. Including these anecdotes helps remind readers that your argument actually affects real people. Personal experience often draws on emotion or pathos.

Paragraphs sometimes include only one or two types of evidence, but it's possible for a paragraph to include all of them. You should choose the kinds of evidence that suit the context and resonate with your audience. Traditionally, academic arguments relied heavily and almost exclusively on logical reasoning. Ethos, or demonstrating personal credibility, played a role too. These days, using a variety of emotional appeals (pathos) will often strengthen your argument and engage your audience. Showing passion about your topic by letting readers know when you feel some sadness, pride, outrage, or skepticism sometimes adds a level of complexity to your writing.

Using multiple paragraphs to support your claim

The claim is only as strong as the supporting paragraphs that follow it. While you may have heard that a proper essay always has a certain number of supporting paragraphs—no more and no less—we encourage you to use as many paragraphs as you need to effectively support your thesis. Keep the following tips in mind as you plan paragraphs in your argument.

- **Limit the focus of each paragraph to one central idea.** Use a topic sentence to focus the paragraph. If material in your paragraph doesn't relate in some way to your topic sentence, it probably needs to be moved to another paragraph or deleted entirely.
- **Arrange paragraphs in an order that makes sense for readers.** Each paragraph performs a rhetorical function that moves your overall argument forward. A paragraph might introduce a supporting subclaim, offer an example to extend an existing supporting claim, analyze information from outside source material, or introduce and address a counterclaim. Arrange paragraphs to deliver relevant information when your readers need it to understand additional paragraphs that will follow.
- **Include at least one paragraph that addresses counterclaims.** A thesis for an argument needs to be disputable. In other words, competing claims can reasonably be made about your topic. These arguments against your claim

shouldn't be ignored. Instead, bring them into your text and demonstrate why they are not as strong as your claim—even if they do have some good points. Your argument and your ethos will ultimately be stronger if you acknowledge these counterclaims and address each one of them.

As you plan and write your paragraphs, remember to use plenty of transition words and phrases to help readers see how your ideas are connected. Look back to Section 4.3 to review how to use transitions effectively.

REFLECT

Consider past experiences with organizing support in an argument

We've been advising you to develop your supporting paragraphs rhetorically. That is, we want you to think about how effectively planning your paragraphs involves considering your audience's need to know. Here, we invite you to reflect on that idea.

You may have never written an academic argument before. That's OK. But we're pretty sure you've had experiences where you needed to make a case for something and you took some time to plan how you'd approach it. Write a paragraph or more about an experience you've had of needing to make a case for something. What was the main thing you were arguing for? What were your reasons? If you had to translate that into an academic argument as we've described it here, what changes would you need to make?

UNDERSTAND

Watch Jay and Li arrange supporting paragraphs

In this video, Jay and Li analyze supporting evidence and decide how paragraphs should be arranged in an essay. They work with the sample paragraphs that follow, taken from the essay "Video Games: Real Women, Real Issues" by Jora Burnett and presented out of order. Look for ways Jay and Li arrange Jora's supporting paragraphs so you can put into action the advice we've given you about arranging support paragraphs in your own academic arguments.

Video: Arranging Supporting Paragraphs

Scrambled paragraphs from a student essay

Jora Burnett

Draft Paragraphs for Essay Assignment

Video Games: Real Women, Real Issues

Introduction and thesis

The rampant misrepresentation of women in the electronic gaming industry may come as a shock to most consumers. Female gamers are a large source of the profits that the thirty-billion-dollar video game industry rakes in, but the industry continues to cultivate sexist stereotypes and tropes in its representation of women. Instead of rehashing and recycling these tropes, the industry would be wise to consider that women come in all shapes, sizes, races, and sexualities, and that proper representation of women is needed. Gamers today should not tolerate the stereotypical, trope-ridden characterization of female characters, and the gaming community needs to take action to combat the intense sexism the industry promotes and the violence directed toward female gamers.

Counterclaim rebuttal

Some people might claim that games with female protagonists are great examples of wonderfully written female power. *Portal* would be one such example, but games that focus on powerful female characters are few and far between. In the past five years, more games have been released that include wonderfully written female characters with varying degrees of representation, but unfortunately, those games still account for only a small number of all video games.

Visuals based on statistics

Women make up a significant audience for the gaming industry. As data from the Entertainment Software Association shows, in 2014 women were only 18 points behind men in the percentage of players (see Figure 1). The video game industry holds the idea of video games being a completely male-dominated community when in fact that is not the case because 41% of gamers in the United States are female. Despite these statistics, only around 4% of video games produced by the industry have a female protagonist who runs the game with her own story (see Figure 2).

Figure 1 Gender of people who play video games

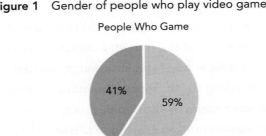

People Who Game

□ Men ■ Women

Figure 2   Gender of protagonists in games

Protagonists in Games

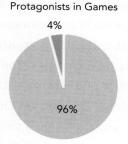

4%

96%

☐ Men   ☐ Women

Outside source (expert opinion and examples)

In video game universes, the damsel in distress is the oldest
trope of all. The damsel-in-distress trope involves a female character
who is rendered completely helpless, usually via kidnapping, and
is used as a plot device for the male character to progress in the
game. Rescuing the damsel can also be the plot. Notable examples
of this trope can be found in the *Mario* and *The Legend of Zelda*
game series by Nintendo, with their two princesses Peach and
Zelda. These series have been around since the 1980s, but the trope
is still popular today. Pop-culture expert Anita Sarkeesian talks
about tropes and women in her three-part *YouTube* series "Tropes
vs. Women in Video Games." In part two she talks in depth about
the modern damsel-in-distress trope. Sarkeesian states, "We've
seen a dramatic increase in the number of games attempting to cut
through the clutter by being as dark and edgy as possible. So we've
seen developers try to 'spice up' the damsel-in-distress cliché by
combining it with other tropes that involved victimized women."
Women's lives are not valued in video games, even if male characters
are supposed to be saving them.

Logical reasoning, outside source, and personal experience

If the video game industry does not change its portrayals of
women, negative issues like the Gamergate movement will be all

the public knows about gamers. In the article "What Is Gamergate, and Why? An Explainer for Non-Geeks," Jay Hathaway explains Gamergate and why it is an online movement no gamer should be a part of. Hathaway states that Gamergate started "as a pernicious attack on one female game developer, Zoe Quinn, and her sex life. Quinn has been the victim of death threats and harassment since she began trying to publish Depression Quest, a text-based game partially based on her own experience with depression, in 2013." Some in the gaming community, primarily males, reacted with hostility against Quinn in online forums such as Reddit and 4Chan, railing against her game and its player experience, noting always that Quinn is too emotional in her game development. These gamers published Quinn's address and phone number and the threats against her became so intense that she had to change her residence and effectively go into hiding for several months. As a female gamer and future game developer, I am afraid that my contributions to this industry will be judged not on their playability but on my own personal life. This is not acceptable.

Personal knowledge and outside source (academic research)

Not only are female characters victimized, but women who play video games are themselves being mistreated. Sarkeesian speaks at universities about the blatant misrepresentation females face in video games. In October of 2014, Sarkeesian had to cancel a speech at Utah State University due to mass-shooting threats the school received via e-mail in response to her visit. The fact that this is happening in 2014 is shocking and makes it clear that something in the video game industry needs to change. Researcher Christopher E. Near writes, "these depictions in video games potentially influence the socialization of young people, who make up a large part of their audience, and thus may transform or reproduce gender representations in the general culture" (p. 253). The video game industry needs to recognize the damage they are inflicting on young female gamers with the gender stereotypes and female tropes they use over and over again.

Complete source information

Works Cited

Entertainment Software Association. "Essential Facts about the Computer and Video Game Industry: 2017 Sales, Demographic, and Usage Data." *Entertainment Software Association,* Apr. 2017, www.theesa.com/wp-content/uploads/2017/09/EF2017 _Design_FinalDigital.pdf.

Hathaway, Jay. "What Is Gamergate, and Why? An Explainer for Non-Geeks." *Gawker*, 10 Oct. 2014, gawker.com/what-is -gamergate-and-why-an-explainer-for-non-geeks-1642909080.

Near, Christopher E. "Selling Gender: Associations of Box Art Representation of Female Characters with Sales for Teen- and Mature-Rated Video Games." *Sex Roles*, vol. 68, no. 3-4, 1 Feb. 2013, pp. 252-69. U.S. National Library of Medicine, www.ncbi .nlm.nih.gov/pmc/articles/PMC3586322/.

Robbins, M. Brandon. "They're Gamers, Not 'Girl Gamers.'" *Library Journal*, 7 Aug. 2014, reviews.libraryjournal.com/2014/08/media/ gaming/theyre-gamers-not-girl-gamers-games-gamers-gaming/.

Sarkeesian, Anita. "Damsel in Distress: Part 2—Tropes vs. Women in Video Games." *YouTube*, 28 May 2013, www.youtube.com/ watch?v=toa_vH6xGqs.

APPLY

Draft a support paragraph for your academic argument

In this section, we've introduced you to strategies for writing paragraphs that support your academic arguments. We've also encouraged you to think about these support paragraphs rhetorically. In other words, we've asked you to think about what your audience needs to know about your argument and have encouraged you to think about when to deliver new information to them.

With all that in mind, write just one paragraph that supports your working claim for your Chapter 6 Project. You'll have plenty of opportunities to improve it and write more paragraphs. But for now, just try to write one.

6.4   Write a persuasive conclusion

In this section, you'll learn what kinds of things to include in a conclusion for an argument and begin making notes on the kind of conclusion you want to write for the Chapter 6 project.

Approaching the conclusion rhetorically

Just as the introduction and supporting paragraphs work best when writers keep readers' needs in mind, concluding paragraphs also benefit from this writing practice. When you think about writing concluding paragraphs, remember that readers of conclusions have specific needs that don't necessarily come into play for other parts of the academic argument.

- **Readers need a concise ending.** Sometimes writers think that a conclusion needs to be really long to capture the full claim and all the evidence that's been presented in supporting paragraphs. In fact, a handful of sentences is fine for most short academic arguments. As the writer, your job in crafting the conclusion paragraph is to reiterate your claim and remind readers of the key support for it.

- **Readers need to see the larger significance of your argument.** As part of your conclusion, consider what impact you want your conclusion to have on readers. How is your argument connected to other issues of concern? In some cases, you might also encourage readers to actively consider your argument by taking an action such as contacting a government representative or local business owner to voice support or concerns.

- **Readers need a memorable conclusion.** So that your argument sticks with your readers, consider including a vivid example or detail, perhaps a quotation or statistic, that will remind readers of why your argument is important.

REFLECT

Write about your experience of writing conclusions

We've suggested you compose your concluding paragraph rhetorically—as a way of connecting with readers who have stuck with you and your argument all the way to the end. The concluding paragraph shows your respect for readers by wrapping up your argument in a concise way and inviting them to participate in the cause you have advocated for.

We imagine this may be a new way for you to think about writing conclusions. Here we invite you to look back on ways you've approached writing concluding paragraphs in the past.

What assumptions have you made in the past about how conclusions should be written? Do you have a go-to method that you use? What parts of writing a conclusion for an academic argument seem challenging for you? Write a paragraph or more to reflect on these questions.

UNDERSTAND

See how to create a rhetorical conclusion

You've learned that an effective conclusion is a concise paragraph that wraps up an academic essay. It reminds readers of your thesis and recaps some of your strongest support for it. Finally, it often invites readers to stay engaged with your topic in some way.

Let's break down one essay's conclusion to see what makes it work effectively. This conclusion is from Jora Burnett's essay "Video Games: Real Women, Real Issues," which Jay and Li discussed in the video "Arranging Supporting Paragraphs." Jora argues that video games don't represent women fairly or accurately and if that issue were addressed, the video gaming industry would attract more — and more diverse — users.

> **(1)** Making the video game industry more diverse and safe for people of all genders is an important transformation that will influence the future of digital entertainment. **(2)** If video game developers add female characters with realistic characterization and tropes that are not based on bias, then all players can find themselves in the game. **(3)** Allowing for female perspectives in game development, the industry will also become a more inclusive culture that can attract both male and female players. **(4)** With the likelihood of more players, the video game industry would profit immensely, and interesting new games would thrive. **(5)** Games and non-gamers alike can make a difference by just paying attention to representations of women in video games and speaking up when they see something they find offensive.

(1) The first sentence in the conclusion recaps the thesis without using exactly the same words as appeared in the introduction. It also points toward a more promising future for gaming.

(2) Here the author restates her point about the gaming industry and how it needs to change to be more inclusive of women's perspectives.

(3) The author reminds readers of a point she developed in the supporting paragraphs of her essay: including female perspectives in game *development* (not just game characters or game playing) will likely increase the number of players.

(4) This sentence recaps one of the strong arguments the writer makes in the essay: making gaming more inclusive also makes it more profitable.

(5) The final sentence leaves readers with a call to action that may help bring about the inclusive future for game development that the writer hopes for.

APPLY

Write plans for a rhetorical conclusion

Now that you've learned about what an effective conclusion does in an academic argument, consider how you might end the argument essay you're writing for the Chapter 6 Project. How might you make your conclusion loop back to your claim? What supporting points should you recap at the end of your argument? How might you suggest larger implications of your argument? How could you make your conclusion memorable for readers? Make some notes to help you plan your conclusion.

Chapter 6 Project
Compose a claim-driven academic argument

Throughout Chapter 6, we've been showing you a rhetorical process for writing an academic argument. Use that information to complete the following writing assignment or a different argument that your instructor assigns.

In her article "The American People Have Spoken: Reform Our Criminal Justice System," Holly Harris argues that an important issue to a majority of Americans is concern about a justice system that jails too many people, incarcerates people unfairly, costs too much, and doesn't always deter enough crime. Finding a way to address these problems should be an issue around which people could unite. As she writes, "Republicans and Democrats are both invested in fixing the justice system, which makes it difficult for either side to politicize this effort. That wouldn't be smart politics anyway. Polls show widespread support for specific reforms that will lower the swelling prison population, save money, and make communities safer."

Take some time to learn more about the concerns driving criminal justice reform. Some good places to start are the websites for the following organizations:

- The Sentencing Project
- The Marshall Project
- The Innocence Project
- Center on Juvenile and Criminal Justice

Once you're more familiar with issues that motivate criminal justice reform, draw on your reading and perhaps your personal experience to write an academic argument on an issue related to criminal justice reform. Your essay should include an engaging introduction, a disputable claim that presents your position on the issue, support paragraphs that give reasons behind your position and that perhaps include some of your personal experience with the issue, and a memorable conclusion that wraps up your argument. If you use outside sources, remember to use in-text citations and include a bibliography page with your sources listed at the end of your argument.

As you're writing, remember that plans can—and often do!—change once you begin planning or writing. As you loop back through your emerging draft, you may think of new ideas, discover a stronger organization for your draft, or realize that you need additional evidence to support your claim. If that happens, just adjust your plan and keep moving forward.

7

Writing for Public, Digital Spaces

 Achieve *If your instructor has assigned them, you can complete the Reflect and Apply activities and work on the Chapter Projects in Achieve.*

7.1 Understand webtexts as academic writing

Academic writing often takes the form of essays, but it can also appear in other types of writing that incorporate public, digital spaces such as online forums, blogs (also known as webtexts), and social media. In this chapter, we will explore popular types of public, digital writing and how authors and audiences shift expectations and use specific tools to connect in these unique spaces.

We'll focus on a few of the kinds of public, digital writing you're likely to use and create during college: webtexts, memes, infographics, and social media posts.

A webtext is an online public document that can be a blog, article, electronic magazine (zine), or other text produced specifically for internet distribution. Most importantly, webtexts are living documents that contain interactive elements that can be revised based on audience feedback. In webtexts, authors share information, thoughts, and ideas they want an audience to read and respond to, often in a series of posts. Somewhat different from academic essays, webtexts are rhetorically successful when their authors are able to generate conversations with readers in real time and draw web traffic to posts. Webtexts serve many of the same purposes as traditional essays and have many of the same structural parts. What's different is that the tools webtexts use to support these parts are multimodal, meaning that they can be videos, audio, images, or hyperlinks.

183

Seeing the similarities between webtexts and academic essays

Webtexts such as blog posts, web pages, and online articles can have many of the same parts as traditional essays—parts such as a title, an introduction, a thesis, evidence, and a conclusion. Let's look at a sample blog by student Eddie Kihara, who is a technical communication major, to see these parts. Eddie's blog (also a webtext) is titled "Ask More Questions," which meets the webtext requirement for a catchy title that will draw in readers.

Webtexts have titles.   Academic blog posts use engaging titles to hook readers. Titles can appear as questions or direct statements, and they usually follow the date and the name of the person writing the post. Titles in blogs are often visually set off by fonts, colors, and text sizes that differ from those used for the rest of the post.

Webtexts have introductions.   In addition to engaging readers through written words, a blog post introduction will also have a visual banner, header, or image "above the fold" (visible on a screen without having to scroll) that invites the reader to engage with your topic. The banner usually also features the blog's title, which needs to be catchy to draw in readers.

Webtexts have a thesis.   Webtexts, especially blogs, use direct language in their introductions to tell readers what they're going to argue. Many times, a

Example of a Blog Post

The banner displays the blog's title, "Ask More Questions."

The title of the post follows the date and appears in a different color than the headings within the post.

In this introduction, the writer states his thesis in the first sentence and states his purpose, to define usability testing, in the last sentence.

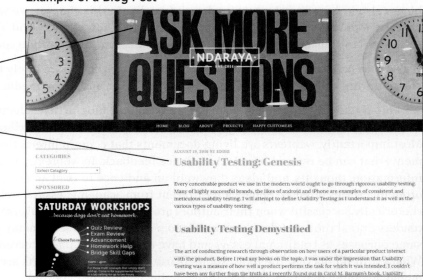

Eddie Kihara

blogger will start an introduction with a thesis statement, then provide some context for it. Near the end of the introduction, a blog post states its purpose outright, to draw in readers and keep them interested in reading. Remember that blogging is a conversation. In a blog post, it's OK to write, for example, "This blog post will attempt to define usability testing." You may explicitly mention the exact points you will make to support your thesis, but often bloggers don't provide this kind of roadmap for readers. So, you must be mindful of your post's organization and make sure you stay on mission with the message you are communicating through your post. Visual elements such as the banner and title will also help convey your purpose to your readers.

Webtexts use evidence. Academic essays have supporting paragraphs, and sometimes images, that provide evidence. So do webtexts, but webtexts also make use of multimodal content such as videos, GIFs (moving images), and links that give readers more information and provide an interactive reading experience. Blog writers, like academic writers, frame each piece of support in their own voices and credit all outside material.

Evidence in a Blog Post

Solutions when announced, will evoke one of three reactions from those affected by the changes, mosity employees. Employee reactions are governed by their perception of solution(s) quality: *High Quality – Low Acceptance, High Quality – Low Acceptance and lastly, Low Quality – High Acceptance.* Needless to say, the most favorable (least resisted) of the three is the high quality and high acceptance solution. This type of reaction is mostly achieved through participative decision making processes where self-directed work teams arrive at a solution though consensus. Assuming the pyramid's bottom two needs are met, let's examine this approach's effectiveness by looking at Maslow's hierarchy of needs.

In this example, support appears as written words, embedded links, and a visual with a source citation.

Maslow Hierarchy of Needs Pyramid (Source: http://bit.ly/1PXJIU3)

When management is seeking to find solutions to problems and implement change, it is always good practice to involve employees in the process. The general idea and goal is to set off a domino effect whereby; employees feel connected to the company as well as the managing group, feel valued since management takes time to hear their voices and opinions resulting in highly engaged work teams eager to fix company issues. Basically, people want to be part of the problem solving group. Additionally, individuals within these problem solving/continuous improvement work teams tend to draw closer to one another which boosts work place interpersonal relations.

Eddie Kihara

Webtexts have conclusions. Webtexts tend to be shorter than academic essays, so their conclusions also tend to be shorter. For example, you might devote several paragraphs to a conclusion in a long essay but only a few sentences to a conclusion in a blog post. And unlike essays, webtexts often include an additional paragraph that invites commenting and feedback—digital audiences expect it. So, in a webtext such as a blog, the conclusion is not the last paragraph; it's the next-to-last paragraph. The final paragraph of a webtext invites readers to engage with the text and includes your contact information for that feedback (i.e., Twitter, Facebook, etc.).

Conclusion of a Blog Post

In this example, Jeanne Bohannon sums up a post on online learning and gives readers her contact information.

> This is just to say… learning best online practices over the past couple of years has taught me to have a growth mindset and to approach new challenges not as drudgery but as opportunities to cultivate my teaching presence as I learn from my communities of teacher-and-student scholars. I really do enjoy being present for all of this amazing growth!
>
> Please provide me feedback and comments below. I look forward to talking with you about democratic, online learning. You may also email me at jeanne_bohannon@kennesaw.edu.

Jeanne Bohannon

Thinking about how webtexts use visuals, links, tags, and commenting

Webtexts such as blogs live online, and by definition they invite feedback, interaction, and conversation. To facilitate that feedback and engage readers interactively, they have features that may not always appear in written academic essays. These features include visual elements, working hyperlinks, and a comments section.

Visual elements. Online readers expect webtexts to be engaging and interactive and tend to get bored by long, unbroken "walls of text." In fact, bloggers who use effective visuals generate more traffic to their posts. When writing a webtext, consider using visuals such as videos, images, memes, or GIFs to strengthen your message and to break up long written passages. You can also use design elements such as color, lines, and different type sizes to add visual interest and enhance your message.

Embedded video breaks up text walls

than anything else, usability testing is a study of various impact a product evokes from a user while trying to understand the motivations, logic, and emotions that drive user behavior while interacting with the product.

Check out the brief video below for a quick run down on what Usability Testing is from a person who is actually a practitioner in this field.

Types of Usability Testing

The greatest advantage to this idea is that testing can be conducted anywhere and with minimal resource investment. **Usability labs** need not run up into the hundreds of thousands in modern times.

Eddie Kihara

The embedded video in this post prompts readers to stop reading and click the play button for a more interactive experience.

Images help frame the text

"P" STANDS FOR PRESENCE: A REFLECTION ON TEACHING IN ONLINE ENVIRONMENTS

I love growing scholars!

Sometimes I have a hard time answering the question: "do you like teaching online?" Colleagues frequently ask me this questions, which is interesting in itself because I teach in a department with the word "digital" in its name. So, when they ask me, I am often slow to answer. I mean, there are so many variables, right? I do like experimenting with my critical-democratic teaching methods in new spaces. I also like providing an alternative to traditional coursework for students who are returning to school. I don't like working on Sunday nights (who does?); I typically don't like modular ANYTHING — I'm an organic kinda gal.

In my second year on the SPSU faculty, my chair asked me to teach a graduate course. Of course, this request also meant teaching online (for the first time), since our department's graduate programs are 100% online delivery. I accepted, because I just can't say no – NO. But, I took on the challenge, primarily because I wanted to teach a grad course. Then came the caveat: "oh by the way, you also have to re/design this course and pass it through TADL (SPSU's legacy online certification protocol. Oh, and you'll also need to get TADL trained by next week." Again, I must practice my "NO's. We were in the midst of consolidation, my chair seemed desperate (which is probably why she asked me in the first place), and I'm a placater. So, I did all of the above.

Yes, of course I will do that!

As I designed my course, I realized early on that many of the same best practices, like:

Jeanne Bohannon

In this blog post, static images are used to illustrate key points and keep readers interested.

Fonts and text-art add visual appeal

The first step to becoming a successful negotiator requires that you meticulously plan the negotiation. Planning involves four main steps as follows: identifying all the issues that you plan to negotiate, prioritizing these issues beginning with 'must haves' then working your way down to issues that you're willing to concede, establishing a settlement range, and lastly, developing strategies and tactics.

Central to your planning stage is the imperative that you find out as much as possible about your counterpart.

The reason why you enjoyed mid to high success rates in your younger age is because you had great insight about the dispositions of your 'opponent'. At times, you knew the degree-of-tantrum needed to sway your mom your way and other times you would use your big puppy eyes to earn yourself a few more minutes doing something you love. To be fair, tantrums and puppy eyes don't quite work as well as they did but, you've grown into a well informed logical being capable of articulating your arguments with charm akin to a baby hedgehog first steps. So, charm away!

Eddie Kihara

Here, larger type and a stylized quotation mark highlight an important point for readers. Quotations used as design elements in this way are sometimes called "pull quotes."

Working hyperlinks.   In webtexts, writers sometimes refer to outside source material via hyperlinks that point readers to those external sources, often other publications or statistics from a reliable source. Unless required for a specific instance, most bloggers don't format their sources as they would in an academic essay. Instead, they provide hyperlinks with keywords for the source, such as author's name, title of the source, and date. Hyperlinks also serve as visual elements and navigation tools to create a multilinear, interactive experience for your audience. If you include hyperlinks in an online academic argument, double-check the links in multiple browsers to make sure they work regardless of the browser a reader is using.

Tags.   After the conclusion of a webtext, readers expect to see tags. Tags are keywords and phrases that describe the main argument and topic of the web-text. When writers insert tags, we help readers find our writing (often called a post) and increase a post's visibility for anyone searching for information on our topic. Think of tags the same way you think of hashtags on Instagram or Twitter. Tags help writers generate meanings that interested readers can discover through web searches. Most public blogging platforms will prompt writers to insert tags.

Example of Tags

Jeanne Bohannon

Comment section.   Webtext authors and bloggers hope and expect that readers will comment on each post. Unlike academic essays, which are often produced for single audiences as final products, webtexts are living documents that need to be monitored by authors so that they can respond to comments posted by readers. Remember: it's all about creating and sustaining a conversation.

Comments on a Blog Post

3 THOUGHTS ON "WIN EVERY NEGOTIATION: STRATEGIZE"

chussey1
MARCH 30, 2016 AT 3:22 PM

I've got to say that you have a gift at blogging about your life stories. I personally would be terrified to challenge your mother to a game of poker after reading about her powers of negotiation. Even if I had a poker face (my face is too open, people can read me like a book), I have a feeling that she would be able to call every one of my bluffs. Your anecdote also illustrated another powerful element of negotiation... the best strategists know their opponent. I really loved this post.

★ Liked by 1 person   REPLY

Kendra
MARCH 31, 2016 AT 11:27 AM

Eddie, I always enjoy your posts, but this one was absolutely great! It was entertaining and I had a smile on my face the whole time I read it. What a great example of negotiation! Your mom seems like an awesome woman and was teaching you powerful lessons at a young age. Your tips about negotiation really resonated with me because I don't think I realized what an important factor fear is when negotiating. The man probably could sense that your mom had no fear of walking away, which contributed even more to his acceptance of her offer. Awesome post!

★ Liked by 1 person   REPLY

samjanea90
MAY 5, 2016 AT 2:04 PM

Let me just start off by saying that you and your mother really photogenic! I really enjoyed how you brought her in your blog. Very touching! You made a great example as far as what it takes to be a great negotiator. When it comes down to negotiating, you really have to know what it takes and strategize. Great post Eddie!

★ Like   REPLY

Eddie Kihara

REFLECT

Consider your experience with webtext successes and failures

As a digital reader, you may have interacted with webtexts that included effective introductions, visuals, and embedded videos. You may also have experienced webtexts that had nonworking hyperlinks, missing tags, or no contact information. Consider what you do as a digital reader when some of these pieces are missing from webtexts. Write a few sentences describing how you react as a reader when authors have been successful with their webtexts and also how you react when they have failed.

UNDERSTAND

Identify elements of a webtext

You've been reading about the ways webtexts should be organized to connect with their readers. In the blog post that follows, student Carson Long makes an argument that texting is not harming the English language. We have annotated Carson's post to identify some of the components of academic writing and webtexts that we've discussed in Section 7.1. As you read Carson's post, we invite you to consider the rhetorical situation: Who is his audience? What is his purpose for writing the post? How successful do you think he is in achieving his purpose?

The "Death" of the English Language: Or How Language Will Never Die

CARSON LONG

Carson hints at his position on the topic in the title, as he would in an argument essay.

Texting and texting shorthand have claims thrown around of people proudly proclaiming that texting is ruining the English language. News sources claiming that "Texting fogs the mind like cannabis" were common in the early 2000s when texting was just growing in popularity. Before texting had entered, even if reluctantly, the more traditional generation, it was seen as a destructive and distracting fad that was ruining the brains of the youth. I think it's safe to say that claims like those stated above would be widely criticized with today's popularization of texting.

The Guardian put out an article in 2012 stating that four billion people were now texting across the world. This is a vast difference from the average of 0.4 texts sent per person per month in 1995. The Guardian also claimed that over six trillion text messages were sent in 2010. Almost no form of technology has had such amazing growth at such an alarming rate. Even the internet took almost twice as long to catch on with the general population. Now, as with any sort of nontraditional advance in technology, there are naysayers claiming that texting will be the death of language. I disagree, and here's why:

> Underlined hyper-links take readers to the sources Carson cites. There is no formal bibliography.

1. Reading is reading, no matter where it's done.

In the past few years, I've noticed a large amount of "book shaming" and "smart shaming" in the youth culture. Book Shaming occurs mainly in the elementary to middle school age, where some children look down on others that enjoy reading. I've personally experienced Book Shaming and been ridiculed because I chose to voice my love for reading. Smart Shaming is nearly the same, but instead of ridicule coming from choosing to read books, it's ridicule caused by succeeding in school. The worst part is that this doesn't end at middle school, as this was very noticeable at a high school level as well.

> Main points are numbered, which is typical in webtexts, not in academic essays.

Leah Warkentin/Design Pics/Getty Images

This is terrifying to me.

Which is one of the reasons that I choose to believe that texting is helpful for developing reading skills in the youth of today who choose to actively not read. Communicating through text is now a necessity in an adult world and children

> Humorous images keep the tone informal and the audience engaged. An argument essay would use a more formal tone.

who choose not to read will be at a disadvantage when they realize this.

Texting, on the other hand, is a great way to develop many skills you would find in reading books. Skills like context clues, interpretation, and rhetorical communication are developing when communicating through text. These are skills that don't require the "right" form of communicating. Texting shorthand is irrelevant when it comes to these skills.

> Logical reasoning is used to provide persuasive evidence.

Reading is practice at communication. Whether it's a book or a text, that skill is being developed. Many kids who choose not to read, yet choose to text, can at least have some practice at reading and communicating through written communication. And that's important to have.

2. Language is a tool and will adapt.

There is no "right" form of language, because we use language to communicate effectively. Whatever form gets our message across quickly and efficiently is how we should use language. Of course, discourse communities each have different dialects to their language. A discourse community that uses hashtags and abbreviations will not communicate the same way as an academic setting. The point is communication is still occurring in a way that is rhetorical to members of that discourse community.

> Carson doesn't discuss the radical changes that English underwent during this time period, which could undermine his argument. Academic audiences expect to see acknowledgment of counterclaims.

Claiming that this or that is "ruining language" is ridiculous. In the past, there have been events that have been dangerous to the English language. In 1066, the Duke of Normandy, called William the Conqueror, took the throne of England. He did not speak any English, but he spoke French and Latin. Effectively, this meant that the royals of England for years to come would speak mostly French or Latin, not English. Somehow English survived in the laborers and peasants of England. For nearly 300 years, English was kept alive only by the peasants and generations of bilingual children. In 1377, King Richard II became the first king to use English exclusively since William the Conqueror, thus bringing English to the house of the royals again.

VCG Wilson/Fine Art/Corbis Historical/Getty Images

King Richard II

What does this mean?

It means that language will develop with the society and culture surrounding it. Our language cannot be killed by our using it in different ways. It is meant to be used in whatever way is most effective between people. There is no "right way." There are right ways for certain discourse communities, but we will all use our language differently.

The conclusion sums up his argument.

APPLY

Analyze a webtext

You've read about the ways in which webtexts are similar to and different from academic writing and considered your own experience with webtext successes and failures. Now we invite you to analyze a webtext. Choose a blog post or short work from a website that interests you and write at least two to three paragraphs in which you analyze its effectiveness. What elements of webtexts does it use successfully (or unsuccessfully)? What elements of academic writing does it include? How well do you think the authors have achieved their purpose with the text and connected with their audience?

7.2 Use effective visual tools to make your point

Writing in public spaces requires authors to consider other elements of rhetoric besides just written text. We've learned about webtexts and how authors use them to generate a conversation in a more conventional, yet still public, space. Webtexts still rely on traditional interplays between text and image. Often, though, digital readers will find meaning in our messages primarily through visuals, such as infographics and memes. But what makes these visuals effective for getting our points across to digital readers?

Reading infographics as meaningful visuals

Infographics are visual images that present complicated information to readers in easy-to-view and easy-to-understand ways. Often, writers use infographics to simplify statistics and numerical data while also providing an engaging way for readers to understand the data.

For example, when the National Education Association (NEA) wanted to inform the public about the dangers of bullying, it used the infographic "Bully Free, It Starts with Me," which also encouraged readers to take a pledge against bullying. This infographic shows a lot of data that we can easily read and understand. We can quickly see that 23 percent of students in American schools are bullied because of their weight, that 58 percent of bullying is verbal, and that 17 percent of the time students are bullied on the internet. The infographic also contains a source that explains how the NEA collected its data. The combination of minimal written text and eye-catching visual elements makes this infographic effective. Notice also that the shapes and colors of visual elements help get the point across. When infographic writers make choices like this, we call it design. An effective design requires thoughtful attention to colors, font size, shapes, and visual placement (where things are on the page) to create meaning for readers. Effective infographics also refer to credible sources for the data they present so that readers know they can believe the information.

Example of an Infographic

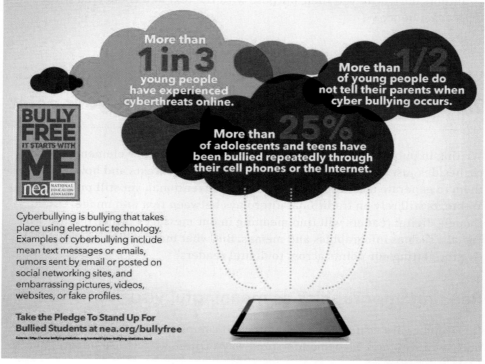

National Education Association

Using memes effectively in public writing

When we write publicly, whether on social media or in online forums, we often use memes to help readers understand what we are trying to say in an entertaining way. Memes are visuals, most often images or GIFs, that describe a timely topic, imitate cultural phenomena, and are shared widely on the internet. Examples of memes include well-known shareables like "Bad Luck Brian" and SpongeBob.

"Bad Luck Brian" Meme

SpongeBob SquarePants Meme

When we make or share memes, we do so because they do such a good job of conveying messages to a large audience. We call this idea *shareability*, and when we're being rhetorical as writers, we understand what makes a visual like a meme have such influence on our readers. When visuals have shareability, it's because they are concrete and timely, meaning they don't depict outdated popular culture events or phenomena. Readers and writers in digital spaces often instinctively know how shareable a meme is in terms of how long it's been circulating online and whether it's meaningful to a large audience.

> **REFLECT**
>
> ## Consider the timeliness of memes
>
> We can loop back to the five components of rhetoric discussed in Section 2.2 (purpose, audience, tone, genre, and context) to learn how our use of memes in public spaces can be effective. Viewing memes through this model will also help us understand how to use memes to be effective communicators in digital, public spaces. For example, we know from our ▶

rhetoric model that memes are a genre, or type, of writing that we generate using just a few words and an image to make a point. We also know that memes have a specific social context, meaning that we make or share memes that have specific cultural meanings in digital public spaces. We also use memes to convey messages for specific purposes for digital (often social media) audiences, also known as our "friends" or "followers."

What does it mean that we must be timely when we want to make or share a meme? List two memes or topics described by memes that you've shared in a digital space and explain whether they were timely or outdated. Why do you think so?

UNDERSTAND

Practice reading an infographic

Now that you know how infographics and memes work, practice evaluating an infographic for design and effectiveness. Look at the infographic on the next page, which was part of former First Lady Michelle Obama's campaign to encourage Americans to exercise more and eat healthy. This infographic was released around New Year's Day, a time when many people make resolutions about improving their health. As you read the infographic, consider the questions in the annotations.

APPLY

Analyze an infographic or meme

Search online for an infographic or meme that interests you. Consider the things that make infographics or memes effective and write a few sentences that provide your opinion on effectiveness of the text you chose. You may want to consider the advice for reading multimodal texts in Chapter 5. For instance, as you view the infographic or meme, try to separate the written words and visuals. How do the words and visuals complement one another? How does the author use colors and fonts in the design to increase the meaning of the message for an audience? How shareable and timely is the message?

What do the design of the title and the image of lights suggest?

What kind of information is presented in this infographic? Who is the audience?

What purpose do the images serve?

Notice the pink lines connecting images and text. Do they serve a purpose? How does the layout reinforce the message?

How does the information at the bottom enhance the infographic's credibility?

7.3   Write and read effectively on public social media

We've already learned how conveying messages in public spaces requires authors and readers to share meaning through nonwritten rhetorical elements. Particularly on social media, readers and authors share meaning through specific strategies that help digital communities communicate effectively with each other.

Sharing effectively on social media

Social media is just that: social. What we mean is that social media spaces are designed for sharing and connecting with followers and friends. What we choose to share in these spaces, however, isn't always effective. We have to choose our words, visuals, and audio mindfully to get our message across in meaningful ways. When we post on social media, especially on common sites like Twitter and Instagram, we intend for our message to be shared with followers, friends, and even a larger audience when a post "goes viral," or spreads rapidly by being shared on social media platforms. Getting to "viral" means that we use elements of rhetoric effectively when we plan social media posts and as we actually write our posts. We should consider how authors and readers generate and share thoughtfully produced posts on social media that don't make us regret hitting the "tweet" or "share" buttons.

We can loop back to the five components of rhetoric (purpose, audience, tone, genre, and context) to learn how our writing on social media can be effective. Thinking of social media through this model will also help us be effective communicators in these digital, public spaces. For example, we know from our rhetoric model that social media is a genre, or type, of writing in which we generate words, visuals, audio, and even genre-specific elements like hashtags for specific purposes and audiences. We also know that social media has different social contexts that both readers and authors must consider when posting and sharing information. Thinking about the five components of rhetoric will help you write effective and meaningful posts that generate productive conversations with friends and followers.

Consider what makes a social media message effective

How do we effectively share information on social media? Thinking about our five-part rhetoric model, as well as elements like images, GIFs, memes, and hashtags, look at one of your own social media posts and write about how well you used these elements to get a point across.

Explore strategies for effective social media writing

When you reflected on your own social media posts, you might have found you're not always effective in getting your intended message across to your audience. You probably thought about ways you could have been more rhetorical. In Chapter 5, we introduced you to multimodal writing, in which authors combine variations of written words, visuals, audio elements, movement, expressions, and gestures to compose texts that are meaningful to readers. In social media writing, there are specific strategies authors can use to make their points and to generate positive audience responses. Remember from Section 7.1 that writing in digital, public spaces is often about generating a conversation. Using the following basic strategies can help you do just that as a social media writer.

- **Think about the words you are using in your post.** Ask yourself if your words are appropriate for your intended audience. What emotions might your words evoke? Do your words accurately represent your message? Have you thought about how your words will be received by followers or friends? How about friends of friends? The general public?

- **Consider what visuals you use in your post.** Are you using images or GIFs? Do they help you increase your ethos (credibility)? Are they an accurate depiction of your intended message? Do they belong to you or someone else? If you are using a meme, is it timely and engaging for your audience?

- **Think about hashtags (#).** Like webtexts, social media posts often feature tags that are keywords for our message. On common social media like Twitter and Instagram, we use hashtags (#) for the same purpose. They usually come at the ends of posts with no spaces between words. If you are using hashtags, they should accurately describe the point of your post, or at least connect your post to a larger topic that you're writing about. For example, if you're advocating to keep the eateries on your campus open for longer hours, you might use: #eatlate or #midnighthunger. Hashtags are searchable on social media, so you want to pay special attention to how you use them effectively.

With a quick web search, you can find many other strategies to help you refine your effective writing on social media. The above basic strategies will help get you started as you engage with audiences in these conversational spaces.

APPLY

Analyze a series of social media posts

Now that you've thought about how you write on social media and learned a few strategies for effective posting, try analyzing a series of Twitter posts for effectiveness. Consider the posts below from a class project on the Atlanta Student Movement (#ATLStudentmovement), which was part of the 1960s American struggle for civil rights. Contemplate all the things you've learned in this chapter about effectiveness on social media. Then, write a couple of paragraphs in which you provide your opinion about the posts' effectiveness.

Post 1

Jeanne Bohannon

Post 2

↻ ATL Student Movement Retweeted

Kennesaw English @KennesawEnglish · Apr 8
In the 1st in a series to promote summer courses, we invite students to check out the WRIT 3150 flyer & enroll in this course, which traces people, places, and events of the @ATLMovement who challenged segregation through political, economic, and legal boycotts during 1960-61.

WRIT 3150-02 SUMMER 2018

Register now For this amazing opportunity

This course traces people, places, & events of the Atlanta Student Movement, focusing on a digital humanities project where students work alongside professors, archivists, and civil rights legends to create content in collaborative, public, digital platforms.

○   ↻ 1   ♡ 1   ✉

ATL Student Movement @ATLMovement · Mar 29
A massive thank you to everyone who joined us yesterday for our finale event of Women's History Month! And our most gracious appreciation to our panelists Dr. Anthony Grooms, Dr. Regina Bradley, and Dr. Sheila Smith McKoy, and our keynote speaker June Davis!
(📷: Casey Etheridge)

Post 3

↻ ATL Student Movement Retweeted

KSU Writing Center @KSUWC · Mar 28
Rise and shine! Today is the finale for Women's History Month. Join our @KennesawEnglish panelists and @ATLMovement alum June Davis for a discussion on women's rights at 10am in Prillaman Hall 2206. #WHM2018

Women's History Month Finale Event

Presented by The Rich Foundation & The Department of English

Stories from the Trenches: Women in Civil Rights Movements from the 1940s to 2018

Keynote Speaker	Wednesday, March 28 10 am-noon Prillaman Hall rm. 2206

Live Streaming on Twitter @KennesawEnglish

June Davis
First Freedom Rider
Atlanta Student Movement Leader
Civil Rights Activist

Panelists

Sheila Smith McKoy
Professor/Chair of English

○   ↻ 2   ♡ 3   ✉

ATL Student Movement @ATLMovement · Mar 27
Can't make it? Don't worry, you can still join us! We'll be live streaming the event on our Instagram page (@ATLStudentMovement) and on the English Department's twitter! @KennesawEnglish

○   ↻ 2   ♡ 1   ✉

Post 4

ATL Student Movement @ATLMovement · Mar 25
Check out our most recent artifacts donated to the project! These are June Davis' jail receipts, a telegram notification of her arrest, and a letter from the President at Spelman College regarding the students' protests. #ATLStudentMovement

FULTON COUNTY JAIL Nº 29429

○   ↻   ♥ 3   ✉

Jeanne Bohannon

Post 5

ATL Student Movement @ATLMovement · Mar 15
Curious to know what the "Ides of March" is?
en.m.wikipedia.org/wiki/Ides_of_M…

○   ↻   ♡   ✉

Show this thread

ATL Student Movement @ATLMovement · Mar 15
"I was trying to do it on the sixteenth, but (the Rev. A.D. King) said 'No, the fifteenth. Beware the Ides of March',"
-Lonnie King Jr. about the launch of the #ATLStudentMovement from his interview with @ajc

Lonnie King: More than five decades later, work rem…
That Lonnie King and a handful of young activists chose March 15, 1960, to launch the Atlanta Student Movem…
myajc.com

○ 1   ↻ 3   ♡ 1   ✉

▶

Jeanne Bohannon

Chapter 7 Projects
Project 7a. Craft a public text advocating or promoting a position on an issue in your community

Public writing is often engaged with communities and involves advocacy for causes, calls to action, and solutions to problems that impact people in their communities. Think about a public issue that influences you or your community. It can be a campus issue, a local issue, a state government issue, or even a national issue. Using our five-point rhetoric model and the tactics of shareability and timeliness, craft a 500-word webtext in which you advocate or promote your position on the issue to a public audience.

Project 7b. Reimagine your Chapter 6 Project (or another assignment) as a public, digital text

Sometimes public writing can be a remix of texts that we have purposed for an academic audience. Think back to the text you composed for Chapter 6, which was a thesis-driven, academic argument. Using the tools you have learned in Chapter 7, reimagine your work as a public, digital text. Revise your text as needed to make it work for the public, digital space you choose. Then, write an editor's note to your instructor at the end that explains your choices on how you would use elements such as infographics, images, GIFs, memes, and hashtags to get across a point. Your note should be around 100 words in addition to your remixed text.

8

Planning Your Research and Evaluating Sources

📚 Achie√e *If your instructor has assigned them, you can watch the video for this chapter, complete the Reflect and Apply activities, and work on the Chapter Project in Achieve.*

8.1 Compose a research question

Many students learn to start a research project by first choosing a topic—for example, how fashion magazines create body-image problems for women or the importance of eating locally produced food. Often the next steps are settling on a thesis and searching for information to help address or support that thesis. In this section, you'll learn to reverse that process by first choosing a question that will drive your research.

Asking a question before giving an answer

We want to challenge you to start the research process by asking questions first and then settling on a thesis or main point only after you have gathered some answers to your questions. It may sound strange to think of the first phase of a researched writing project as asking questions rather than settling on a research topic, but inquiring into those questions helps you arrive at an argument that is personally meaningful to you and more likely to reach its target audience.

Working in this inquiry-based approach means developing a curious mindset. Don't settle for the first five sources you find just because they are the first to appear in a Google search. Dig deeper. When you find some answers to your original questions, think about new questions this information leads you to. The table below illustrates the differences between a topic-driven approach and the inquiry-based approach we are encouraging you to use.

Topic-Driven Research Focus	Inquiry-Based Research Approach
Day care on campus	Why is there no day care facility for young children of adult students on our campus?
Gun control	What, if any, common ground exists between pro-gun and anti-gun groups in our country? How could we tap into that common ground to design gun policies that a majority of citizens would support?
Online pet pharmacies	Should online pet pharmacies be government regulated? How can I be sure that prescription drugs I order online are safe for my pets?

Creating a question that invites interesting answers that matter to you

As we all know, some questions can be answered with a simple one-word response. If we were to ask "What's your favorite color?" then a simple "red" or "yellow" would do as an answer. But that kind of back-and-forth doesn't make for a very interesting conversation, does it?

Instead, we encourage you to create research questions that lead to some really interesting, in-depth answers to explore in your projects. So how would that work? Think about the following two questions and the different responses each would invite:

1. Should the speed limit on federal interstates be raised to 95 miles per hour?

2. US senators will soon vote on a bill that allows individual states to raise the maximum speed limit on interstates that run through their states to 95 miles per hour. What information related to this issue—pro, con, or otherwise—should your senators consider before deciding how to vote? Based on that information, how would *you* want your senator to vote and why?

Question 1 requires only a one-word answer—yes or no. As it's written, it doesn't even invite an answer that includes evidence or reasoning that supports a yes or no answer. In contrast, Question 2 invites an in-depth response that considers a variety of viewpoints and lines of reasoning. As you think about the research question you want to pose, aim for an open one like the Question 2 example above. To help you remember, consider Bill in the meme below.

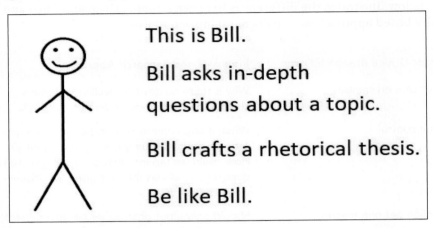

This is Bill.

Bill asks in-depth questions about a topic.

Bill crafts a rhetorical thesis.

Be like Bill.

Watch Meg develop a research question

In the following video, you'll see how Meg's life circumstances prompted her to compose a research question that addresses a critical issue in her own life.

Video: Developing a Research Question

REFLECT

Develop your own potential research questions

Coming up with inquiry-based research questions may sound daunting. But we've found that if you focus on real problems that you want to address, the process is much easier. Take a look at some hypothetical examples in the chart below.

Your Personal Experience	Preliminary Research Question Inspired by Your Experience
Your aunt was recently diagnosed with breast cancer, and you are wondering if alternative therapies might help her.	What alternative treatments are available to breast cancer patients (i.e., meditation, diet, herbal therapies), and how effective and safe are they?
Your boss insists that you go through a security search after your shift ends that can take up to thirty minutes, but he doesn't pay you for that time. You think this is unfair and possibly illegal.	How long, and under what conditions, can employers require employees to work without pay?
Your family is convinced your gaming hobby is making you anti-social and warping your mind.	How does playing first-person shooter video games affect the people who play them?

Now we invite you to give the process a try. Make a list of five potential research questions that—if answered—might somehow impact your life or the life of someone you care about. Your questions could focus on your community, your personal relationships, your family, your concerns about global or environmental issues that affect your community, your education, or anything in your everyday life. Remember to write questions that invite interesting, in-depth responses rather than questions that invite a simple yes or no answer.

Learn how to transform basic questions into compelling research questions

Now that you've thought about an inquiry-based approach to research, let's look more closely at how to change a simple yes or no question into an inquiry-based research question that invites interesting, in-depth responses.

Suppose you have several visible tattoos and you recently interviewed for a job for which you were very well qualified. As you were interviewing, you noticed that the person interviewing you often glanced at your tattoos. You didn't get a call back after your interview, and you're suspicious that this employer might have decided not to consider you for the job because of your tattoos. Your experience has led you to the following yes or no question:

> Can an employer refuse to hire workers because they have visible tattoos?

You're not an expert in employment law, so you don't have a simple yes or no answer to this question, even if one existed. But you do have a strong sense that something is wrong if a potential employer holds tattoos against you, and you believe that illegal discrimination might be happening. Because you need to gather more information, a yes or no answer doesn't work for this question. You'd need to ask lots more questions.

For starters, you might ask what employers can and can't legally consider when they're interviewing potential workers. You know that employers can't legally discriminate on the basis of sex or race. Obviously, having tattoos doesn't fall into one of those categories. So, as much as you disapprove, maybe discriminating against someone because of their tattoos is fair game. Later, as you've thought about it more, you might wonder if your tattoos should be treated as free speech under the Constitution. After all, some of your tattoos express controversial positions that are protected under the First Amendment.

Once you've thought about it more deeply, you arrive at a more nuanced and interesting research question:

> Under what, if any, conditions can an employer refuse to hire workers who have visible tattoos?

APPLY

Compose your best research question

Look back at the five potential research questions you wrote for the Reflect activity. From this group of questions, choose the two that really interest you most. For each potential research question, write a couple of informal paragraphs to discover what you already know about the issue. Feel free to revise your original research question as you write about it. Use the following prompts to help you think about what drives your interest in the research question.

- What exactly do I know about this issue?
- What's my history with this issue?
- When did I first learn about it?
- Why does it interest me?
- Who are some key people that I associate with this issue?
- What are some of the major controversies related to it?

After you've written at some length about your top two questions, choose the one that you think will be most interesting to pursue.

8.2 Find and evaluate credible sources

Just like you, when we want a quick answer to a question, we head to Google. In this section, you'll learn that Google and Wikipedia are good places to start, but you need to dig deeper to develop credible sources. In this section, we encourage you to take what you learn from a Google or Wikipedia search and turn to more academic sources to help you focus your topic and lead you to useful search terms. And we encourage you to connect with your campus librarians. The sooner you involve your library resources, the better your research efforts will turn out.

Finding sources that suit your purpose and work in context

The key to finding a really good source is to find one that is appropriate for *your* purpose and audience. Context is everything. Many types of texts can potentially be an appropriate source for a researched argument. The key is to determine how the source might contribute to your purpose and whether the audience will accept the source as credible. Rather than asking yourself or your instructor, "Can I use _____ as a source?" with the blank being filled in with an unconventional source such as Reddit or "my Uncle Malcolm," ask yourself why you think this source will enhance your argument. What is the purpose of citing something you saw on Reddit or learned from your Uncle Malcolm?

The sources you choose should help you accomplish a rhetorical purpose, so you should pick the right tool (source) for the job. If you want to explore our culture's fascination with celebrity, for example, you certainly could refer to the sheer number of reality shows and magazine covers that feature one of the Kardashians to provide background context. But it may not be appropriate (or very convincing) to quote Kim Kardashian as an expert on the deeper psychological, philosophical, or sociological underpinnings of celebrity. For that purpose, you'd want to cite an actual psychologist, philosopher, or sociologist to provide that expertise.

Using Google or Wikipedia to find sources

When is it OK to turn to Google and Wikipedia? We're going to be completely straight with you: despite what you may have heard to the contrary, Google and Wikipedia *can* provide respectable sources for your research. If you are looking for basic information such as "When did the United States enter World War II?" or "Who was the first Supreme Court Justice?" by all means, trust Google or Wikipedia. These search engines/databases are at their best when they are delivering noncontroversial, nondebatable facts.

But in the case of Wikipedia especially, you have to move beyond it to find a variety of sources and perspectives that speak to your research question. Because Wikipedia allows anyone to edit its entries, someone who has a vested interest in a subject can easily edit the entry to reflect that interest. In turn, this creates biased information about the issue at hand.

Even if you start your search using Wikipedia, look at the sources Wikipedia editors have footnoted. If those sources seem sketchy or clearly biased, don't rely on the Wikipedia "fact" supported by this questionable source. Take what you learn from your Google and Wikipedia searches, then turn to your library's research databases. That's where you'll find the most reliable information for your project.

Including library resources in your research

The simple truth is that involving the library in your search, especially meeting your local librarians and consulting your library databases, can save you time and give you access to a greater number of credible sources. When you conduct a general internet search with a search engine like Google, you might end up with hundreds or even thousands of results. If you refine your search by date or domain extension (.edu and .org, for example), your chances of retrieving a reasonable number of results improves dramatically, but you will still likely have to spend time weeding out unreliable or irrelevant sources. Worse yet, results that look promising in a general internet search sometimes require a subscription or charge a fee for access. Here's where the library can help.

Your college or public library already pays fees for many reliable publications, which you can access for free through library databases. For many academic writing purposes, sources are considered credible only if they come from *peer-reviewed* academic sources. These sources are written by scholars, sent to their peers (fellow scholars in the discipline) who review the piece to make sure the research is solid, then published in an academic journal or book.

Your college also provides librarians, people who are specially trained to help you find what you need. Libraries spend time and money on quality resources so you don't have to. It makes sense to take advantage of those resources early and often in your research process. Instead of wading through hundreds or thousands of Google results, some of which you can't even access, rely on librarians and your library's databases and other resources to jump right into a vast pool of curated texts that have been vetted by experts and fact-checked by editors.

Making sure your sources are credible using the C.R.A.P. test

Regardless of where you find a source, you need to be able to determine on your own if it's credible. Google and Wikipedia may get blamed for leading you to questionable sources, but even library databases can turn up sources that aren't a good fit for your project. Many librarians recommend that you submit each potential source to the C.R.A.P. test by asking questions about the following areas.

1. Currency.   Is the information up to date for your purposes? For some issues, like scientific research, newer information is often better information. For a historical topic, however, you may want to consult a source published near the time of the event to understand how it was perceived when it occurred.

2. Reliability.   Does the source rely on expert opinion or published research? Does it include references that you can track to verify information? A source that cites an expert opinion rather than a random person is more reliable. Likewise, sources that refer to published information are transparent, and thus more credible, than those making claims based on evidence readers can't examine on their own.

3. Authority.   Who created this source? Does the author have the experience or expertise to provide trustworthy information? Some sources provide a biography of the author. If no biographical information is included, a quick Google search of the author will reveal whether the author is well-known and respected for his or her expertise.

4. Purpose or point-of-view.   What is the intent or purpose of the source? Does the source have a sponsor? If so, how might that affect potential bias? Say you are researching ways to increase safe practices for high school football players and you find a source that questions recent reports about the dangers of concussions that players get in football games. You would need to look carefully at who published that research. If you find it was posted on a website called ConcussionsAreNoBigDeal.com and is sponsored by a lobbying organization that supports treating head injuries lightly, you should question its objectivity.

R E F L E C T

Determine a source's credibility in context

So far, we've argued that a source's credibility depends on how you want to use it. If you're just having a conversation with a trusted friend, a statement doesn't need a lot of evidence to back it up. You tend to trust your friend and take what she says at face value. In that casual context, you don't expect your friend to provide loads of evidence, and you're certainly not going to put what she says to a formal C.R.A.P. test. If you did, your friendship might be on shaky ground.

In an academic context, however, it takes more to determine if a source is credible. To be credible in an academic argument, it has to convince your audience, help you achieve your purpose for writing, and pass your C.R.A.P. test.

Following are a list of claims in academic arguments. For each claim, consider the possible sources to be used to support them. Which ones would you consider most credible and why?

1. Claim 1: Sodas that contain real or artificial sugars should not be sold as fundraisers for K-12 schools.

   Potential source a: opinion of the PTA president

   Potential source b: peer-reviewed journal article about the impact of consuming soda on teens

   Potential source c: website of a major soda company such as Coca-Cola or Pepsi

2. Claim 2: By the year 2040, there will be more electric charging stations for cars than gas stations.

   Potential source a: a blog post from a car hobbyist

   Potential source b: an article in the popular magazine *Autoweek*

   Potential source c: a published statement from the US Department of Transportation endorsing this claim

3. Claim 3: On average, students who sit in the front row of a classroom tend to earn higher grades than students who sit in the back.

   Potential source a: a peer-reviewed journal article on how classroom temperature affects student learning

▶

Potential source b: a peer-reviewed journal article on how many current college students are studying to be teachers

Potential source c: a quote from an interview you conducted with an education professor on your campus who is a recognized expert in increasing student engagement and achievement

4. Claim 4: Despite increased awareness campaigns, the rate of domestic violence incidents continues to rise in the United States.

Potential source a: a flyer posted in a dorm lobby stating "Every day more than 50,000 American women are beaten by their husbands or boyfriends."

Potential source b: a book about domestic violence that was published in 2018 by a university press and purchased by your college library

Potential source c: a statement from a domestic violence survivor and advocate

UNDERSTAND

Evaluate a website using the C.R.A.P. test

As an exercise in understanding what a credible source is, let's consider *The Hechinger Report*. This organization, based at Teachers College, Columbia University, describes itself as "an independent, nonprofit newsroom" that produces "deep and incisive journalism that uncovers the real problems facing our education system and examines the evidence supporting proposed solutions" (hechingerreport.org). Some academic writers would not consider this site a peer-reviewed source of information because it doesn't appear in a scholarly journal. Is there any reason to push back against that opinion? In other words, could this be a credible source to use in academic writing? Let's put it to the C.R.A.P. test to find out.

When you explore *The Hechinger Report*'s website, you will find lots of up-to-date, researched articles about contemporary issues facing public education in the United States. Even at first glance the site appears to pass the C.R.A.P. test, but let's look more closely to make sure.

Is it current?   During a recent search of the site, we found articles such as "Teachers are first responders to the opioid crisis." The articles we found had been published earlier the same month, suggesting that *The Hechinger Report* passes the currency section of the C.R.A.P. test.

Teachers are first responders to the opioid crisis

In some schools in McDowell County, W.Va., as many as 40 percent of kids don't live with their parents

by **REBECCA KLEIN**   **November 3, 2018**

This article was published in November 2018, a few weeks before our search.

This story about the opioid crisis and foster care was produced as part of a series, *"Twice Abandoned: How schools and child-welfare systems fail kids in foster care,"* reported by HuffPost and The Hechinger Report, *a nonprofit, independent news organization focused on inequality and innovation in education.*

WAR, W.Va. — Middle school teacher Greg Cruey can explain the most harrowing details of his students' lives with matter-of-fact precision.

That smart sixth-grader who had her hand raised last period? She's homeless and has, in the past, been suicidal. That middle school student who seemed on edge during class? As a young

Is it reliable?   In another section of the website, a series of special reports focuses on the concept of "the future of learning"—exploring how cutting-edge schools are using innovative ways to close the achievement gap. Not only are these articles current, but they also contain expert opinions, credible research, and cited sources. Looks like *The Hechinger Report* passes the reliability part of the C.R.A.P. test.

Future of Learning

The factory model of education is out. Now more schools are personalizing learning and trying to motivate students by empowering them in the classroom. Will this improve academic outcomes? Will it close achievement gaps? The Hechinger Report explores the innovations at the core of today's cutting-edge schools.

Using teacher-leaders to improve schools

"Opening the door for innovation" by extending the impact of the best teachers to more students

FUTURE OF LEARNING   by Tara García Mathewson – November 29, 2018

Designing accessible ed tech can be costly, but demand is on the rise

Schools are putting more pressure on developers to think about access

FUTURE OF LEARNING   by Tara García Mathewson – November 15, 2018

Is it authoritative and what is its purpose and point of view?   *The Hechinger Report*'s mission statement says that it "cover[s] inequality and innovation in education with in-depth journalism that uses research, data and stories from class-rooms and campuses to show the public how education can be improved and why it matters." Further, as part of the mission statement, the site states in bold font: "Content published in *The Hechinger Report*—or content produced and disseminated by any of its collaborators with funding from the Hechinger Institute—is editorially independent of its funders, and does not necessarily reflect the views of Teachers College, its trustees, administration or faculty." Based on this statement, we think it passes the C.R.A.P. test for authority, purpose, and point of view.

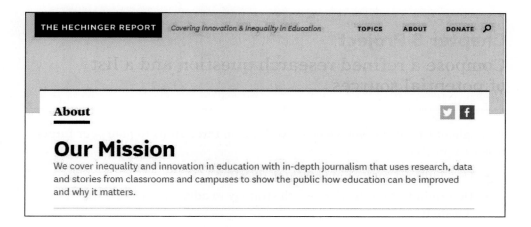

So, even though *The Hechinger Report* isn't a traditional academic source, it passes the C.R.A.P. test. Its information is current. The research it publishes is reliable because it includes expert opinion and provides clear citations for the research it references. It's an authoritative source backed up by a major university (Teacher's College, Columbia University). And its purpose is to provide detailed, well-researched journalism about contemporary issues in American education without being beholden to sponsors.

APPLY

Put your sources to the C.R.A.P. test

Using one or more library databases recommended by your instructor, find five potential sources that might address the preliminary research question you developed in Section 8.1. Using the C.R.A.P. test criteria, determine whether each source would be credible in an academic setting and explain why or why not.

For each source, record *at least* the author, title, publication date, and the database you used to locate the source. If your source has page numbers, record those, too.

Many library databases will provide a citation in the documentation style you need. If that function is available, give it a try. Keep in mind that citation generators aren't perfect, but they are a quick way to capture the details you'll need in the citation—even if you have to tweak them later.

Chapter 8 Project
Compose a refined research question and a list of potential sources

Throughout Chapter 8, you've been working on three steps to plan your future research project:

- Developing a compelling research question
- Determining an effective search strategy to address your research question
- Finding credible sources that address your research question

For your Chapter 8 Project, you will finalize your research question and locate ten sources (or the number of sources your instructor specifies) that address your research question and pass the C.R.A.P. test.

These sources might provide background information, discuss controversies related to your question, or present evidence to support one or more answers to your research question. You may want to start with a general internet search to gain background knowledge, but the most credible sources are likely to be the ones you will find using your library's research databases.

We want to let you know up front that some of the sources you collect for this project may not end up in a research paper you write later. That happens often. As you write, you learn. And as you learn, your developing thesis may evolve or expand. Some of what you researched may not work to defend your argument. In fact, your position may have changed completely. For now, let's focus on getting to a workable research question and collecting credible sources to help you address your research question.

1. First, record your research question from 8.1 Apply or a revised version of it. This will likely be the research question you use in Chapters 9 through 12.

2. Next, list the sources you've identified as credible texts that may be worth exploring in more depth to address your research question. Your instructor may ask you to use a standard citation style such as MLA or APA, which are described in the Appendix, Understanding Academic Citation Styles. The sources you collect will be the ones you'll consider including in the work you write in later chapters.

For each source, include the following information, which you'll also need to include later in your formal citations:

	Example	Keep in Mind
Authors' Names	Holly Scott and Heather Cleland Woods Anti-Defamation League	Sources may have multiple authors. Others seem to list no author or list an organization as the author. Include as much information as you can about your source's author.
Title of Source	"Fear of Missing Out and Sleep: Cognitive Behavioural Factors in Adolescents' Nighttime Social Media Use" *Thinking Machines: The Quest for Artificial Intelligence and Where It's Taking Us Next*	Credible sources often have titles that include a colon (:) followed by an extension. Record the entire title.
Title of Publication in Which the Work Appears (journals or websites, for example)	*Journal of Adolescence* *Salon* *The Washington Post*	For a book with only one author, you can skip this step. But for short works from websites and articles that appear in magazines, newspapers, or academic journals, include the name of the publication.
For Books, the Publisher and Year of Publication	TarcherPerigee, 2017 Harvard UP, 2018	The publisher's name can be found on the title page or copyright page at the front of the book. (In MLA style, omit words like "Press" and "Publishing Company" and abbreviate "University Press" as UP.)
Volume and Issue Numbers, If Any	Vol. 68 Vol. 52, No. 4	Journals will often have volume and issue numbers. ▶

	Example	Keep in Mind
Date of Publication	12 May 2017 October 2018 Spring 2019	Depending on the type of source, it may have an exact date, a month and year, or a season and year—such as "Spring 2019." Books will have only a year of publication.
Page Numbers, If Available	pp. 61-65 pp. 152-57	If the source doesn't have page numbers, skip this step.
Link to Your Source	https://doi.org/10.1016/j .adolescence.2018.07.009 ProQuest Arts and Humanities Database, www.proquest.com /products-services/Arts _and_Humanities.html	Links to sources that turn up in your library search are never as simple as www .articletitle.com. They often look like gobbledygook and are accessible only from computers located on your campus or if you log in to your library from off campus. Check to see if your source offers a "stable URL," a "permalink," or a "DOI." If it does, use that one. That's the URL that anyone can access to view your source. If it does not have such a link, record the name of the database and the URL of the database's home page.

GOAL ▼
To create an annotated
list of credible sources
that address your research
question.

9

Managing, Annotating, and Summarizing Sources

⚏ Achieve *If your instructor has assigned them, you can complete the Reflect and Apply activities and work on the Chapter Project in Achieve.*

9.1 Use critical reading skills to take notes from sources

In Chapter 5, you learned about reading actively with a three-phase process so that you're engaging with the text before, during, and after you read. In this section, you'll learn to deepen those skills as you prepare to read multiple potential sources you are considering using in your own writing.

Why take notes on sources?

In Chapter 8, we focused on the need to locate multiple potential sources that might address your research question in some way. Now that you have some sources, it's time to really dig into them and evaluate them more carefully to determine whether and how they might be useful for your project. One of the best techniques you can use to critically read potential sources is to take notes on them.

Even if we had photographic memories and could recall perfectly all the sources we viewed in our research, we would still need to make notes on how all the research fits together. Keeping notes while conducting research is important for several reasons. Most simply, it helps you recall accurately what the original source said. Beyond that, it reinforces critical reading because it creates an ongoing dialogue between you and the source's author. Finally, it can help you make connections between multiple sources. Because you've created notes about one source, you're likely to have retained information about it that you can recall as you read a related source. Beginning to see connections among your sources is a crucial step for planning a piece of writing that relies on multiple sources.

What should I record in my notes?

People use all sorts of methods for taking notes. Some people like to write on the source itself with comments and questions in the margins and important passages underlined or highlighted. Others prefer to keep detailed notes on index cards, in a notebook, or in an electronic file. Most of us arrive through experimentation at our own unique combination of methods.

What's more important than *how* you take notes is *what* you actually keep track of in your notes. To see how this works, take a look at different ways that Meg, Li, and Gabby took notes on the same article, "Sense of Smell Is Strictly Personal, Study Suggests," which appeared in the magazine *Science News* in June 2015. Read the full article below at least once along with the notes taken by the three students.

Although Meg, Li, and Gabby have different notetaking methods, you'll notice each student's notes focus on some common areas. Each student indicates the main point in some way, each records important details that support the main point, and each notes the conclusions drawn by the writer, in this case the significance of the "olfactory fingerprint" experiment. In addition, in a variety of ways, each student indicates important terms (such as *olfactory fingerprint*) and keeps track of personal questions and insights about the reading.

Meg's notes.   Meg's annotations consist of underlining in the text and comments and questions in the margins.

Sense of Smell Is Strictly Personal, Study Suggests

SARAH SCHWARTZ

"Olfactory fingerprint" could be tough target for identity theft

A person's sense of smell may reveal a lot about his or her identity.

A new test can distinguish individuals based upon their perception of odors, possibly reflecting a person's genetic makeup, scientists report online June 22 in *Proceedings of the National Academy of Sciences.*

Main idea

Most humans perceive a given odor similarly. But the genes for the molecular machinery that humans use to detect scents are about 30 percent different in any two people, says neuroscientist Noam Sobel of the Weizmann Institute of Science in Rehovot, Israel. This variation means that nearly every person's sense of smell is subtly different. Nobody had ever developed a way to test this sensory uniqueness, Sobel says.

Important scientific breakthrough!

Sobel and his colleagues designed a sensitive scent test they call the "olfactory fingerprint." In an experiment, test subjects rated how strongly 28 odors such as clove or compost matched 54 adjectives such as "nutty" or "pleasant." An olfactory fingerprint describes individuals' perceptions of odors' similarities, not potentially subjective scent descriptions.

Key term

All 89 subjects in the study had distinct olfactory fingerprints. The researchers calculated that just seven odors and 11 descriptors could have identified each individual in the group. With 34 odors, 35 descriptors, and around five hours of testing per person, the scientists estimate they could individually identify about 7 billion different people, roughly the entire human population.

100% of subjects had an individual O. F. Impressive.

People with similar olfactory fingerprints also showed similarity in their genes for immune system proteins linked to body odor and mate choice. This finding means that people with similar olfactory fingerprints probably smell alike to others, says study author Lavi Secundo, also a neuroscientist at the Weizmann Institute.

Um, OK, but why is this important?

It has been shown that people can use smell to detect their genetic similarity to others and avoid inbreeding, says neuroscientist Joel Mainland of Monell Chemical Senses Center in Philadelphia.

Oh! That's why!

Sobel says that the olfactory fingerprint could someday be used to construct smell-based social networks. The test could also become a diagnostic tool for diseases that affect the sense of smell, including Parkinson's disease, he says.

What's a "smell-based social network"? People with similar genes share other qualities besides smell?

Administering scent tests can be cumbersome, so it will be hard to use such tests in the clinic without scent-generating electronic devices, Mainland says. But using scent perception to identify genetic markers is interesting, and from a security standpoint, he adds, an olfactory fingerprint would be very hard to copy or steal. "There might be applications of this that we haven't thought of."

CITATIONS

L. Secundo et al. Individual olfactory perception reveals meaningful nonolfactory genetic information. *Proceedings of the National Academy of Sciences.* Published online June 22, 2015. doi: 10.1073/pnas.1424826112.

Li's notes. Li uses a mix of marginal notes and drawing on the text for his annotations. He also takes time to define words that are unfamiliar to him.

Sense of Smell Is Strictly Personal, Study Suggests

SARAH SCHWARTZ

→ *related to the sense of smell*

"Olfactory fingerprint" could be tough target for identity theft   *look for info about identity theft in the article*

A person's sense of smell may reveal a lot about his or her identity.

A new test can distinguish individuals based upon their perception of odors, possibly reflecting a person's genetic makeup,

central idea—new smell test may reveal a person's genetic identity

scientists report online June 22 in *Proceedings of the National Academy of Sciences.*

Most humans perceive a given odor similarly. But the genes for the molecular machinery that humans use to detect scents are about 30 percent different in any two people, says neuroscientist Noam Sobel of the Weizmann Institute of Science in Rehovot, Israel. This variation means that nearly every ⟵ person's sense of smell is subtly different. Nobody had ever developed a way to test this sensory uniqueness, Sobel says.

Sobel and his colleagues designed a sensitive scent test they call the "olfactory fingerprint." In an experiment, test subjects rated how strongly 28 odors such as clove or compost matched 54 adjectives such as "nutty" or "pleasant." An olfactory fingerprint describes individuals' perceptions of odors' similarities, not potentially subjective scent descriptions.

All 89 subjects in the study had distinct olfactory fingerprints. The researchers calculated that just seven odors and 11 descriptors could have identified each individual in the group. With 34 odors, 35 descriptors, and around five hours of testing per person, the scientists estimate they could individually identify about 7 billion different people, roughly the entire human population.

People with similar olfactory fingerprints also showed similarity in their genes for immune system proteins linked to body odor and mate choice. This finding means that people with similar olfactory fingerprints probably smell alike to others, says study author Lavi Secundo, also a neuroscientist at the Weizmann Institute.

It has been shown that people can use smell to detect their genetic similarity to others and avoid inbreeding, says neuroscientist Joel Mainland of Monell Chemical Senses Center in Philadelphia.

Sobel says that the olfactory fingerprint could someday be used to construct smell-based social networks. The test could also become a diagnostic tool for diseases that affect the sense of smell, including Parkinson's disease, he says.

potential value of new test

Administering scent tests can be cumbersome, so it will be hard to use such tests in the clinic without scent-generating electronic devices, Mainland says. But using scent perception to identify genetic markers is interesting, and from a security standpoint, he adds, an olfactory fingerprint would be very hard to copy or steal. "There might be applications of this that we haven't thought of."

Ah! Identity theft angle— sense of smell can't be hacked?

CITATIONS

L. Secundo et al. Individual olfactory perception reveals meaningful nonolfactory genetic information. *Proceedings of the National Academy of Sciences.* Published online June 22, 2015. doi: 10.1073/pnas.1424826112.

Gabby's notes.   Gabby took a completely different approach and wrote a detailed paragraph summarizing the article's main points and her questions and insights about the article. She stapled her written notes to the printed article, so her notes will always stay with the original text.

Main idea was clear at the beginning of the article: a new "olfactory fingerprint" test can be used to identify people. Article is interesting because the researchers think there are important social and security implications for this new smell test, but the article doesn't go into detail about the significance of the findings. Yes, identities would be hard to steal, but how complicated would it be to create this test? Would it be practical? The author's name was listed as well as the date. Comes from a reputable science news magazine, so the evidence is logos-based. I need to look up the author (Sarah Schwartz) to make sure she's the real deal, too.

Remember these eight elements to address in notes

However you choose to take notes, make sure these eight elements are reflected in them.

1. **Author and title.** Write down both author and title so that you can find the source again if you need additional information. If both author and title are clearly visible on your copy of the source, highlight them so that you can easily find them later.

2. **Thesis or main idea.** What claim is this text making, or what main point is it attempting to convey?

3. **Evidence and support.** What key pieces of information or lines of reasoning are the most important for supporting the argument or main point? How does the support rely on logos, pathos, and ethos?

4. **Significance of the source.** How or why is this source important for your research? How or why is it significant within the body of research available to address your research question?

5. **Questions you have.** Note any questions or concerns you have about the strength of the evidence, line of reasoning, the meaning of specific words or phrases, and even questions about what the source is actually saying.

6. **Additional ideas or responses you have.** Make notes about connections you see with other sources, doubts you may have about something in the source, or additional areas you want to check. This is a way to "talk back to the text," an essential skill for active reading.

7. **Indication of conflicts of interest or possible bias.** Is the source sponsored by an organization that might benefit from its message?

8. **Page numbers.** If page numbers aren't visible on your copy of a print source, be sure to jot down the starting and ending page numbers. Also, if you have found a particular quote in the source that you may want to include in your own writing, definitely record the page number(s) where it appears. Some sources, of course, won't have page numbers. If you are using academic blog posts, websites, or other online sources, you may not find page numbers for them. In these instances, you may want to write down possibly usable quotes or save the page to your desktop for later.

> ### REFLECT
> ## Reflect on your notetaking habits
>
> This process of recording eight elements during your notetaking may be quite new to you. How have you traditionally taken notes on information you read? What are some strategies or methods you use? What new information or ideas you've encountered in *The Writer's Loop* might be helpful? Write a paragraph that describes how you typically take notes and how you might focus on these eight elements as you take notes on texts moving forward.

UNDERSTAND

Learn how to take notes that address the eight elements

Because you are researching a question that you're interested in, reading sources to help you answer the question shouldn't be a chore. Still, we understand that not every source you read is going to be super easy beach reading! Our students find that focusing on the eight elements we discussed is a good way to stay engaged with what they're reading and grapple with how the information might address a research question.

Eight elements to take notes on

1   **Author and title**

2   **Thesis/main idea**

3   **Evidence and support**

4   **Significance of source**

5   **Questions you have**

6   **Insights you have**

7   **Conflicts of interest/possible bias**

8   **Page numbers (if included)**

Consider what an annotation including all eight elements would look like. The first thing you should know is that addressing these eight elements doesn't mean you'll have only eight annotations. You might have more or less, but as a whole, your annotations will hit these eight targets.

Let's look at notes and questions written in the margins of a news article published by ProPublica, a nonprofit investigative journalism organization. The article reports on the response of the Orlando Fire Department after the Pulse nightclub shooting in June 2016. Despite having worked on a plan to respond to a mass shooting, including purchasing vests for first responders that were filled with tourniquets and other equipment needed to treat trauma victims, paramedics were unprepared to cope with the emergency scene.

Orlando Paramedics Didn't Go In to Save Victims of the Pulse Shooting. Here's Why.

1 **2** Thesis is stated in the title.

ABE ABORAYA

1 Author is respected health news reporter.

This article was produced in partnership with WMFE, which is a member of the ProPublica Local Reporting Network.

8 No page numbers because this was published as an online article.

4 ProPublica is an award-winning journalistic organization—reliable source.

Stan Lim/Digital First Media/The Riverside Press-Enterprise/Getty Images

"I need the hospital! Please, why does someone not want to help?"

The man's screams inside the Pulse nightclub pierced the chaos in the minutes after the shooting stopped on June 12, 2016. With the shooter barricaded in a bathroom and victims piled on top of one another, Orlando police commanders began asking the Fire Department for help getting dozens of shooting victims out of the club and to the hospital.

"We need to get these people out," a command officer said over the police radio.

"We gotta get 'em out," another officer responded. "We got him [the shooter] contained in the bathroom. We have several long guns on the bathroom right now."

A few minutes later, the Orlando Police Department's dispatch log shows the police formally requested the Fire Department to come into the club. "We're pulling victims out

3 Uses info from dispatch log as evidence.

the front. Have FD come up and help us out with that," one officer said.

The Orlando Fire Department had been working on a plan for just such a situation for three years. Like many fire departments at the time, Orlando had long relied on a traditional protocol for mass shootings, in which paramedics stayed at a distance until an all-clear was given. The department had tasked Anibal Saez Jr., an assistant chief, with developing a new approach being adopted across the country: Specialized teams of medics, guarded by police officers and wearing specially designed bulletproof vests, would pull out victims before a shooter is caught or killed.

6 Not starting from scratch— building on others' rapid response plans.

After a recommendation from Saez in 2015, the department bought about 20 of the bulletproof vests and helmets. The vests had pouches filled with tourniquets, special needles to relieve air in the chest, and quick-clotting trauma bandages.

None of that equipment was used at Pulse. Emergency medical professionals stayed across the street from the club. And the bulletproof vests filled with life-saving equipment sat at headquarters.

5 Inertia? = inactivity in this context.

In the three and a half years before the shooting, bureaucratic inertia had taken hold. Emails obtained by WMFE and ProPublica lay out a record of opportunities missed. It's not clear whether paramedics could have entered and saved lives. But what is clear is Saez's plan to prepare for such a scenario sat unused, like the vests.

7 No bias against first responders, just saying that the plan wasn't followed.

His effort had sputtered and was ultimately abandoned after a new fire chief, Roderick Williams, took over the department in April 2015. Williams named another administrator to finalize and implement the new policy. That administrator declined multiple requests to comment for this story. Saez said he offered to help but never heard back.

"There was a committee that was responsible for the [policy], however, I am not sure whether one was created and approved," one fire official emailed another on March 30, 2016.

In April 2016, two months before Pulse, Williams emailed his deputy chiefs asking for a progress report: "Update on Active Shooter?"

3 Quotes from emails used as evidence.

The only response was an email asking if anyone had responded. No one did.

Ultimately 49 people died during the Pulse attack, one of the worst mass shootings in modern history.

Saez, a 30-year veteran of the Orlando Fire Department, a paramedic and a member of the bomb squad, has been haunted by the possibility that things didn't have to turn out the way they did. "I wonder sometimes if I should've done something else," he said in an interview.

"In my mind I'm thinking, 'Man, if I would have had that policy, if I could have got it done, if I could have pushed it, maybe it wouldn't be 49 dead. . . . Maybe it would be 40. Maybe it would be 48. Anything but the end result here,'" he said.

A study published this year in the journal Prehospital Emergency Care concluded that 16 of the victims might have lived if they had gotten basic EMS care within 10 minutes and made it to a trauma hospital within an hour, the national standard. That's nearly one third of victims that died that night.

"Those 16, they had injuries that were, potentially were survivable," said Dr. Edward Reed Smith, the operational medical director for the Arlington County, Virginia, Fire Department, who reviewed autopsies of those who died with two colleagues. Smith, whose department was one of the first in the country to allow paramedics into violent scenes with a police escort, has reviewed more than a dozen civilian mass shootings using the same criteria. "How would they be survivable? With rapid intervention and treatment of their injuries."

A separate Justice Department review last year concluded "it would have been reasonable" for paramedics to enter after 20 minutes, a different time frame from the one Smith analyzed. Orlando's mayor, as well as the Police and Fire chiefs, dispute that they could have done anything differently. They say it was impossible to know at the time that there was only one shooter at Pulse or that he wouldn't resume shooting after he barricaded himself in the bathroom. It was also impossible to know whether a bomb threat he later made was real. All of that, they say, would have kept victims from getting care in time.

3 Two separate studies support the position that earlier intervention could have saved lives.

6 The people in charge sound very defensive.

Williams, the fire chief, said he still believes the inside of Pulse nightclub was a "hot zone," or a place of direct threat, which would have stopped first responders from going in.

"We're not prepared to go in hot-zone extraction. That's just not what we do as a fire department," Williams said. "It was active fire, active shooting."

But not everyone who responded that night is sure the Fire Department had done all it could. They say some victims might have had a chance had Orlando finished what it started.

Orlando Fire District Chief Bryan Davis was in charge of his agency's response the night of the Pulse shooting. In an interview, he said his department had done active shooter drills, but it wasn't enough.

"We didn't have formalized training," Davis said. "We didn't have a policy. We didn't have a procedure. We had the equipment [bulletproof vests]. But it was locked up in EMS in a storage closet. . . . And unfortunately, we were a day and a dollar too late."

When you look at all the annotations (eleven of them in this case), you'll see that together they address all the eight elements we've encouraged you to focus on. But the reader didn't take notes by checking off eight specific boxes. Instead, this is a holistic approach that considers how the eight elements might appear in different places in different sources.

APPLY

Practice taking notes on one of your own sources

You have read through the annotated version of "Orlando Paramedics Didn't Go In to Save Victims of the Pulse Shooting. Here's Why." Now try your own hand at taking notes on a text as you read it.

Choose one source you have located that addresses your research question. As you read through it, take notes that include the following elements as they apply to your specific source.

1. Author and title

2. Thesis or main idea

3. Evidence or support

4. Significance of the source

5. Questions you have

6. Additional ideas or responses you have

7. Any conflicts of interest or possible bias

8. Page numbers, if used

When you're done making notes on your source, write a brief paragraph discussing how easy or difficult it was to identify all eight elements in your notes. Include any questions you have about the notetaking process now that you've given it a try.

9.2   Keep track of source information and avoid plagiarism

To complete a research project successfully, you need to manage the sources you find in real time. Without careful attention, managing sources can quickly turn into a disorganized mess. In this section, you'll learn how to organize the sources you find and make sure you have clear notes on all the information about them you may need if you decide to include them in your writing.

Creating a process to manage source materials

When you find a new source, you decide if it *might* be helpful or it's definitely *not* helpful. During the first phase of reading a text, we usually make those judgments based on skimming the source's abstract or introduction, the headings, and the conclusion (see Section 5.1 to review reading a text in three phases). If the source is definitely *not* relevant to your research question or topic, move on. It's OK to set it aside and not return to it. For those sources you *might* find helpful, though, you need a system for categorizing them as you review and sort sources into useful and less useful sources. We suggest the process shown in the flowchart "Process for Managing Source Materials."

Process for Managing Source Materials

At every stage, librarians can help you adjust keywords to get better search results.

Source
— initial review —
Possibly helpful → Not relevant

after a closer look

Definitely! → MAYBE → Not relevant

Definitely!
These are rare and wonderful finds!

after a more thorough review

Definitely! → Possibly still useful → Not relevant

Definitely!
You discover that the source has important relevant info.

Possibly still useful
Hold on to these. Maybe a source is really dense and you need more time or help to understand it. But something feels promising about it.

Not relevant
Let it go.

Along with this process of evaluating and sorting sources, decide how you want to keep track of your sources in each category. You might use a color coding system, keep sources in different physical folders, or group them in digital folders on your computer.

Avoiding plagiarism when taking notes

In our everyday exchanges online, we frequently share funny memes or posts without necessarily giving credit to the person who created them. Academic writing works differently: it requires that you give credit to whoever created the quote or intellectual property.

In academic writing, using an original source's words or ideas as if you wrote them yourself is considered plagiarism—a form of cheating with serious consequences, including being expelled from your school. To avoid plagiarism, use quotation marks in all your notes to indicate that you're copying original text. Even if you are copying only a couple of words, a longer phrase, or a short sentence, always use quotation marks and include the source author and the page number where the quote appeared, if applicable. This practice will help you differentiate your words from your sources' words. Also keep track of any ideas you take from a source in the form of a paraphrase or summary (see Sections 11.4 and 11.5).

Formalizing your list of sources

You have now gathered some sources to address your research question and made notes about the basic publication information for all of them: author's name, title of source, and date of publication, at least. You also included page numbers when available. And you did it in a way that felt right for *you*, creating your own unique method of highlighting, underlining, and annotating.

Now it's time to formalize your list of sources. This process is similar to changing from sweaty workout clothes to getting dressed up for a night on the town. When you're headed to the gym, you care about a few basics: did you remember your water bottle, do you have your music? But you don't really worry about what your hair looks like. Likewise, when you are first gathering your sources, you want to make sure you have enough information about them that you can find all the important details when you need them, but you don't have to write them in perfect academic citation style.

However, when you are formalizing your list of sources, just as when you're getting ready to go out for a special night, you're moving from an audience of yourself to an audience of other readers. You have to pay very careful attention to details, making sure that every word is properly italicized or in quotation marks or in parentheses, and that the publication date and all the other details you're supposed to include are there and in the right place. We'll consider this in more detail in the Understand component of this section.

REFLECT

Consider your thoughts on the source-management process we advise

Write a paragraph that describes how you anticipate managing source information using the process we've described. In your reflection, you might consider how your past experience of collecting and keeping track of sources is similar to or different from the process we've suggested. What are some challenges you have faced when starting to find sources for a research project? Looking back, how might you have more efficiently dealt with those challenges? How might our process help you save time and avoid problems?

UNDERSTAND

Learn the basics of MLA and APA citation styles

There are many different academic citation styles, and as you get deeper into your major, you'll learn the ins and outs of the style expected in your field. For now, we're going to focus on only two: MLA (Modern Language Association) and APA (American Psychological Association), the most widely used styles in first-year college courses. MLA style is used in literature, foreign language, and other humanities courses, while APA style is used in social science courses like psychology and sociology. We're also going to focus on citations for just a handful of specific kinds of sources—ones you're likely to use for the Chapter 9 Project. (See the Appendix for more examples of citations for other kinds of sources.)

When you need to cite additional types of sources, check a resource your instructor has recommended or assigned. If nothing's been assigned, ask your college librarian to help you find the latest edition of the *MLA Handbook* or *Publication Manual of the American Psychological Association*. Automatic citation methods such as EndNote and the auto-citations available via your library's databases can be really helpful, but use them with caution. As with spellcheckers, these technologies can be a big help, but they're not right 100 percent of the time. You'll want to check any auto-generated citation models against the format provided in an instructor-recommended resource. If you have additional questions, you can always ask a librarian, your instructor, or a fellow student. You can also ask a tutor at the Writing Center if your school has one.

Understanding MLA-style citations.   MLA expects authors to convey specific information about a source by listing nine "core elements" that are relevant to virtually all sources, in order, followed by a period or comma. As you build your MLA citations, the table below may help you recall the order of information and the specific punctuation that follows each element. Not all sources have all nine core elements, so skip it in your citation if it doesn't apply to your source.

Elements of MLA-Style Citations

Author.	"Author" is the person or entity that created the source. List the author in this format: Last name, First name followed by a period.
Title of Source.	Use the title on the title page of the specific source you're using. Put titles of self-contained sources (books, journals, websites) in *italics*. Put titles of sources that appear as part of a larger source in "quotation marks." Think about essays within a book, articles within journals, or pages on a website. Capitalize all the main words in the title.

Title of Container,	Containers are larger venues that contain the source. Academic journals and databases can be containers for articles. Websites can be containers for blog posts, videos, articles, etc.
Other Contributors,	If a person other than the author participated in creating this source—perhaps as an editor, director, narrator, or illustrator—acknowledge that person here. Many of your sources will not have other contributors.
Version or Edition,	If multiple versions of the source exist (such as editions), indicate the version of your source. Version is another core element that is not always needed.
Volume and Issue Numbers,	If the source is part of a multi-volume, multi-issue, or multi-episode larger work, list its number. For journals, abbreviate "volume" as "vol." and "number" as "no." Separate volume and number with a comma.
Publisher,	The publisher is the organization or company responsible for making the source available.
Publication Date,	Publication dates will include at least the year, and, in some cases, also the date, month, or season. Write the publication date with the day of the month first, then month, then year. Months are abbreviated.
Location of Source.	Location is information that tells readers where the source can be found. The location format is often page numbers, a DOI (digital object identifier), or a URL. If the article does not have a DOI, write *Retrieved from* followed by the URL of the journal's home page.

The examples below illustrate expectations for citing four frequently used types of sources. These examples follow the guidelines in *MLA Handbook*, 8th edition (2016).

Book by a Single Author

Author Last Name, First Name. *Title of Book*. Publisher, Publication date.

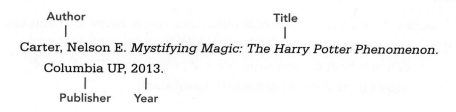

Work in an Anthology (a book that is a collection of chapters written by different people)

> Author Last Name, First Name. "Title of Essay." *Title of Collection*,
>   edited by Editor's Name(s), Publisher, Year, pp. page range of entry.

Author   Essay title   Book title

Miller, DeVaughn P. "Working in the Minefields." *New Perspectives*

Editor

on Post-War Existence, edited by Roberta Williams,

Publisher   Year   Page range

University of Georgia Press, 2010, pp. 246-69.

Journal Article from a Library Database

> Author. "Title of Article." *Title of Journal*, vol., no., date, pp. page
>   range. Database, DOI number or permanent URL.

Author   Article title

Holfeld, Brett, and Bonnie J. Leadbeater. "The Interrelated Effects of
    Traditional and Cybervictimization on the Development of Internalizing
    Symptoms and Aggressive Behaviors in Elementary School."

Journal title   Vol. and No.   Date   Pages   Database

Merrill-Palmer Quarterly, vol. 64, no. 2, Apr. 2018, pp. 220-47. *JSTOR,*

DOI

doi: 0.13110/merrpalmquar1982.64.2.0220.

Website or Section of a Website

> Author (if available). "Title of Section." *Site Name.* Name of institution/
>   organization affiliated with the site (sponsor or publisher) if
>   different from the site name, date of publication, URL. Date of
>   access (if no date of publication is available).

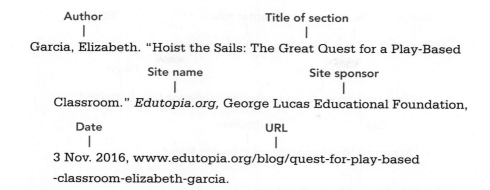

Author   Title of section

Garcia, Elizabeth. "Hoist the Sails: The Great Quest for a Play-Based

Site name   Site sponsor

Classroom." *Edutopia.org,* George Lucas Educational Foundation,

Date   URL

3 Nov. 2016, www.edutopia.org/blog/quest-for-play-based
-classroom-elizabeth-garcia.

Understanding APA-style citations. Although APA citations include similar information, the format of APA citations is very different from MLA citations. For starters, APA style uses only initials for the first names of authors. The year the source was published appears right after the author's name in parentheses. Journal article titles do not appear in quotation marks and only the first word of the title is capitalized, along with any proper nouns. The city of publication is included along with the publisher's name for books.

Below are examples of the same four types of sources we presented in MLA style, but this time we present them as they would be cited in APA style. These examples follow the guidelines in the *Publication Manual of the American Psychology Association* (2010).

Book by a Single Author

> Author, A. A. (Year of publication). *Title of work: Capital letter also for subtitle.* City: Publisher.

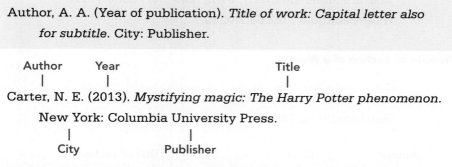

Author   Year   Title

Carter, N. E. (2013). *Mystifying magic: The Harry Potter phenomenon.*
New York: Columbia University Press.

City   Publisher

Work in an Anthology (a book that is a collection of chapters written by different people)

> Author, A. A., & Author, B. B. (Year of publication). Title of chapter. In A. A. Editor & B. B. Editor (Eds.), *Title of book* (pp. pages of chapter). City: Publisher.

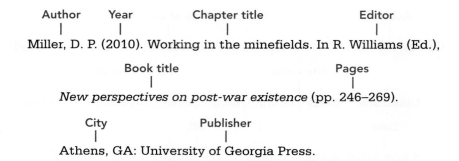

Author   Year   Chapter title   Editor

Miller, D. P. (2010). Working in the minefields. In R. Williams (Ed.),

Book title   Pages

New perspectives on post-war existence (pp. 246–269).

City   Publisher

Athens, GA: University of Georgia Press.

Journal Article from a Library Database

Author, A. A., & Author, B. B. (Date of publication). Title of article.
Title of Journal, volume number(issue number), page range.
DOI or Retrieved from URL.

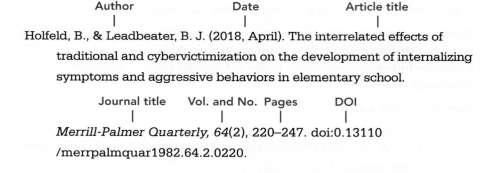

Author   Date   Article title

Holfeld, B., & Leadbeater, B. J. (2018, April). The interrelated effects of
traditional and cybervictimization on the development of internalizing
symptoms and aggressive behaviors in elementary school.

Journal title   Vol. and No.   Pages   DOI

Merrill-Palmer Quarterly, 64(2), 220–247. doi:0.13110
/merrpalmquar1982.64.2.0220.

Website or Section of a Website

Author, A. A., & Author, B. B. (Date of publication). *Title of section*.
Retrieved from URL.

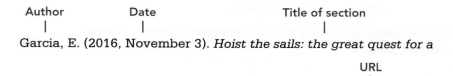

Author   Date   Title of section

Garcia, E. (2016, November 3). *Hoist the sails: the great quest for a*

URL

play-based classroom. Retrieved from https://www.edutopia.org
/blog/quest-for-play-based-classroom-elizabeth-garcia.

APPLY

Practice working with citation styles

1. The following citation for a work from an anthology is in APA style. What would you change to reformat it in MLA style? Rewrite the example and write a sentence or two explaining what you changed.

> Miller, D. P. (2010). Working in the minefields. In R. Williams
> (Ed.), *New perspectives on post-war existence*
> (pp. 246–269). Athens, GA: University of Georgia Press.

2. The following citation for a short work from a website is in MLA style. What would you change to reformat it in APA style? Rewrite the example and write a sentence or two explaining what you changed.

> Enzinna, Wes. "Syria's Unknown Revolution." *Pulitzer Center
> on Crisis Reporting*, 24 Nov. 2015, pulitzercenter.org/
> projects/middle-east-syria-enzinna-war-rojava.

9.3 Summarize sources to use in your writing

Earlier in Chapter 9, you practiced taking notes on your sources. In this section, you'll move beyond those notes to a formal summary of each source.

What's the difference between notes and a formal summary? It comes down to audience and purpose. The audience for your informal notes is you—the note taker. The audience for a summary is another reader, perhaps your instructor or classmates. When you took notes on your sources, you were able to use all sorts of marks that meant something to you. Maybe you underlined, added comments or questions in the margins, drew arrows from one part of the text to another, or drew stars to remind you that something was important to you.

Those notes make complete sense to you, but they wouldn't convey much meaning to another reader. For outside readers such as your peers and instructor, you need to compose a formal summary that pulls your notes together into a coherent, organized message that explains the main claim(s) of the source and the evidence it includes to support those claims. Summarizing a source requires you to slow down and focus on what the writer is really trying to tell readers. That's where your purpose comes in.

In this section, you'll learn what readers typically expect from a summary and the process for creating a summary.

Understanding what readers expect from a summary

Writing an effective summary requires you to follow some simple rules of thumb:

- **Clearly identify the source.** In most cases, readers need to see the author's last name and the title of the piece in the first paragraph of your summary. Otherwise, they won't know what you're summarizing.

- **State the main ideas.** The summary has to convey *all* the main ideas or points that are essential to understand the text's argument or message.

- **Keep it brief.** A summary includes all the texts' main points, but it needs to convey that information in the most compact way possible. Leave out nonessential details and examples. A summary of a short article should take no more than a few sentences. Likewise, a summary of a book may require a full paragraph.

- **Accurately represent the source.** When you are trying to convey the full meaning of the text in a much smaller space and in many fewer words, accuracy can get lost. Always check and double check to make sure your summary accurately reflects the content of the original piece.

- **Remain objective.** A summary always has an objective tone. It is not the place to tell readers how you feel or what you think about the text. Keep a "just the facts, ma'am" tone in mind as you write to avoid including your personal perspective on the text's message. A summary is your report of the main points, not your opinion of them.

It's not enough to address only some of these tips. You need to address them all to write an effective summary.

Some texts will come with built-in clues to help you summarize. Use them to your advantage. For example, the piece may include an *abstract*—a paragraph at the beginning that gives an overview of the text. In longer pieces, the author may include a paragraph near the beginning, though not necessarily the first paragraph, that explains what the piece will argue and what the key evidence will be. In other cases, you may see headings that break up the text and identify what each section will address. And sometimes, you'll see a summary or concluding paragraph that attempts to give an overview of the main claim and support. Although these clues may be helpful, none of them is a substitute for a careful summary that you produce based on your own careful reading of the text. Use these elements as tools to help you write your summary in your own voice.

Seeing the summary rules of thumb in action

Now, we want to show you two summaries. First, you'll see a summary that doesn't follow one or more of our rules of thumb. Second, you'll see a summary that incorporates all the rules of thumb we suggest.

Before you read the summaries, read the following article to see what the student writers were summarizing. This article appeared on the website *CNET* in November 2018.

Don't Obsess Over Your Follower Count

SEAN KEANE

Jack Dorsey doesn't want you to worry about your follower count.

The Twitter CEO said that emphasizing the number of followers you've gathered isn't the best idea, Slashdot reported Monday.

He and fellow founders Noah Glass, Biz Stone and Evan Williams didn't consider "all the dynamics that could ensue afterwards" as they prepared Twitter for its 2006 launch, Dorsey noted during a talk Monday in New Delhi.

"It is actually incentivizing you to increase that number. That may have been right 12 years ago, but I don't think it is right today," he said. "I think what is more important is the number of meaningful conversations you're having on the platform. How many times do you receive a reply?"

Twitter has been thinking a lot about meaningful conversations in recent months. Like Facebook, it has faced scrutiny and criticism about the ways in which social media networks get abused by trolls, bullies and disinformation. Those companies have also drawn fire because of the perception that they censor certain voices, especially conservative ones.

For the record, the most popular Twitter accounts have tens of millions of followers. The top three as of August, according to Statista, are singer Katy Perry

(107 million), singer Justin Bieber (104 million) and former US president Barack Obama (102 million).

Dorsey, meanwhile, confirmed that the company is still looking at letting you edit your tweets, according to The Next Web.

"We have been considering this for a while and we have to do [it] in the right way. We can't just rush it out. We can't make something which is distracting or takes anything away from the public record," he said.

Twitter declined to comment beyond an October tweet in which the company said it is hard at work trying to incentivize "healthy conversation."

Last week, Williams told a Web Summit audience that showing the follower count is "detrimental" because it turns Twitter into a popularity contest, Recode reported, even though those counts generated huge publicity for the social media platform in its early days.

And people do pay close attention to those numbers. Last month, for instance, President Donald Trump (55 million followers) slammed Twitter, suggesting it had a political bias after his follower count dropped by about 300,000 in July.

But Twitter says that its occasional user purges stem from its focus on the "health of the service," as it tries to remove bots and fake accounts.

Every aspect of the platform is under review, including the "like" button, Twitter noted last month.

Summary 1 ignores the rules of thumb.

① This article is talking about what people should think about their **②** Twitter followers. **③** Counting your followers used to be important when Twitter got started, but it's not important now. **④** I agree with this article because **⑤** I think keeping up with how many followers people have is just a big competition to see who can get more people behind them.

① This summary includes neither the author nor the title of the source.

② The first sentence is so vague that it doesn't tell us what the author actually reports about the Twitter CEO's comments and thoughts.

③ The second sentence is accurate about one point in the article, but it inaccurately represents the whole source because it doesn't convey all the main points of the full article.

4 The writer inserts personal opinion that doesn't belong in a summary.

5 The summary is brief but inaccurate, and it includes too much personal opinion.

Summary 2 follows the rules of thumb.

1

In "Twitter CEO Jack Dorsey says you shouldn't obsess over your follower count," Sean Keane reports Dorsey's opinion that Twitter **2** users should focus more on having "meaningful conversations" on the **3** platform than gaining as many followers as possible. The article also documents some criticism Twitter has faced over allowing trolls and bots to post false or hateful information and confirms that Twitter is considering additional modifications such as letting people edit their tweets, but wants to take its time to consider the broader impacts of **4 5** any changes.

1 Clearly identifies the author and title.

2 Clearly states the main idea of the article.

3 Stays faithful to the original source without embellishing or misrepresenting the author's ideas.

4 The summary doesn't include any of the student's personal opinion about the article.

5 Summary conveys the main points of the article in only two substantial sentences.

REFLECT

Decide what's essential information

Now that you've seen an example of how to effectively write a summary, practice it yourself. Carefully read one of the sources you've gathered and make notes about information you definitely want to consider including ▶

in a summary. Next, reread your source and revise your notes to narrow what will appear in your summary. Later you'll use these notes to write a brief but accurate summary of your source that uses the rules of thumb we discussed earlier.

UNDERSTAND

Manage sources with an annotated bibliography

Once you've collected several sources to use in your researched writing project, it can be daunting to move straight to writing the whole paper. A really valuable interim step is to create an annotated bibliography, a more formal listing of your sources that summarizes and evaluates them individually. In an annotated bibliography, each source's citation is followed by a paragraph (the "annotation" part of annotated bibliography) that carefully summarizes the source and evaluates its usefulness for your project. You'll have an opportunity to compose your own annotated bibliography for the Chapter 9 Project.

For now, let's take a look at a sample annotated bibliography entry for the article "Student Evaluations of Teaching Are Not Valid" by John W. Lawrence. A student located it as a potential source for her research question: "How should college professors' effectiveness be measured?" Notice that the annotation paragraph doesn't repeat the author's full name or the title because that information is available in the citation.

Sample annotated bibliography entry (MLA style)

Lawrence, John W. "Student Evaluations of Teaching Are Not
   Valid." *Academe*, vol. 104, no. 3, 2018, pp. 16-18. *ProQuest*,
   www.proquest.com.

   In this review of published studies of student evaluations
of teaching (SET), Lawrence states that SET scores are invalid
measures of teaching effectiveness for a variety of reasons. First,
SET scores have statistical problems, including a response rate
that is often low. Beyond that, SET scores often reflect students'
opinions about things not related to a teacher's effectiveness,
including the teacher's gender or appearance. Lawrence also
notes that SET scores can result in easier coursework and inflated

grades. He says that colleges still use them despite these problems because they are fairly simple to give students and they appear to be completely objective. He concludes by saying that a better evaluation system would shift the focus from evaluating teachers to evaluating teaching and involve studying teaching materials and multiple observations written by other faculty in the same field. This article could help me explain the argument for getting rid of course evaluations completed by students.

APPLY

Collaborate on writing an entry for an annotated bibliography

We've selected a source that could potentially help a student address the following research question: "Did the Healthy, Hunger-Free Kids Act of 2010 actually improve children's health, or should it be changed or repealed?" Working with a small group, read the following article and create an annotated bibliography entry that includes an accurate citation and a paragraph in which you summarize and evaluate the source's value for addressing this research question. Use your instructor's guidance about which citation style to use.

The Potentially Negative Consequences Associated with the Healthy, Hunger-Free Kids Act

CRAIG GUNDERSEN

Craig Gundersen is a professor of agricultural strategy at the University of Illinois and the executive director of the National Soybean Research Laboratory. This article was published on Policy Matters, a website published by the University of Illinois's Department of Agricultural and Consumer Economics to "communicate research-based analysis on current issues to help inform policy and policy makers."

The National School Lunch Program (NSLP) is a core component of the social safety net for low-income children in the United States. The proposals ▶

implemented through the Healthy, Hunger-Free Kids Act of 2010 have the potential to reduce the effectiveness of the NSLP in improving the well-being of low-income children.

The NSLP operates in over 100,000 public and nonprofit private schools across the United States and, in the process, has the potential to reach almost all children attending school. In 2012, approximately 30 million students participated in NSLP and over 70 percent of these participants received free or reduced-price meals. A child is eligible for a free meal if his or her family income is less than 130 percent of the poverty line (for a family of four in 2013 this was $30,615) while a child is eligible for a reduced price meal (40 cents) if his or her family income is between 130 percent and 185 percent of the poverty line. In some cases, schools in high-poverty areas can provide free school lunches to all children without the requirement of family incomes. The total cost of the program to the federal government was about $11 billion in 2012.

The benefits associated with receiving a school meal are substantial—the average benefit for a child receiving the meals is about $60 per month. In light of the size of the program for the government and for children, research has examined whether or not the program is successful with a particular emphasis on whether it has improved the well-being of children in low-income households. Recent work has concentrated on this over two dimensions. First, children who receive free or reduced-price lunches are between 2.3 and 9.0 percentage points less likely to be food insecure than eligible non-participants. While this is not as large as the effect of the Supplemental Nutrition Assistance Program (SNAP, formerly known as the Food Stamp Program), this is a large effect. Along with this direct evidence there is indirect evidence that NSLP leads to reductions in food insecurity insofar as there are increases in food insecurity over the summertime when most children are not in school. Second, research has examined the impact of NSLP participation on childhood obesity. This research is especially instructive insofar as at least some people believe that the NSLP is associated with increases in childhood obesity. Research has found, though, that low-income participants in the NSLP are no more likely than eligible non-participants to be obese or overweight.

Despite the proven benefits associated with NSLP participation, the Healthy, Hunger-Free Kids Act of 2010 called for a total restructuring of the standards of the program. This includes, among other things, caloric downsizing; major decreases in allotted sodium, trans fats, and saturated fats per meal; offering of fruits and vegetables daily as two separate meal components; all grains must contain at least 50 percent whole grain; the establishment of daily minimum and maximum ranges of grains and meats/meat substitutes; stipulating that milk must be fat-free (flavored and unflavored) or 1 percent reduced fat (unflavored). In addition, standards for snacks and foods distributed outside of the lunch line have also been implemented.

On the surface, this restructuring of the NSLP seems like a good idea. After all, who is against healthier meals? However, concerns exist regarding what might happen to childhood hunger in the United States due to these new rules. The following are three probable consequences of the policy changes for consideration. First, schools are faced with higher expenses due to these requirements and declines in participation among students and, hence, fewer meals sold. In response, some schools have chosen to opt out of the NSLP so they do not need to abide by the new rules. In the process of doing so, NSLP-eligible children who attend these schools will no longer have access to free or reduced-price meals, putting them at heightened risk of food insecurity. Second, children may be less likely to eat what is served through the revised guidelines and, hence, a decline in the receipt of school meals. This is consistent with a study that showed a marked decline in milk consumption after flavored milk was removed from some school meal programs due to the perceived negative characteristics of flavored milk and, as a consequence, the health benefits associated with milk consumption were not realized. Something similar is likely to occur when "healthier meals" are introduced. Third, for many students, the main meal they eat might be lunch due to limited food availability at home. Children with sufficient food at home can make up for the reductions in calories of the new school lunches but this is not an option for many low-income children. As a consequence, these children will be more likely to be food insecure and/or put greater demands on their family's already limited food budget.

There are some in the United States who may be willing to accept more hunger among children if this were paired with a decline in childhood obesity. However, a decline in obesity may not occur due to these "healthier meals" for two main reasons. First, there is evidence that persons will compensate for the loss of calories in one meal with additional calories in other meals. So, for children in households with sufficient resources, the reduction in calories in school meals may be replaced with calories in other meals. Second, as noted above, many schools have reported declines in participation in the NSLP. If these children are being given even healthier meals through sack lunches or through consumption of foods at local retail food outlets, this may then mean these children would not be at higher risk of obesity. But, if their sack lunches or alternative outside-school meal options are not healthier, they could be at higher risk of obesity. ▶

The Healthy, Hunger-Free Kids Act of 2010 does appear to be a well-intentioned policy change. It is worthwhile, though, for policymakers and program administrators to continue to evaluate the negative consequences associated with this change, especially since these consequences are most likely to be borne by children in low-income families.

APPLY

Write your own annotated bibliography entry

Now that you've collaborated with classmates to practice creating a sample annotated bibliography entry, turn back to the sources you collected for your potential research project and write an annotated bibliography entry for one of those sources. Be sure to include a full citation and a paragraph that carefully summarizes the source and explains how the source might help you address your research question.

Chapter 9 Project
Compose an annotated bibliography

In Chapter 8, you determined a research question and collected several sources that address it in some way. Now, create an annotated bibliography of those sources.

Start by revisiting the work you did for the Chapter 8 Project. Review the research question you wrote and the credible sources you found to address it. List your citations for each source in alphabetical order by author. For each of your sources, write a paragraph of about four to six sentences that states the main point or claim of the source and explains the specific evidence or line of reasoning the author provides to support that claim. Then, comment on how you think this source will help you address your research question. Your annotation may also address how the source complements or offers a different position from one or more other sources you've gathered. Finding those connections at this stage can help prepare you for planning to write your paper.

10

Crafting a Thesis for a Substantial Writing Project

≈ Achie√e *If your instructor has assigned them, you can watch the video for this chapter, complete the Reflect and Apply activities, and work on the Chapter Project in Achieve.*

10.1 Explore thesis options in response to your research question

In this section, you'll learn how a process of making notes on the sources you've gathered can help you move toward a thesis that addresses your research question.

Listening to your sources

Once you've carefully read, evaluated, and summarized the sources you collected to address your research question, you have become a bit of an expert on your chosen subject matter. You know the main issues, you understand the different approaches other writers have taken to address the central problem, and you recognize the specific disagreements people have about the topic. But how do you move from understanding the issue to making your own argument about it?

We like to think about this process as "listening to your sources." What are they telling you about your issue? When you really understand your sources, you've likely already begun grouping them in your mind according to how they relate to one another: this group supports one approach, that group supports a different solution. Because you've become an expert yourself, however, you have your own perspective on the issue. It's important that your voice is clear in the thesis you ultimately compose.

REFLECT

Consider your process for creating a thesis

As you begin to consider the advice we're giving you about creating a source-inspired thesis, it's important to think about how this advice meshes with your own experience of writing thesis statements. In the past, when you've needed to formulate a thesis, how did you do it? What was your process?

Write a paragraph that discusses your experiences with thesis writing. You may want to discuss advice (helpful or not!) that you got from teachers, peers, or writing center tutors. How has your prior experience with writing a thesis statement affected your confidence in your ability to write an effective thesis? In other cases, you may have had little experience writing a thesis statement. If that's your situation, explain in your paragraph what questions you have about writing an effective thesis or what you hope to learn about thesis writing as we go forward. In your response, feel free to include both positive and negative experiences.

UNDERSTAND

Consider one student's process: A case study

In the following case study, you'll see how one student developed a draft thesis by thinking through her own ideas and those expressed in her sources.

Amy Minton is a college student who hopes to get certified to teach both math and English in middle school. People often ask her how she can possibly be interested in teaching two subjects that seem completely different from one another. But Amy has always believed that the two subjects were more connected than they get credit for; she feels it shouldn't surprise anyone that people can excel in both math and English as she has.

So when Amy's writing class was working on a research-based argument paper, she knew she wanted to focus on the connections she sees between writing and math. Amy's process of developing a draft thesis included the following steps.

Developing a research question. When Amy was assigned to develop a research question, find credible sources that related to her question, and then ultimately write an argument using those sources, she decided she wanted to explore connections between math and English in some way. After brainstorming, here is the research question she developed:

How can writing be used to help students learn math?

Taking notes on sources to focus ideas. To address her research question, Amy consulted more than a dozen credible sources. When she settled on the most useful ones, she wrote summary paragraphs for each of them. Below, we've reproduced four representative summary paragraphs she used to decide what her thesis would be. In the margins, you'll see comments that show her thought process.

Research Question: How can writing be used to help students learn math?

Source 1
The authors argue that students succeed in problem solving only when their mathematical thinking skills are developed first. The authors believe integrating writing into the curricula is the answer to this. To test this hypothesis, ninety-six middle school students took part in a STEM (science, technology, engineering, and math) course during the summer. Half of the students were placed into a class that focused on the writing process and math, and the other half were put into a class that taught high-stakes testing skills. The result was that the students who went through the writing skills class were better problem solvers than the other children. This paper is important for my research

Students who write develop problem-solving skills. Crucial for learning math.

because it provides a rationale for why students should write in the first place, not just for mathematics. It also has some ideas about how to do this, and it tells you how to be effective.

Source 2

This author believes that writing within math will help build problem-solving skills, in turn building better prepared college-ready seniors. In the study, the author observed twenty-five intermediate algebra college students. The students went through a sixteen-week course, where the first half of the week was lecture and the second half was recitation. In the last ten lecture sessions, the students were given writing assignments that required them to think critically and explain their answers, and their observations were recorded. It was found that the process of writing everything down definitely helped the low students. Many students also noted that writing it down and thinking it out allowed them to see what they didn't know or needed more help with. While this study isn't unique in topic, it is unique in subjects. The students are college level, and they are remedial students. This article also has some interesting ideas about how writing to learn math (WTLM) allows students to become better metacognitive thinkers and eventually their own teachers.

Having to explain in writing their answers/process for solving a math problem helps students, especially the ones who struggle with math, understand where they are making mistakes or what they don't get yet.

WTLM (writing to learn math) results in more reflective students who can learn to solve their own problems.

Source 3

The authors attempt to prove to a group of pre-service teachers that writing to learn mathematics (WTLM) is necessary for the success of students within the K-12 classroom. The hypothesis was that by introducing pre-service teachers to WTLM, they would better understand the diverse ways that students learn, allowing them to be better differentiators. In this article, the authors examine

Implies that current teachers don't respect WTLM? Trying to get them young?

preexisting opinions of WTLM and present two prompts for the teachers to complete, in an effort to change their opinion. It was proven that when the pre-service teachers saw the effects of WTLM many of them changed their opinions and became much more open minded about using WTLM. While this article is about pre-service teachers, I believe that it will be beneficial for my research because it provides a lot of background to answer the question, "Why do we need to teach our students this way?" The article also includes some examples of ways that we can incorporate WTLM.

So WTLM could be more successful/ effective if new teachers learn about it in school before they are in charge of their own classrooms?

Source 4

This source argues that expository writing within the mathematics classroom in the form of formative assessment will create better students. They investigate four eighth-grade students while they completed two different questions as a group, analyzing their interpretation, justification, and representations. They could conclude after their study that the combination of expository writing and formative mathematical assessment can deepen both the student's understanding of the questions presented to them and the quality of the expository writing. This article is useful for my research because it quotes the National Council for Teachers of Mathematics on the importance of communication within math, which can be done in writing. Justification is also something that I find very important to teaching math, so I enjoyed reading the results on studying the role of justifying answers to math problems.

Writing while solving math problems helps students' math and writing abilities.

From the notes Amy made about her annotations, she came to two important conclusions:

1. *Writing helps students learn math. No question about it.*

2. <u>*Future educators may embrace the concept of writing to learn math*</u>*—as well as specific strategies for doing it—more easily than current teachers who have taught for many years.*

Drafting a working thesis.   Based on the conclusions she'd learned from her notes, Amy wanted to develop a thesis that advocated for both using writing to learn math *and* teaching this concept to future educators in their college courses as they prepare to become teachers.

Here's what she wrote for her first-draft working thesis:

> All education majors should study WTLM (writing to learn math) because research shows that it helps students learn their math.

Amy knew that her thesis would probably change as she read more sources and further examined her own ideas about the subject. But having a working thesis helped her focus her ideas. Knowing that writing—even writing a thesis—happens in a series of recursive loops, she was prepared to revise it later if needed.

APPLY

Sharpen your notes on sources

Like Amy, you created a list of potential sources and wrote annotation paragraphs for each of them when you wrote your annotated bibliography in the Chapter 9 Project. Turn back to your draft annotated bibliography and make brief notes to reflect your most important insights from your sources. As you make these notes, you might find that you're moving closer to being able to settle on a thesis statement or claim in response to your research question.

APPLY

Create some potential thesis statements or claims

Now that you've made notes about your sources, write two or three possible thesis statements or claims to address your research question. Remember, a thesis statement, as explained in Section 1.2, reflects your take on an issue, defines the scope of the draft, and appears early in the draft. If you want to write an argument in response to your research question, consider claims that go beyond stating an obvious fact and offer a debatable position that others could reasonably disagree with.

10.2 State a specific type of claim and support it

In this section, you'll learn that the thesis of your researched argument is not only a claim but also one of several specific types of claims. Furthermore, we'll introduce you to a variety of types of evidence you might use to support your argument, and we'll help you think through choosing different kinds of evidence to support your claims.

Determining your purpose for writing

When you're writing to persuade or prove a point, think of your claim as the central argument you want to make. It answers the question "What am I trying to convey?" and clarifies the purpose of your argument. Without a clear claim, or purpose, you'll have trouble reaching your audience.

Consider the following situation: Carlos's boss reprimands him in front of his coworkers for breaking an office rule by texting during a work meeting. However, Carlos wasn't texting. Angry and humiliated, he sits down during his next break to compose the first draft of an email to his boss, Maggie:

> Dear Maggie,
>
> Calling me out in front of the whole office today was wrong of you. Not only was it humiliating, but I wasn't even texting. I was looking at my phone to see if Dan had emailed me the new numbers you'd just asked for. And besides, everybody thinks your rule against texting during meetings is ridiculous. You yap at us so much in meetings that it's hard for anyone else to get a word in, so texting is a quick and quiet way to get some answers to our questions before the meeting is over. We are adults and should be allowed to do anything work-related during meetings if we want to.
>
> Sincerely,
>
> Carlos

Carlos's first draft is like many people's emotionally charged first drafts: it lacks a clear purpose. In this case, Carlos begins with the purpose of asserting that his supervisor's behavior was inappropriate, but then quickly moves to challenging the rule banning texting in meetings. To send a clear message to his supervisor, Carlos first needs to determine exactly what purpose he wants his message to achieve (what claim he wants to make). He then needs to make sure all of his statements support that single message. Once his purpose is clear, he needs to further revise his email to express his message in a way that is not insulting to his supervisor.

Recognizing five types of claims

Generally, rhetoricians—people who study argument—agree claims come in five basic types, although these types may overlap.

Fact claims.   Fact claims argue whether something happened, whether it exists, or whether it is true.

> **Examples**
>
> Most college students hold part-time jobs.
>
> Most cars will be driverless by the year 2050.
>
> Studying penguins, who mate for life, could teach humans how to be monogamous.

Definition claims.   Definition claims argue what something is or how we should or could define it.

> **Examples**
>
> A family can be more than blood relatives.
>
> Executing convicted killers is not murder.
>
> Digital media can be credible sources for academic writing.

Cause/effect claims.   Cause/effect claims focus on the causes of an event or phenomenon or the effect of an event or phenomenon.

> **Examples**
>
> Legalizing and taxing marijuana sales would strengthen our economy.
>
> Gene targeting research will lead to a cure for cancer in the next two decades.
>
> Fake news affected the outcome of the 2016 US presidential election.

Value claims.   Value claims determine whether something is good or bad, moral or immoral.

> **Examples**
>
> The Powerball lottery is a good way to fund public education.
>
> Political Facebook posts stir up drama and arguing between friends.

Policy claims.   Policy claims argue for a course of action or a specific process to be followed.

> **Examples**
>
> Our class should consider the Adopt-a-Brick program for its senior project.
>
> DNA testing should be used whenever possible to determine the guilt or innocence of a criminal defendant.
>
> Students should use only their school email address when communicating with professors.

Considering six types of evidence to support claims

Evidence to support your claim can come in a variety of forms. As you think about how you want to make your argument most compelling, consider how you could use each type of evidence to support your claims.

- **Statistics and numerical data.** Providing numbers in an argument communicates objective fact that's hard to dispute. These data can come from your own investigations or from credible sources you've collected to address your research question.

- **Quotations from credible texts.** Including a particularly memorable quotation, especially one that speaks in a powerful voice, can be an effective way to make a strong point.

- **Expert opinion.** Drawing on the advice or insight of a recognized expert often helps reinforce your claims.

- **Personal experience.** Sharing a personal story that illustrates your connection to your claim or the reasoning behind it can be a powerful and memorable way to humanize your claim and connect with your audience.

- **Examples.** Citing specific incidents that illustrate the specifics or scope of an issue can help you explain the issue to your audience.

- **Visual evidence.** Adding images such as graphs, charts, or photos can often make information easier for your audience to process. In addition, images can be helpful for breaking up long blocks of written text.

A single text can include more than one of these types of evidence. For example, a newspaper article might include a photo, a quote from an expert, and an interview with a community member who relayed a personal story that creates empathy or an urgent call to action. When you consider types of evidence to use in your researched writing, think about how you want each one to support your claims.

Consider how to support a claim using a variety of evidence

We've suggested that all sorts of evidence can be used to support a specific claim. The most important thing is to consider the impact the evidence will have on your audience.

To test this, let's look at a single claim. This one is a claim of definition:

> A person's family shouldn't always be limited to blood relatives and may include close friends.

Take some time to reflect on the types of evidence a writer could use to support this claim. Write a paragraph that describes at least three specific pieces of evidence someone could provide to support this claim. For example, if your paragraph wanted to claim that visual evidence would be useful, you'd need to explain what would appear in the visual. Would it be a meme? If so, what would be the message? Would it be a photo of a group of people or a family reunion? If so, why is the specific image important?

See how to recognize and address counterclaims

As much as we'd all like to think that what we write is perfect on the first try, we also know that credible arguments against our claims are out there. So, heed the words of dearly departed Grumpy Cat.

You will be most successful when you consider the arguments against your claim and address them. Think of tackling counterclaims as an opportunity to strengthen your own argument by getting out in front of readers who might dispute your claim with their own evidence.

The key to addressing counterarguments is to acknowledge the limited parts about them you find acceptable, and then to explain in more detail why you believe these counterarguments aren't persuasive enough to undermine your own argument.

Let's look at an example of this in action. Each year around Halloween, people talk about how a Halloween costume can be offensive if it involves cultural appropriation. As a general rule, most people acknowledge that white people wearing blackface is ignorant, insensitive, and wrong. But we're not so clear on where the boundaries are for outsiders wearing the traditional dress of cultures not their own. In October 2018, Malaka Gharib wrote an opinion piece for NPR arguing that in a very specific situation, it was OK for her non-Filipino husband to wear traditional Filipino clothing to celebrate her elderly Filipino grandfather's ninetieth birthday. In the piece, Gharib acknowledges and addresses counterclaims that criticize her non-Filipino husband for wearing her uncle's Filipino *barong*. Then she argues that, despite these counterclaims, her husband should still be allowed to celebrate her grandfather by wearing traditional Filipino dress.

When Is It OK to Wear the Clothing of Another Culture?

MALAKA GHARIB

> To draw in readers from all sides, the title doesn't state a position.

For my grandpa's 90th birthday, our family threw him a *barrio fiesta*-themed bash.

We decorated the backyard with colorful bunting so it would look like the neighborhood parties that Tatay grew up with in his home country of the Philippines. We ordered a big *lechon*, a roasted pig. And the guests were asked to wear *filipiniana*, traditional Filipino costume.

While I was jazzed to don a bright orange and yellow *patadyong*—a sarong-like skirt and wrap—my white, thirty-something husband Darren, from Nashville, Tennessee, felt nervous in his *barong*, an embroidered shirt woven from

> Introduces implicit contradictory positions on the issue.

pineapple leaf fibers. My aunt had told all the guests to dress in traditional clothes.

"I feel like this is cultural appropriation," he said, tugging at the collar and looking around nervously. "I honestly feel uncomfortable."

Introduces the concept of cultural appropriation and her husband's discomfort with it.

I could understand Darren's trepidation. Just over this past year, a number of prominent people have gotten into hot water for donning the dress of other cultures. In February, Canadian Prime Minister Justin Trudeau and his family were criticized for wearing over-the-top Indian attire on his state visit to India. "We Indians don't dress like this every day . . . not even in Bollywood," wrote one person on Twitter.

Introduces examples of nods to different cultures that were perceived as alternately offensive and respectful.

In August, Madonna sported a mishmash of accessories from the Amazigh tribe in North Africa while performing at the VMAs. Some found her jewelry "insulting," although Addi Ouadderrou, a Moroccan Amazigh, told NPR that her getup didn't bother him. "If someone comes to Morocco and wants to wear our clothes, to me, that's an honor; that's not an insult," he said.

But wearing a *barong* to Tatay's birthday party—this, I felt, was not appropriation. It filled me with pride to see my white husband in the clothing of my heritage. I know my family was excited, too. My uncle lent his shirt, which he had dry-cleaned and pressed before giving to Darren. My cousins wanted to take selfies with him.

Shows that Filipino family wasn't offended by white family member wearing Filipino dress for this event.

I reassured him that he was expressing support and a sense of unity with my Filipino family. And we were wearing these outfits as an act of kindness to Tatay. He is losing his memory—but *barong* and *patadyong* and *lechon*, these are some of the things that remain in his mind. Still, I wasn't sure who was right. Was Darren appreciating? Or appropriating? I turned to the experts for advice.

Erich Hatala Matthes, an assistant professor of philosophy at Wellesley College who studies the ethics of cultural heritage, told me that there's no clear definition of cultural appropriation: "It's a really messy thing."

Expert acknowledges this is a case of cultural appreciation, not appropriation.

Listening to my story, he says it was OK that Darren wore a *barong* to my family party. "He's been invited by you and your family. He has a good reason to do it. It's an act of cultural solidarity," he says.

But there are times when it's not OK, says Matthes: If you are wearing the clothing of another culture to intentionally offend or make fun of the group or to assert power over them (for example, if Darren was wearing the *barong* to make a point that America once occupied the Philippines—yikes!). And the folks I interviewed urge caution when it comes to dressing up in the garb of another ethnic group for Halloween. "If you're [not] wearing it as part of a cultural exploration or education, you should be hesitant," Matthes says.

Each culture gets to give permission to share a cultural tradition—or not, says C. Thi Nguyen, an associate professor of philosophy at Utah Valley University. He is the co-author of a paper titled "Cultural Appropriation and the Intimacy of Groups."

imagegallery2/Alamy Stock Photo

That's because not all groups within a culture have the same views, he says. In May, a white high school student in Utah ignited furor for wearing a Chinese-style dress to prom because she liked its look. In a viral tweet, one person on Twitter wrote, "my culture is NOT . . . your prom dress." Another wrote, "I am a Chinese woman. I support you!"

The student, Keziah Daum, told ABC News that the backlash was unexpected. "My intention was never to cause any commotion or misunderstanding," she said.

If you want to wear a cultural outfit to an event, say a *qipao* to a party hosted by Chinese friends, or a sari to a South Asian wedding, but you are not a member of either of these groups, what should you do?

"Listen to the cultures involved," says Nguyen. "Ask the most relevant representatives of the culture, in this case the family, whether they want you to participate."

And it's not up to outsiders to decide. "It imposes *your* singular view from the outside without consulting that particular cultural group"—and it can come off as dismissive and presumptive. You're basically deciding on behalf of a group that you're not part of, says Nguyen.

Lastly, be aware that donning a culture's dress comes with great responsibility, says Mayra Monroy, an adjunct professor at Baylor University and the author of a paper called "An Analysis of Cultural Appropriation in Fashion and Popular Media." Don't just wear something "because it looks nice," she says.

Let's say you've been gifted a piece of jewelry from Afghanistan or bought a traditional embroidered shirt from Mexico and are wondering whether to wear it. Find out what that clothing, design, print or jewelry symbolizes within the culture and what it might mean for an outsider to wear it, says Monroy.

The conversations I had with the researchers hit a big point home for me: What we choose to wear has real power.

Seeing Darren in that *barong*, standing next to my Tatay in his, showed me that he was making an effort to understand and connect with my family.

And that, to me, was a beautiful thing.

APPLY

Identify the type of claim your thesis makes

Now that you've learned about different types of claims, seen some examples of each type, and examined how a writer addressed counterclaims in her argument, it's time for you to think more deeply about the type of claim you want to make in your upcoming argument.

Consider the evidence presented in the sources you included in your annotated bibliography in the Chapter 9 Project. Now reread the draft thesis statements you created in Section 10.1. After reviewing your potential thesis statements and considering the evidence you've gathered, choose one thesis statement that seems most promising. You may want to revise it.

Consider what type of claim your thesis statement makes. Does it primarily address facts, definition, cause/effect, value, or policy? Write your full thesis statement, then follow it with a paragraph that explains what type of claim it makes and why you believe that the sources you've gathered will help support that type of claim.

10.3 Qualify your claim

At some point, we've all been on the receiving end of someone's complaint that we *always* do something annoying or *never* do something thoughtful.

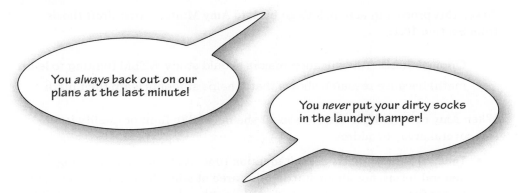

These kinds of complaints are exasperating because they are generalizations. For example, even if your friend Joel has a bad habit of cancelling plans at the last minute, it would be inaccurate to say that he backed out at the last minute on *every single* plan he'd ever made with you.

Likewise, a thesis or claim can be too broad if we're not careful to make good rhetorical choices. In this section, you'll learn strategies for making your thesis more specific.

Refining your thesis by considering time, scope, degree, and absolutes

Consider tightening your thesis by looking especially at these areas.

Time. Should your claim include a time frame such as "in the next ten years"? Does it need to state that one event should happen before or after another?

Scope. Limit your claim to the specific topics or groups it actually addresses. Rather than saying "people," for example, should you say "Americans" or "college students"?

Degree. How might words that indicate degree strengthen your claim? Is the solution you offer "better," "simpler," "less expensive," or "more reasonable" than other alternatives?

Absolutes. Words such as "always," "never," "all," and "none" can really box you into a corner. Think carefully about whether absolute words apply to your writing situation. You may be better off avoiding them.

Refining a sample thesis

To see this process in action, let's go back to Amy Minton's first-draft thesis from Section 10.1:

> **Original thesis:** All education majors should study WTLM (writing to learn math) because research shows that it helps students learn their math.

When Amy reviewed her thesis to see if she needed to limit or qualify it, she saw several areas to address:

- **Time.** Her draft thesis doesn't mention time at all. She was thinking in general terms, not about starting this area of study before a certain time. Going forward, she could consider adding the phrase "as soon as possible" if it strengthens her claim.
- **Scope.** When she reread her thesis, Amy realized that she'd forgotten to mention that WTLM (writing to learn math) also helps students improve their writing, so she needed to expand the scope of her claim.

> **Revised thesis:** All education majors should study WTLM (writing to learn math) because research shows that it helps students learn their math <u>and improve their writing</u>.

- **Degree.** Based on her research, Amy was convinced that teachers who use WTLM could be somewhat more effective than teachers who do not. She revised her thesis to reflect that point:

    Revised thesis: All education majors should study WTLM (writing to learn math) because research shows that <u>it is more effective than traditional methods for helping</u> students learn math and improve their writing.

- **Absolutes.** Amy realized that *all* is a pretty unforgiving word, and she wondered if every single education major really needs to learn WTLM. Science teachers? Music teachers? She decided to further revise her thesis to reflect more accurately what she wanted to claim:

    Revised thesis: <u>Students planning to teach math or writing</u> should study WTLM (writing to learn math) because research shows that it is more effective than traditional methods for helping students learn math and improve their writing.

REFLECT

Consider how to refine your own thesis

Now that you've seen Amy's process for considering time, scope, degree, and absolutes, how could you improve your own working thesis by qualifying your claim? Look back at the working thesis you developed in Sections 10.1 and 10.2. What specific words or phrases would you change or add? Write a few sentences to explain your thoughts. You don't need to provide a fully revised thesis just yet. Just describe what you think might need to change to adjust for time, scope, degree, and absolutes.

UNDERSTAND

Watch Gabby revisit her sources and revise a thesis

Sometimes it's hard to think through revising your thesis on your own. Sharing your work with a teacher, peer, or writing center tutor can help you revisit your sources and working thesis with a fresh eye. Sometimes just explaining your thinking to another person provides new perspective and fresh insights. If you're stuck, see if having a conversation about your work helps you revise.

Check out how Gabby works through the process in the following video. Gabby has gathered sources, made notes about them, considered her own ideas about her topic, and written a draft thesis.

> **Gabby's working thesis:** The government should implement emergency preparedness procedures for the US.

She's still not sure, though, whether her draft thesis responds effectively to the ideas in her sources. So she decides to meet with Jay in the Writing Center to talk about what she has so far. Notice how Gabby and Jay consider each part of the process and loop back to make Gabby's thesis more rhetorical.

> **Gabby's revised thesis:** Although state and federal governments have some emergency preparedness plans in place, those plans need to work together and local residents should understand how those plans impact them in an emergency such as a terrorist attack.

Video: Revisiting Sources and Revising a Thesis

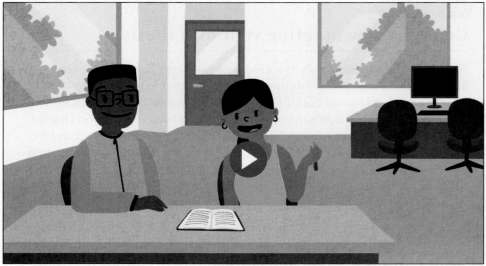

APPLY

Revise your working thesis

You've seen Gabby revise her working thesis into one that is limited and more accurately represents a claim her sources will support. And you've done some writing about how you think your own working thesis could be improved.

Look back at the working thesis you developed in Sections 10.1 and 10.2. Using what you've learned about qualifying or limiting a claim to account for concerns about time, scope, degree, and absolutes, write a revised, qualified thesis.

Chapter 10 Project
Develop an approved thesis for a researched project

Write a thesis that you plan to support in a written, researched argument. If you have completed the Reflect and Apply activities in this chapter, you have already done most of the work for this project. You have drafted a thesis that addresses your research question, offers a debatable position, makes a specific type of claim, and acknowledges counterclaims. You have also revised that thesis considering time, scope, degree, and absolutes.

Review your thesis one more time and repeat any of the above steps you feel are necessary. When you are satisfied with your revised thesis statement, submit it for your instructor's approval. You might continue working with this thesis in the Projects in Chapters 11 and 12.

11

Integrating Ideas from Sources

📻 Achieve *If your instructor has assigned them, you can watch the video for this chapter, complete the Reflect and Apply activities, and work on the Chapter Project in Achieve.*

11.1 Use sources to provide context, showcase evidence, and address counterclaims

In this section, you'll learn about different ways to use sources to support your arguments.

Considering what sources can do for you

To write an effective research paper, you'll want to think strategically about how you can best use the source material you've gathered to support your thesis and compose a rhetorically effective argument. One way to do this is to think about sources as doing a variety of "jobs" to support your argument. Some of the jobs your sources can do include the following:

- **Offer context or supply background information.** Put your argument in context by providing a historical framework, noting related statistics, or referencing pop culture moments that speak to your topic.

- **Provide evidence to support your main claim (thesis) and subclaims.** You can locate passages, quotes, or concepts from notes you made on your sources to help you support your claims.

- **Boost your credibility or ethos.** Include support from acknowledged experts to help you establish trust and authority with your audience.

- **Introduce potential objections to your argument so you can address them first.** Imagine reasons that readers may have to doubt your argument. Why might they think your argument is limited or ignores important factors? What would they argue instead? Anticipate those counterclaims and use your sources to address them.

REFLECT

Put sources to work

Consider the sources you've collected in response to your research question in Chapter 9 along with the thesis you developed in Chapter 10. How might you use them in the jobs you need your sources to perform in your paper?

For each of the following jobs, provide the author and title of at least one source that could potentially perform that job in your essay. Explain how or why that source—or part of that source—will serve that function.

1. offers context or supplies background information

2. provides evidence to support your thesis and subclaims

3. boosts your credibility or ethos

4. introduces potential objections to your argument so you can address them first

UNDERSTAND

Watch Gabby use sources for multiple purposes

Some sources can perform more than one job. You may find that you have a "multitasking" source that can support your claims in multiple ways. Perhaps one part of the source provides historical background that will help readers understand your argument; perhaps another part helps you build your ethos.

Another source might include both a fact that supports your thesis and information that can help you counter an opposing argument.

In the video that follows, you'll see how one student mines her sources to make them work for her in multiple ways. After drafting a working thesis for a political science paper, Gabby is considering how her sources could work for the four purposes described in this section. As you watch and listen, note how Gabby uses the same sources to do multiple jobs.

Video: Using Sources for Multiple Purposes

APPLY

Apply what you've learned to a sample source

Imagine you are a student writing a research essay on combating identity theft. Your working thesis is "The United States needs to invest in developing new technologies to combat the problem of identity theft." The following press release, issued by the Alaska Department of Law in 2018, is one of the sources you have collected. Read the press release to see how it could be used to support your thesis. Next, write a paragraph that explains whether and how the press release as a whole or a passage from it could potentially perform the jobs that sources need to fulfill in your writing:

1. offers context or supplies background information

2. provides evidence to support your thesis and subclaims

3. boosts your credibility or ethos

4. introduces potential objections to your argument so you can address them first

Alaska Attorney General Announces Settlement with Uber over Data Breach

ALASKA DEPARTMENT OF LAW

Alaska Attorney General Jahna Lindemuth announced that she, along with the other 49 states and the District of Columbia, has reached an agreement with California-based ride-sharing company Uber Technologies, Inc. (Uber) to address the company's one-year delay in reporting a data breach to its affected drivers.

Uber learned in November 2016 that hackers had gained access to some personal information that Uber maintains about its drivers, including drivers' license information for approximately 600,000 drivers nationwide. Uber tracked down the hackers and obtained assurances that the hackers deleted the information. However, even though Alaska law requires a company to notify affected Alaska residents when their personal data, such as drivers' licenses, has been breached, Uber failed to report the breach in a timely manner, waiting until November 2017 to let people know. Uber's conduct also violated Alaska's Unfair Trade Practices and Consumer Protection Act.

"In this technological age, data breaches are a real threat to personal security," said Attorney General Lindemuth. "It is vital that companies like Uber let the public know as soon as possible, while they work to remedy the situation. Waiting a year before disclosing this type of information is unacceptable."

As part of the nationwide settlement, Uber has agreed to pay $148 million to the states. Alaska will receive $584,000. In addition, Uber has agreed to strengthen its corporate governance and data security practices to help prevent a similar occurrence in the future.

▶

Alaska will provide each Uber driver impacted in state with a $100 payment. Eligible drivers are those drivers whose driver's license numbers were accessed during the 2016 breach. Some of those drivers may no longer be driving for Uber. Eligible Uber drivers will be contacted via mail and email to confirm their address before receiving any payment.

The settlement between the State of Alaska and Uber requires the company to:

- Comply with Alaska data breach and consumer protection law regarding protecting Alaska residents' personal information and notifying them in the event of a data breach concerning their personal information;

- Take precautions to protect any user data Uber stores on third-party platforms outside of Uber;

- Use strong password policies for its employees to gain access to the Uber network;

- Develop and implement a strong overall data security policy for all data that Uber collects about its users, including assessing potential risks to the security of the data and implementing any additional security measures beyond what Uber is doing to protect the data;

- Hire an outside qualified party to assess Uber's data security efforts on a regular basis and draft a report with any recommended security improvements. Uber will implement any such security improvement recommendations; and

- Develop and implement a corporate integrity program to ensure that Uber employees can bring any ethics concerns they have about any other Uber employees to the company, and that it will be heard.

All 50 states and the District of Columbia are participating in this multistate agreement with Uber.

11.2 Focus on your own ideas as you synthesize sources

One of the major challenges of writing an essay that uses sources is making sure your own voice and perspective stay in charge of the discussion. In this section, you'll learn how to strike an appropriate balance between the sources you rely on and your own voice.

Creating a conversation with your sources

It's tempting to include a lot of outside source material, but the downside of doing that is that it can drown out your own voice. And your voice is always the most important one in your own work. We want to encourage you to find ways to use your sources effectively without having them take over your essay. You can do that by including source material in various ways that echo the ways you have conversations with people.

"Wait, what?" you may be thinking. Here's what we mean. Conversations start with one person speaking and another person responding. As the conversation progresses, each speaker has a number of options that direct how the conversation will go. Sometimes we agree completely with the first speaker. Sometimes we agree really enthusiastically or with only a few objections. In other conversations, we respond with a flat *no* or a *no* with conditions. We encourage you to think about a conversation with your sources in this way — as a conversation that deepens the more you engage with it.

To engage conversationally with your sources, we encourage you to think about how your sources might respond to your thesis. We suggest you might think about six ways your sources could "talk with" or "talk back to" your thesis. Each source you reference in your writing is basically saying one of the following things to your thesis:

1. **Yes.** These sources completely validate your perspective.

2. **Yes, and.** These sources validate your perspective and enhance it by adding additional support or information.

3. **Yes, but.** These sources generally support your perspective, but they introduce information that needs to be considered before adopting your perspective completely.

4. **No.** These sources completely oppose your perspective.

5. **No, but.** These sources have problems with your claim, but they are willing to accept parts of it.

6. **No, and.** These sources reject your claim and present a different solution to the problem.

REFLECT

Firm up your case

Once you've immersed yourself in your sources and have a deep understanding of the issue your research question addresses, write a short version of your argument without citing a single source. Just write what you think. Explain your position in your own words.

Once you've written that mini-argument, consider how your sources can strengthen it. Make a list of sources (include the author and title for each source) that might work for each of the roles below.

1. List one or more sources that say **Yes** to your argument and validate your viewpoint.

2. List one or more sources that say **Yes, and**. These sources validate your perspective and enhance it by adding additional support or information.

3. List one or more sources that say **Yes, but**. These sources generally support your perspective, but they introduce information that needs to be considered before adopting your perspective completely.

4. List one or more sources that say **No**. These sources completely oppose your perspective.

5. List one or more sources that say **No, but**. These sources have problems with your claim, but they are willing to accept parts of it.

6. List one or more sources that say **No, and**. These sources reject your claim and present a different solution to the problem.

UNDERSTAND

Use signal phrases to integrate source material

Source material in a researched argument will have more persuasive power if it is integrated seamlessly into your own writing. Quotations or summaries that stand alone with no introduction can be disorienting; readers don't know where your idea ends and a borrowed idea begins. To make your writing more fluid, introduce the borrowed information using a *signal phrase* such as "According to..." or "Thompson argues that..."

Signal phrases help readers keep track of the difference between your ideas and the ideas of the person you are citing. To understand better how this works, take a look at the following problematic sentences from a student essay about food safety:

> According to Vani Hari, a controversial blogger and author known as "The Food Babe," big food companies use dangerous food additives to extend the shelf life of processed foods. These companies are deliberately poisoning American eaters with the chemicals they add to our food.

The first sentence has a clear signal phrase—"According to Vani Hari, a controversial blogger and author known as 'The Food Babe,'"—that attributes the ideas in the sentence to someone other than the writer and makes that person's position clear. But the second sentence lacks such a cue to readers. Without that attribution, readers might assume that the writer holds the pants-on-fire belief that these "companies are deliberately poisoning American eaters," a situation that could alienate and stoke fear among readers. A clearer way to write that paragraph would be to add a signal phrase to the second sentence, such as "In Hari's view, these companies are deliberately poisoning American eaters..." so readers know without a doubt that the statement reflects the beliefs of Vani Hari, not the student writer.

Using signal phrases to clarify your use of a source.   Signal phrases also give writers the opportunity to help readers understand how a source functions in your paper. One way you can help readers recognize the value of your source and increase ethos is to include credentials in the signal phrase. If you want to cite an expert to support your claim, make sure readers have some sense of the source's expertise. Compare these two signal phrases:

> *According to Michael E. Mann,* climate change increases extreme weather events.

> *According to University of Texas climate expert Michael E. Mann,* climate change increases extreme weather events.

The first statement offers no clue as to why the writer has chosen to mention Michael E. Mann. The second statement makes it clear that the writer calls on Mann as an expert in the field and someone who is affiliated with a major academic institution.

Using verbs effectively in signal phrases.   The most important part of a signal phrase is the verb because it tells readers how they should interpret a cited author's words. If you write "Smith *assumes* that there is life on other planets," you are saying something much different than if you were to write, "Smith *proves* that there is life on other planets." In the first sentence, you are suggesting that readers consider Smith's point with some skepticism. In the second sentence, you imply that readers should accept Smith's point without question. The table below contains just some of the verbs that would indicate to readers how you are using borrowed material.

Possible verbs in signal phrases

acknowledges	disagrees	proposes
advises	discusses	questions
agrees	embraces	recognizes
allows	emphasizes	regards
analyzes	explains	remarks
answers	expresses	replies
appreciates	holds	reports
argues	implies	responds
asserts	interprets	reveals
assumes	leaves us with	says
believes	lists	states
charges	objects	suggests
claims	observes	supports
concurs	offers	tells us
considers	opposes	thinks
criticizes	points to	wants to
declares	points out	wishes
describes	presents	wonders

Positioning signal phrases rhetorically.   Signal phrases often appear at the beginnings of sentences, but they can land in other parts of a sentence, too. Sometimes they fall in the middle of a sentence or appear as a tag at the end. Inserting signal phrases rhetorically helps readers separate your words from those of your sources. The following passage, a paragraph referring to Eric Schlosser's 2001 book *Fast Food Nation: The Dark Side of the All-American Meal*, contains summary, paraphrase, and quotation, supported by a variety of signal phrases. Look for the underlined signal phrases to help you see many different ways a writer can distinguish the difference between ideas from others (quoted or not) and the writer's own thoughts.

In addition to raising concerns about the spread of disease through travel, Schlosser attributes the spread of *E. coli* to changes in meat production and distribution over the last century. Schlosser observes that

> the nation's industrialized and centralized system of food processing has created a whole new sort of outbreak, one that can potentially sicken millions of people. Today a cluster of illnesses in one small town may stem from bad potato salad at a school barbecue — or it may be the first sign of an outbreak that extends statewide, nationwide, or even overseas. (195)

Such outbreaks are potentially deadly and, according to Schlosser, potentially preventable. Through his interviews with individuals in all facets of the meat industry, from the feedlots and slaughterhouses to the packing plants and distributors, Schlosser argues that the motivation to keep the outdated system of meat inspection in place is largely political. He reports that some of the largest donations to some Republican politicians come from the meat packing industry. He also suggests that many of President Reagan's and President Bush's appointments to top seats in the United States Department of Agriculture (USDA) occupied positions of power in the meat packing industry as well (206). Such a suggestion implies that the politicians' best interests would be served by throwing support behind legislation that would benefit the meat packing industry, which Schlosser claims they did. He supports his claim by highlighting legislation impeded by the Republicans in Congress. He contends that "the Clinton administration's efforts to implement a tough, science-based food inspection system received an enormous setback when the Republican Party gained control of Congress in November of 1994" (210). He goes on to say "the meatpacking industry's allies in Congress worked hard in the 1990s to thwart modernization of the nation's meat inspection system" (210). Though Schlosser's harsh critique of the Republican effect on the meat inspection legislation would suggest his Democratic alliance, <u>he does admit that</u> legislation passed under Clinton "had been significantly watered down," though <u>he credits</u> this to the "negotiations with the meatpacking industry and Republican members of Congress" (215).

APPLY

Practice identifying signal phrases

In Section 11.2, we've shown you why signal phrases are important for readers and how you can include them in your writing to make it more effective. Signal phrases *literally* tell readers that you are including material from a source that is not you. Often, they work best at the beginning of a sentence, but you can also insert them in the middle or at the end of a sentence to help your text read more rhetorically.

To practice recognizing signal phrases—a first step in gearing up to use them in your own writing—read the paragraphs below, excerpted from an online journal article titled "Buy-It-Yourself: How DIY Got Consumerized." In the article, author Elizabeth Chamberlain argues that DIY (do-it-yourself) fashion bloggers should actively resist corporations' deceptive techniques to infiltrate the bloggers' online presence. She writes,

> This essay is a warning tale for online social activism. It will examine how a small handful of DIY fashion blogs flashed in the anti-consumption pan, how that movement became co-opted by corporations through a series of technological and social shifts, and how a small group of bloggers has managed to keep the anti-consumptive vision alive. Corporations have long, sometimes invisible tendrils that snake through online communication. For Internet activists to be successful, they must learn to recognize and resist those tendrils. (Chamberlain)

For each of the passages from the essay, identify the signal phrases you see.

1. It's the age-old struggle of counterculture: subversive movements want to get big, get noticed, get so loud and proud that people at the top start to get itchy. Yet getting popular means getting potentially

profitable, and the mainstream likes money. Dick Hebdige—in his famous 1979 analysis of punk fashion, *Subculture: The Meaning of Style*—calls this "incorporation." Incorporation is the melting of subculture into the mainstream, a process that always "ends with the simultaneous diffusion and defusion of the subcultural style" (93).

2. This is how deviant movements get reconciled: they are first reviled, then situated within dominant culture in a way that's recognizable to everyone. Punk rockers become children playing dress-up. Finally, Hebdige says, "the fractured order is repaired and the subculture incorporated as a diverting spectacle within the dominant mythology from which it in part emanates: as 'folk devil,' as Other, as Enemy" (94). And once the trappings of a counterculture are no longer frightening (just a little avant garde), they become marketable.

3. Sociologist Lisa Wade has similarly described "the commodification of rebellion." Wade explains, "When tokens of resistance can be bought and sold, rebellion becomes something you purchase and perform [...], which] can actually connect you deeper to the very structures you want to resist." We don't defeat our cultural demons by destroying them; we just call them cute, pat them on the head, and fill our magazines with their "edgy" clothes.

4. Like punk clothing, DIY products also now line the shelves. DIY kits. DIY tools. DIY guides and handbooks. DIY is attractive to companies in a wide variety of areas; it's a way of adding a human touch to a product, of making us participate in corporate culture. When we participate, we feel better about the things we buy. There's the famous story of Ernest Dichter, the General Mills cake mix marketer who conducted a survey of 1950s housewives. Women, he found, felt better about using boxed cake mix if the mix required them to add an egg—it was as if they'd made it themselves. If a mix required nothing but water, women were more likely to feel self-indulgent. Of course, as Snopes.com points out, the triumph of "add an egg" mixes over "just add water" mixes probably had as much to do with the fact that a fresh egg made for a better-tasting cake. Nevertheless, Dichter's point stands and has become practically a marketing axiom: participating in our purchases makes us feel better about them.

11.3 Use quotations effectively and keep the emphasis on your own writing

In this section, you'll learn how to use quotations strategically to incorporate outside source material while maintaining your own voice in your writing.

Using quotations: Why and how

Quotations are word-for-word excerpts of a text that you enclose with quotation marks (" ") and include in your own writing to help support your argument or illustrate a point. To integrate quotations into your paper, you'll want to use signal phrases and possibly explain why the quoted information connects to your own ideas. If the quotation is a bit complex, you may also need to further explain it to your readers.

Novice writers sometimes believe that the more quotations in a paper, the better. Not true. Because a quotation is someone else's words, using too many quotations too close together creates the impression that the paper is a patchwork of other writers' ideas, rather than a product of your own ideas. Furthermore, because quotations are written in the distinctive style of each of the original authors, stringing quotations together can make your own writing seem incoherent and disjointed. Take a look at the following paragraph a student wrote to include in her researched essay about Americans' fondness for fast food:

> Even though many fast food restaurants offer low-fat items, most of the food is high in calories and fat. "Relatively few fast food chains offer truly healthy options" (Rodriguez 187). According to food writer Dan Myers, "Supercharged burgers break the 700-calorie mark, giant milkshakes contain astronomical levels of dairy fat, and macho-man breakfasts take the prize as the unhealthiest items on the entire menu, tipping the scales at more than 1,000 calories" ("Unhealthiest Items"). A recent article in *The New Yorker* reports that "each month, more than two hundred million people eat at least one meal at one of the hundred and sixty thousand fast-food restaurants in the United States" (Specter).

The heavy use of quotations in this paragraph creates a number of problems. First, notice that of the three sentences in this paragraph, only one—the opening sentence—is crafted by the student. After the lead sentence, every other sentence is a quotation from another writer. Such heavy borrowing from others' work weakens the student writer's ethos by creating the impression that she has nothing original to say about this topic. In reality, if she has visited restaurants enough to be interested in this topic, she probably has plenty of her own ideas to share about the issue.

When quoting from your sources, think "less is more." Use a quote only if:

- **The quotation preserves clarity or accuracy.** If paraphrasing would muddy or misrepresent the writer's point, you should quote directly.
- **The quotation captures a phrase the author coined.** For example, if your source created a new word or phrase to explain a cultural phenomenon, and it doesn't appear anywhere else, you should quote it.
- **You want to discuss the language of the quotation itself in your own paper.**
- **The quotation uses especially memorable language that expresses the author's style.**

All quotations must end with an appropriate citation to acknowledge the original source and to alert readers that the quotation is over and your own original ideas follow.

REFLECT

Reflect on using quotations in your writing

We've encouraged you to use quotations in your writing with a "less is more" attitude in general. Specifically, we've advised you to use quotations in four writing situations:

- The quotation preserves clarity or accuracy.
- The quotation captures a phrase the author coined.
- You want to discuss the language of the quotation itself in your own paper.
- The quotation uses especially memorable language that expresses the author's style.

How does this instruction echo or contradict earlier advice you've gotten about including quotations in your writing? In a brief paragraph, comment on how you can use this advice in your future writing. Feel free to include questions in your response as well.

UNDERSTAND

Choose the most effective quotations

Let's return to our student's essay about fast food. The quotations she has chosen contain useful information, but not all of them include compelling language worth preserving in the final draft. The exception is the Myers quotation, which uses memorable figurative language to help readers visualize the calorie-packed fast food menu items. When the student realized this, she looped back to revise and put more of the paragraph in her own words. After she revised, the only quote remaining was the Myers quotation, so its powerful language really stands out even more.

Original paragraph

Even though many fast food restaurants offer low-fat items, most of the food is high in calories and fat. "Relatively few fast food chains offer truly healthy options" (Rodriguez 187). According to food writer Dan Myers, "Supercharged burgers break the 700-calorie mark, giant milkshakes contain astronomical levels of dairy fat, and macho-man breakfasts take the prize as the unhealthiest items on the entire menu, tipping the scales at more than 1,000 calories" ("Unhealthiest Items"). A recent article in *The New Yorker* reports that "each month, more than two hundred million people eat at least one meal at one of the hundred and sixty thousand fast-food restaurants in the United States" (Specter).

Revised paragraph

Even though many fast food restaurants offer low-fat items, most of the food is high in calories and fat. Restaurants get good publicity for including healthy food on their menus, but most people still associate chain restaurants with their unhealthy signature items like Burger King's Whopper or Taco Bell's Burrito Supreme, not the new healthier items they have added. As food writer Dan Myers explains, fast food restaurants are best known for their "supercharged burgers [that] break the 700-calorie mark, giant milkshakes [that] contain astronomical levels of dairy fat, and macho-man breakfasts" ("Unhealthiest Items").

To use quotations most effectively, use as few as possible so that the focus remains on your own writing.

> **APPLY**
>
> ## Choose quotations strategically
>
> Now that you've spent some time thinking about using quotations in your writing, let's take a look at how that applies to the sources you've gathered for your own writing. Select one quotation you intend to use in your paper and write a signal phrase with it that names and provides credentials for the author. Then, write a brief explanation of why you want to include this information as a quotation. Was the language particularly striking or effective? Is the quotation necessary to convey meaning accurately?

11.4 Use paraphrase to discuss ideas from a source

If heavy use of quotations isn't acceptable, how can you incorporate substantial amounts of the research you've collected into your research-based argument? The answer is through paraphrase and summary. We'll consider paraphrase in this section and take a look at using summary in the following section.

Using paraphrase: Why and how

A paraphrase restates someone else's ideas using your own words and approximately the same amount of words as the original passage. The key to good paraphrasing is to accurately represent the content of the original writing while using words and sentence structures that are truly your own. Writers who paraphrase well:

- Represent the original content accurately
- Maintain the level of detail contained in the original passage

- Translate difficult material into clearer language
- Create consistency of tone for their arguments

As with quotations, all paraphrases must end with an appropriate citation to acknowledge the original source and to alert readers that the paraphrase is over and your own original ideas follow.

REFLECT

Explore your history with paraphrasing

The key to paraphrasing is putting your source material into your own words. While that sounds easy enough to do, lots of us have trouble doing it well. Sometimes we may not feel confident we understand the original source in the first place. Or maybe we've heard that bad paraphrasing can lead to accusations of plagiarism. Whatever your experience with paraphrasing has been—positive, negative, or nonexistent until now, we invite you to reflect on it. Write a paragraph that explores your history with paraphrasing and your thoughts about how you are feeling about it if you've never tried it before.

UNDERSTAND

Avoid common problems with paraphrasing

In our experience, students who are learning to paraphrase often run into two main issues:

1. The paraphrase is too similar to the original text.

2. The paraphrase misrepresents the meaning of the original text.

The first problem occurs when writers inadvertently use many of the same words that are in the original text, they follow the original word order of sentences too closely, or they change only one or two words and leave the rest of the original sentence intact. This results in accidental plagiarism. The second problem occurs when writers are so focused on not using the original text's exact words that their paraphrase actually changes the meaning of the original text.

Let's take a look at how this can happen. First, read a brief passage from Eric Schlosser's book *Fast Food Nation*. In this excerpt, Schlosser explains why

E. coli, the microorganism responsible for some of the most serious cases of food poisoning, is such a dangerous pathogen.

Original text

Efforts to eradicate *E. coli* 0157:H7 have been complicated by the fact that it is an extraordinarily hearty microbe that is easy to transmit. *E. coli* 0157:H7 is resistant to acid, salt, and chlorine. It can live in fresh water or seawater. It can live on kitchen countertops for days and in moist environments for weeks. It can withstand freezing. It can survive heat up to 180 degrees Fahrenheit. To be infected by most foodborne pathogens, such as *Salmonella,* you have to consume a fairly large dose—at least a million organisms. An infection with *E. coli* 0157:H7 can be caused by as few as five organisms. A tiny uncooked particle of hamburger meat can contain enough of the pathogen to kill you. (Schlosser 200–201)

Now let's look at two *unsuccessful* paraphrases of the passage to understand some of the most common problems writers have when trying to paraphrase. In this first paraphrase, too much original text has been copied verbatim, synonyms have been dropped into the sentences to substitute for an original word, and the sentence structure follows the original too closely:

Unacceptable paraphrase 1

Attempts to eliminate *E. coli* have been complicated by the fact that it is an easily transmittable bacteria. It is resistant to salt, chlorine, and acid. It can live in lakes, rivers, or oceans, and even on countertops for several days. It cannot be harmed by freezing or heating up to 180 degrees Fahrenheit. Some foodborne pathogens, like *Salmonella,* require you to eat a large dose, but with *E. coli,* even a tiny piece of uncooked hamburger meat can kill you. (Schlosser 200-201)

1 synonyms
2 word-for-word copying
3 words or word order changed only slightly

This second paraphrase is written in the student's language, but it distorts the original meaning of the passage, making the paraphrase inaccurate and therefore unacceptable. We have underlined the content that is not in the original passage.

Unacceptable paraphrase 2

> *E. coli* is the most dangerous of the foodborne pathogens, worse than *Salmonella*, which is also fatal. Even though they are both fatal, only *E. coli* is fatal in every case. *E. coli* is also more common than *Salmonella* and is found in freshwater rivers and streams as well as in the ocean. Almost nothing can kill it and it can be found in most kitchens where hamburger has been prepared. (Schlosser 200-201)

The facts about *E. coli* that the student attributes to Schlosser's paragraph may be true statements, but they are unacceptable in this paraphrase because they are not in the original source material—a paragraph on pages 200–201 of *Fast Food Nation*.

In contrast to the previous paraphrases that used language that was too close to the original passage or included information not in the original source, the paraphrase below accurately captures the meaning of the original passage, conveying the same level of detail in about the same amount of space—all while using the student's own language.

Better paraphrase

> Destroying the *E. coli* microbe is difficult because of its strength; it can survive in most situations, including exposure to extreme cold and heat, and is unharmed by many toxic agents. *E. coli* is a powerful toxin itself with the ability to infect a person who has consumed only a very small amount of it. The power *E. coli* has to infect in such small doses differs from other foodborne microbes, like *Salmonella,* which are toxic only when large doses have been ingested. (Schlosser 200-201)

APPLY

Try your hand at paraphrasing

Now that you've seen some examples of effective and less effective paraphrases, try writing one yourself. Recall the advice we gave you earlier for paraphrasing a passage:

- Represent the original content accurately.

- Maintain the level of detail contained in the original passage.

- Translate difficult material into clearer language.

- Create consistency of tone for your argument.

The paragraph below is excerpted from the book *Parenting Out of Control: Anxious Parents in Uncertain Times* (2010) by Margaret K. Nelson. Using what you've learned in this section, write a paraphrase of this paragraph.

> When I compared parenting styles among the professional middle-class respondents with those of their less privileged peers, I found quite distinctive differences. Among the former, parenting includes a lengthy perspective on children's dependency without a clear launching point for a grown child, a commitment to creating "passionate" people who know how to find a "proper" balance between working hard and having fun, personalized and negotiated guidance in the activities of daily life, respectful responsiveness to children's individual needs and desires, a belief in boundless potential, ambitious goals for achievement, and an intense engagement with children who in previous generations might have been encouraged to begin the process of separation. Privileged parents also put child rearing front and center: even in the midst of extremely busy lives, they highlight the significance and meaning they find in this activity, and they avoid shortcuts (such as playpens) that could make their job easier. Parents who view themselves as being alone in the task of raising children and as having sole responsibility for their children's safety and psychological well-being readily embrace these burdens. (Nelson 6)

11.5 Use summary to condense ideas from a source

In Section 9.3, you learned how to write summaries when taking notes on your sources. In this section, you'll learn how summaries differ from paraphrases and how using them in your writing can strengthen your arguments.

Using summary: Why and how

A summary is a brief statement of another writer's main point and key supporting ideas. Summaries themselves are not arguments, but they can support a researched argument by offering evidence to support your claims or showing an audience that other writers have come to the same conclusions you want to offer.

Unlike a paraphrase, which attempts to maintain the same level of detail as the original source, a summary aims to communicate the main point in a very short space—usually just a sentence or two for a short article and a paragraph or two for longer sources such as books or documentary films. But like both a quotation and paraphrase, all summaries should be integrated with a signal phrase and must acknowledge the original source with an appropriate citation.

Use summary when:

- The details are not necessary to understand the main point.
- You want to communicate a main idea in a short space.

REFLECT

Distinguish between summary and paraphrase

Both summaries and paraphrases attempt to capture the original meaning of a source you want to use in your writing. But they are different in some important ways. Based on what you've learned in this section and the previous one on paraphrasing, write a short paragraph that explains the differences between the two. Your paragraph should include at least three differences between a summary and a paraphrase.

UNDERSTAND

See summary in action

A student who is researching the ethics of spouses keeping secrets from each other discovered a book she thinks may be helpful for her research: Sissela Bok's *Secrets: On the Ethics of Concealment and Revelation* (1983). As she writes her paper, she wants to include a summary of a section from page 25 called "The Dangers of Secrecy" to bolster her claim that keeping secrets is harmful.

After reading this passage, the student made notes about the main claim and the essential supporting points.

The Dangers of Secrecy

Secrecy can harm those who make use of it in several ways. It can debilitate judgment, first of all, whenever it shuts out criticism and feedback, leading people to become mired down in stereotyped, unexamined, often erroneous beliefs and ways of thinking. Neither their perception of a problem nor their reasoning about it then receives the benefit of challenge and exposure. Scientists working under conditions of intense secrecy have testified to its stifling effect on their judgment and creativity. And those who have written about their undercover work as journalists, police agents, and spies, or about living incognito for political reasons, have described similar effects of prolonged concealment on their capacity to plan and to choose, at times on their sense of identity.

Secrecy can affect character and moral choice in similar ways. It allows people to maintain facades that conceal traits such as callousness or vindictiveness—traits which can, in the absence of criticism or challenge from without, prove debilitating. And guilty or deeply embarrassing secrets can corrode from within before outsiders have a chance to respond to be of help. This deterioration from within is the danger Acton referred to in his statement, and is at the root of the common view that secrecy, like other exercises of power, can corrupt.

Main idea

Reason 1: harms judgment

Reason 2: leads to bad decisions/ behavior

Reason 3: eats away at secret-keeper

From these notes, the student is able to write a brief summary in her own words with an in-text citation giving the page number of the source:

> Keeping secrets—including very embarrassing ones—is dangerous because it leads to impaired judgment and bad decisions, along with damage that comes from trying to conceal a shameful or embarrassing truth (Bok 25).

APPLY

Try your hand at summarizing

Now that you've seen an example of an effective summary, try writing one yourself. Recall the advice we gave you earlier about when and how to use a summary:

- Use a summary if the details are not necessary to understand the main point.

- Use a summary to communicate a main idea in a short space.

- Include an appropriate in-text citation to distinguish the summary from your own ideas.

In Section 11.4, you paraphrased the paragraph below from the book *Parenting Out of Control: Anxious Parents in Uncertain Times.* Now write a summary of the paragraph that follows the advice you've learned in this section.

> When I compared parenting styles among the professional middle-class respondents with those of their less privileged peers, I found quite distinctive differences. Among the former, parenting includes a lengthy perspective on children's dependency without a clear launching point for a grown child, a commitment to creating "passionate" people who know how to find a "proper" balance between working hard and having fun, personalized and negotiated guidance in the activities of daily life, respectful responsiveness to children's individual needs and desires, a belief in boundless potential, ambitious goals for achievement, and an intense engagement with children who in previous generations might have been encouraged to begin the process of separation. Privileged parents also put child rearing front and center: even in the midst of extremely busy lives, they highlight the significance and meaning they find in this activity, and they avoid shortcuts (such as playpens) that could make their job easier. Parents who view themselves as being alone in the task of raising children and as having sole responsibility for their children's safety and psychological well-being readily embrace these burdens. (Nelson 6)

Chapter 11 Project
Compose the first draft of a research paper

In Chapters 8 through 10, you conducted research to address your research question, gathered credible sources, and formulated a thesis to guide your argument. In Chapter 11, you've learned to integrate sources into your writing by using quotations, paraphrase, and summaries. You're ready now to write the first draft of your researched writing.

Your draft should provide background context, showcase evidence, and address counterclaims. Consider which sources can help you do that work. When you use source material—whether you are summarizing, paraphrasing, or quoting—be sure to add an in-text citation so that you'll avoid accidental plagiarism. For this first draft, aim to write five to seven double-spaced pages.

Take time to make some notes or plans about how you want to shape your argument, then get started. Remember as you write to loop back as often as you to reread, add or delete content, or rearrange your information. Later, you ise this draft for your Chapter 12 Project.

12

Tightening Your Argument

📰 Achieve *If your instructor has assigned them, you can watch the video for this chapter, complete the Reflect and Apply activities, and work on the Chapter Project in Achieve.*

12.1 Reevaluate your sources

Congratulations—you have finished a first draft of your research project! In some ways, the hardest part is complete. You have conquered the dreaded flashing cursor on a screen and produced actual text that you can add to, move around, delete, or replace with *better* text—better ideas, paragraphs, sentences, words, or phrases.

In this section, you'll learn how to review your current sources to see if they're reaching their full potential in your draft.

Examining your sources rhetorically

Your work now should focus on ensuring that the sources you've included are doing the job you enlisted them to do. Keep in mind that sources can perform several different "jobs" or purposes for your paper:

- **Offer context or supply background information** through statistics and facts that provide a historical framework for your argument.
- **Provide evidence to support your thesis and subclaims** by including quotes, paraphrases, or summaries of sources to support your claims.

- **Boost your credibility or ethos** by including support from acknowledged experts.
- **Introduce potential objections to your argument so you can address them first** and respond fully to counter those objections.

Going forward, you'll need to ask yourself if the sources you've used are fulfilling their roles. In metaphorical terms, are you missing "employees" or "team members" needed for important jobs in your essay?

REFLECT

Critically reread your first draft

We all have moments when we need to sit down with a friend or family member and tell them something that may be difficult for them to hear, but we know—and they come to know—that it's in their best interest to hear the news from someone who cares about them. Revising a first draft is a bit like having that uncomfortable discussion. In this case, though, the "friend" getting the hard news is the first draft you've just completed. By definition, first drafts are not our best work. They are messy works in progress. They sometimes have holes in their arguments, leave important points unstated, or provide weak or unconvincing support for major points. Your first draft probably has these features, and if so, you're just like every other writer on the planet. Welcome to the club!

Read through your first draft as an audience who might be skeptical about the argument you are making. Be honest. This is a safe space in which to push against everything you're pushing *for* in your draft. The goal is to find the places in your draft where you need to offer more or stronger evidence. Review the first draft you completed for the Chapter 11 Project. Read through it skeptically and make notes in the margins where you need to strengthen your evidence. Be sure to note *why* you need better evidence at each point.

UNDERSTAND

Watch Meg reevaluate sources in a draft

You've spent some time thinking about where your draft needs more compelling evidence or a stronger argument. As you continue this process, you'll also need to consider whether your sources are doing the work you want them to do in your argument. Watch as Meg rereads her draft, rethinks how to use existing sources she's gathered for the project, and determines where she needs additional research to support her claims.

Video: Reevaluating Sources in a Draft

Incorporate stronger sources

Throughout this section, you've been thinking about ways to locate and include stronger support for your argument. You've thought about how you can use sources in several ways to strengthen your work:

- **To offer context or background information** through statistics and facts that provide a historical framework for your argument.

- **To supply evidence or supporting lines of argument** in the form of quotations, paraphrases, or summaries of sources to support your claims.

- **To boost your credibility or ethos** by including support from acknowledged experts.

- **To introduce potential objections to your argument so you can address them first** and respond fully to counter those objections.

You've also had the opportunity to critically reread your first draft and make some notes about where source material needs to be added or used

for a different job. Now, we invite you to work with your notes to create a revised passage of one to three paragraphs that uses source material more effectively. Write a brief separate paragraph to explain why you believe the revised passage is more effective than what appeared in your first draft.

12.2 Anticipate and address competing claims

We've explained that one important job for sources in a research paper is to address positions that run counter to your own. Are we suggesting that you deliberately bring up opposing arguments in your paper? Yes! In this section, we'll explain why.

Recognizing that important issues have more than two sides

Careful readers approach an argument with a bit of critical skepticism. They aren't going to accept that your argument is valid just because you wrote it. Instead, a voice in their heads provides running commentary as they read, noting when they agree with or question your argument, evidence, or reasoning. That inner voice is saying things like "OK, that sounds reasonable" when they read something they agree with and "But what about...?" when they see another potential way to deal with an issue. Knowing that careful readers will respond in a variety of ways, your job as the writer has three angles:

1. Imagine ahead of time what those "But what about...?" questions might reasonably be.

2. Address those questions in your work and acknowledge that other approaches may have some appeal or merit.

3. Offer evidence showing that your approach is better *even if* other approaches do have some merit.

Addressing other possible approaches head-on strengthens your ethos by showing readers that you are confident about your position and you're not afraid to bring counterclaims into the conversation. Ignoring them, on the other hand, can suggest to readers that you are not sufficiently informed about the issue you're discussing.

Addressing competing claims fairly and effectively

So how might you go about acknowledging claims that are different from the one you are advocating in your paper? Two general moves are important.

1. **Acknowledge the claim's merits or the good intentions of the people who would make the claim.** Just because you are arguing for one way to address an issue doesn't mean that you think other approaches are horrible. You build goodwill with your audience when you can say that a position that is different from your own presents some good ideas or that the people who want to solve the problem in a different way share your belief that this is a problem that needs to be addressed.

2. **Explain the claim's limitations.** Use logical reasoning to demonstrate why the counterclaim is not an effective solution or accurate representation of the issue. You can also bring in outside evidence to support your statements about the claim's limits.

The paragraph below, from a paper arguing to start middle and high school days no earlier than 9:00 a.m., illustrates how a writer acknowledges the good intentions of a counterclaim *and* explains the claim's limits or weaknesses.

Acknowledges good intentions of the counterclaim.

Explains the claim's limits or weaknesses.

It is true that a later start time will probably require a later end time each school day, and thus, will reduce the time students have to work after-school jobs. These part-time jobs do help teenagers learn responsibility and they supplement family incomes. However, according to a report by the Annie E. Casey Foundation, only about 25% of American teens currently hold after-school jobs (4). With all the research we now have about teens' circadian rhythm (the time when our bodies naturally want to fall asleep and wake up), we can't sacrifice the health of all our teens by starting school so early just to make it easier for some to work after school.

Work Cited

The Annie E. Casey Foundation. *Youth and Work: Restoring Teen and Young Adult Connections to Opportunity.* The Annie E. Casey Foundation, 2012, https://www.aecf.org/resources/youth-and-work/.

REFLECT

Anticipate objections

Your thesis states your reasoned perspective on the issue at the center of your research paper. After some research and drafting, you probably feel like you're taking a reasonable stance on the issue you've chosen to explore. A strong thesis is not only reasonable but also debatable. What other positions might people take on the issue you're writing about? Have you come across counterarguments in your research? To explore possible competing claims that your paper may need to address, list five alternate positions that others might have on this issue.

UNDERSTAND

Consider your audience's perspective

To make an argument effective, you must anticipate how your audience will react. One way to figure out what your audience might be thinking is to consider who they are and how they might engage with your text. What kinds of counterclaims might they make? Consider the following possible audience profiles as you research and build your argument.

Audience Profiles

Audience	Who are they?	What will persuade them?
The Novice	The Novice is interested in your topic but doesn't know much about it. Without enough information about key points, he might not be able to accept or even follow your reasoning.	For readers who might be unfamiliar with your topic, make sure you provide enough context to make your claims understandable and persuasive. Define key terms and try to provide background information wherever you think readers might get lost without it. ▶

Audience	Who are they?	What will persuade them?
The Skeptic	The Skeptic is inclined to disagree with you, even before she starts reading, probably because she has already formed her own opinion about the issue. What might her opinion be?	To anticipate the needs and counterpoints of readers who might be skeptical of your argument, you'll want to read what others have written about your topic, especially those with whom you disagree. Consider their arguments carefully and offer persuasive, respectful counterclaims to support your own argument. Data and reasoning will probably be more persuasive than emotional appeals for a skeptical audience.
The Sympathizer	The Sympathizer is inclined to agree with you, but even a sympathetic audience will be looking for something interesting to think about.	You'll need to engage sympathetic readers by providing a well-researched argument that addresses positions counter to your own. The Sympathizer may find emotional appeals engaging, too, when combined with sound reasoning and data.
The Unpersuadable	No matter how strong your argument is, some readers will never agree with your position. Their minds are already made up on this issue, and they are completely unpersuadable.	Spend as little time as possible worrying about an unpersuadable audience and focus on readers who are open to considering your perspective.

UNDERSTAND

Approach your own writing as a skeptical reader

In the following example, a student named William Lewis imagines how readers might respond to his work as he reviews an early draft of an essay about free speech on college campuses. His goal is to strengthen his argument, so even though it might feel like he's torpedoing his own draft, he does his best to poke holes in his own writing that he can address during revision.

In a sense, he's fact-checking his draft. At this point, he's looking only at the effectiveness of his source material. He'll loop back later to review how well the draft engages his audience and adheres to sentence and punctuation conventions.

Lewis 1

William Lewis

Professor Bohannon

ENGL 1010

November 17, 2018

Speak Up! Making Free Speech a Central Goal

of Higher Education

What exactly is the goal of higher education? Some students think of college as only a job training center, but I think college should have higher goals. Colleges should also introduce students to new ideas, make us step out of our comfort zones, and deepen our critical thinking abilities. Different ideas and forms of expression should engage one another, and civil discourse should reign. Colleges and universities often claim that they value this civil exchange of ideas, but too often, campuses fail to live up to these ideals. To create a conducive environment for learning and critical thinking, colleges must not simply tolerate the free exchange of ideas and speech, they must actively encourage it.

Lewis 2

Does my draft really prove that "many people" share this concern? To make sure it does, I'll have to include specific numbers or at least lots of different types of sources that share this point of view.

<u>Many people</u>, including the Foundation for Individual Rights (FIRE), an organization whose mission is "to defend and sustain individual rights at America's colleges and universities," <u>believe that free speech is under serious threat in America's higher education institutions</u> ("Mission"). One core part of FIRE's work is to rate colleges' speech policies using a traffic light metaphor. Campuses that do not appear to threaten students' free speech rights are given a "green light." Colleges that have vague speech policies that could threaten free speech are given a "yellow light." Those that "clearly and substantially" — in FIRE's view — violate free speech rights get a dreaded "red light." In its 2017 annual report about the state of college speech codes, FIRE reported that 39.6% of rated schools earned a red light, 52.8% earned a yellow light, and 6% earned a green light ("Spotlight").

This whole paragraph discusses only one school in a small state. People who disagree with my point might say that these incidents happened only at U of D. I need more examples from other schools to prove my point.

One school that consistently gets a "red light" from FIRE is the University of Delaware. To celebrate Freedom Day 2017, students at U of D encouraged others to write whatever was on their mind on a large inflatable "free speech ball." After someone wrote the word "penis" and added an image, a college police officer told the students that they had to remove the word and drawing. If they didn't comply, they had to take down the entire free speech ball (Simon). <u>In 2007, the University of Delaware tried to implement what FIRE called an "ideological reeducation program" to force students to align with university-approved views on topics ranging from race to environmental issues</u> ("University of Delaware").

I need more recent examples to show that this is an ongoing problem.

College administrators are not the only ones who are insisting on restrictive speech practices; in some cases, students are demanding them as well. To demonstrate the

Lewis 3

power that vocal students have, <u>FIRE's president Greg Lukianoff</u> points to a 2013 incident at Brown University in which Raymond Kelly, New York City's former police commissioner, was shouted down by students over his support of stop-and-frisk practices (Simon, "Fighting"). This response from students shouldn't be completely surprising. According to a November 2015 Pew Research Center poll, forty percent of American Millennials support government censorship of speech that is offensive to members of minority groups (Pouschter). Because most college students are Millennials, it makes sense to infer that college students who support legal restrictions on speech would also advocate for those same ideas at the college-level, both by pressuring administrations and by taking direct action, like ousting controversial speakers.

The benefits of unregulated speech are not limited to allowing civil discourse and expression; educational curriculums benefit when students and faculty are allowed to speak freely when discussing sensitive topics from a historical and scholarly viewpoint. The case of Brandeis University professor Donald Hindley is a perfect example of what happens when free speech is truncated. Hindley used the term "wetback" in his Latin American Politics course in order to explain the origins of the term. When using it, he denounced and criticized the derogatory term during his lecture. <u>After a student reported Hindley's use of the slur, Brandeis administrators found him guilty of violating the school's nondiscrimination policy, put a university staff member in his class to monitor his speech, and denied his attempts to appeal the university's decision</u> ("Brandeis University").

I'm relying too much on statements from FIRE and other news stories that report on FIRE's work. I need to look for sources that offer a different perspective on the campus incidents my FIRE sources mention.

Once again I'm using only FIRE's version of events. I should look at other sources to see if they back this up or have a different perspective on how this all went down.

Lewis 4

Discussing sensitive topics in class is important because it brings academic value and debate to courses. If simply uttering a term to explain that term is deemed unacceptable, as in the Hindley case, then how will those sensitive topics be discussed? Walking on thin ice and using vague, neutral terms doesn't seem to be a productive way to do it. Imagine if a history teacher was labeled a Nazi and faced disciplinary action for showing a swastika during a discussion of Nazi symbols and propaganda. Hindley's case is fundamentally identical to the hypothetical history teacher's situation. Educators should be free to use tools to better their curriculum, even if that is done via addressing uncomfortable ideas.

The freedom to exchange different ideas, even controversial ones, is one of the best and most beneficial components of American society. When colleges limit it, schools and their students lose out on civil debate and disagreement, causing self-contained bubbles of forcibly like-minded individuals on campuses and sterile educational materials. The actions of some college administrators and students to eliminate unsavory elements from campuses have been at the expense of those whom the actions were intended to protect: the students. If colleges strive to advance intellectual discovery, the free exchange of ideas, and evidence-based decision making, then they must allow individuals to express their differing ideas, especially if those notions are controversial. After all, controversy spurs debate, and debate drives people to solve problems around them.

Lewis 5

Works Cited

"Brandeis University: Professor Found Guilty of Harassment for Protected Speech." FIRE: Foundation for Individual Rights in Education, 5 Feb. 2008, https://www.thefire.org/cases/brandeis-university-professor-found-guilty-of-harassment-for-protected-speech/.

"Mission." FIRE: Foundation for Individual Rights in Education, 2017, https://www.thefire.org/about-us/mission/.

Poushter, Jacob. "40% of Millennials OK with Limiting Speech Offensive to Minorities." Pew Research Center, 20 Nov. 2015, http://www.pewresearch.org/fact-tank/2015/11/20/40-of-millennials-ok-with-limiting-speech-offensive-to-minorities/.

Simon, Cecilia Capuzzi. "Fighting for Free Speech on America's College Campuses." *The New York Times,* 1 Aug. 2016, https://nyti.ms/2aGulRz.

---. "Want a Copy of the Constitution? Now, That's Controversial!" *The New York Times,* 6 Aug. 2016, https://nyti.ms/2aGuaFZ.

"Spotlight on Speech Codes 2017." FIRE: Foundation for Individual Rights in Education, 2017, https://www.thefire.org/about-us/mission/.

"University of Delaware: Students Required to Undergo Ideological Reeducation." FIRE: Foundation for Individual Rights in Education, 29 Oct. 2007, https://www.thefire.org/cases/university-of-delaware-students-required-to-undergo-ideological-reeducation/.

> **APPLY**
>
> ## Identify and address competing claims in your draft
>
> Throughout this section, we've explained the importance of acknowledging competing claims in your research paper. You have identified five potential competing claims and experienced William Lewis's process of identifying places in his draft where he needed to consider competing claims about free speech on college campuses. Now it's your turn.
>
> For each of the five competing claims you identified earlier in this section, use research you've gathered to write a sentence or more to respond to each of them.

12.3 Consider how to integrate competing evidence

In earlier sections, you worked on addressing competing claims by acknowledging their merits and the good intentions of those who offer arguments different from yours. You also identified counterclaims and worked on plans to address them. In this section, we'll introduce you to three specific strategies for accomplishing that work.

Learning strategies to incorporate competing evidence

Deliberately bringing in evidence that supports a claim that runs counter to yours sounds a little nuts, we know. But it really can help you build a stronger argument that appeals to a wider audience. Following the principles below is a good way to get started.

1. **Try to find common ground.** As odd as it may sound, finding something that your claim and a counterclaim have in common can help you. The effort builds your ethos and helps to set a respectful tone.

2. **Avoid "attack" language.** "Attack" words characterize an audience's position as extremely unappealing, even delusional. Although you want to show the limits of counterclaims, attack words alienate people who have an important stake in the issue you want to discuss. The language can also damage your ethos by suggesting to your audience that you would rather use name-calling than substantial evidence and clear thinking to build support for your position.

Some Attack Words to Avoid
cowardly
crazy
dubious
incompetent
self-seeking
stupid
unreasonable
untrustworthy

3. **Refer to the counterclaim in a dependent clause and your claim in the independent clause.** Dependent or subordinate clauses often appear in front of independent clauses in a sentence. They contextualize the more important information contained in the independent clause. In the sentence below, the dependent clause with the counterclaim appears in **boldface**, and the independent clause with the writer's claim is <u>underlined</u>.

> **Although converting downtown streets from one-way to two-way may be confusing at first,** <u>the conversion will boost business in the area and strengthen our city's economy in the long run.</u>

You don't have to use this sentence format every time you refer to a counterclaim, but it can be helpful if used strategically.

REFLECT

Examine attack words in context

Consider the two examples below written by writers who oppose reinstating the military draft in the United States. While both writers oppose the draft, they want to address the position of others who support the draft, but they do it in very different ways. The first paragraph addresses pro-draft positions without using attack words. The second example ▶

definitely uses attack words to describe the opposing position. After reading both examples, write a short paragraph that identifies some of the attack language used in the second paragraph and explain why it weakens the argument being made. How do the attack words get in the way of finding common ground with others?

Without attack words

Some draft proponents believe it would act as a great leveler, ensuring that military demographics would more closely mirror the US population. If all classes were equally represented in the military, the thinking goes, our government might be more contemplative about going to war. Moreover, our citizens would be more likely to support war efforts if the children of our leaders were among those putting their lives on the line.

With attack words

Bringing back the draft is the latest crazy talk rearing its ugly head once again. The people who support this position are warmongers who just want to have a fresh pool of innocent young people ready to send into battle whenever they want to start another war.

UNDERSTAND

See how a successful argument addresses competing claims

Take a look at the following short essay written by Gregory A. Smith of the Center for Education Research, Analysis, and Innovation at the University of Wisconsin-Milwaukee. In it, he argues that small neighborhood schools provide the best way to reform public education, despite other claims that promote voucher programs or charter schools. As you read, you'll see notes that indicate how he effectively deals with opposing positions.

Small Public Schools: Returning Education to Families and Communities

GREGORY A. SMITH

Troy Aossey/Taxi/Getty Images

In debates over vouchers or charter schools, many educators generally focus on the threat these innovations pose to the integrity of public schools. They rarely acknowledge the good sense behind these efforts, however. People drawn to charters or vouchers hope to place their children in educational settings that are more personal, supportive, and academically demanding. Some also seek to achieve a higher level of control over their children's education than is possible in most public schools. Critics need to give credence to these legitimate desires.

> Praises rather than derides the idea of vouchers, calling them "innovations."

> Characterizes charter and voucher supporters as people with respectable goals.

State mandates to consolidate schools and standardize student assessment have contributed to the problems these people are fleeing. Since the 1940s, school consolidation has reduced the number of elementary and secondary public schools in the United States by a startling 69 percent—from about 200,000 to 62,000—even as the national population has *grown* 70 percent. The schools children attend today are increasingly distant from their homes and neighborhoods, and are, on average, five times as large as those their grandparents attended a half-century ago. As schools have ballooned, students and parents find it more and more

> Uses facts, not personal attacks, to establish the reasons behind troubled public schools.

difficult to feel that they are known and cared for by teachers or administrators. Large schools also tend to leave more students on the margins, unable to find a place where they can discover and share their talents and interests.

National efforts since the 1980s to increase the accountability of individual schools and districts for student achievement have increased the distance between schools and those they serve. No longer can school boards shape curriculum to meet local needs or determine appropriate levels of student performance. These decisions are now being made by state-level elected officials or bureaucrats influenced by federal and corporate leaders.

So it should come as no surprise that increasing numbers of Americans want to reverse this situation, either by using tax dollars in the form of vouchers to attend private schools, or by creating charter schools freed from bureaucratic requirements. These strategies, however, risk undermining public education itself. Privatizing this essential institution threatens to widen the gap between schools that serve economically privileged students and those whose families are just getting by or worse. Left unchecked, markets tend to reward people with resources and ignore those without. There is no reason to assume that education is immune from this fact.

> Characterizes the voucher movement as understandable, not a knee-jerk response to an imagined problem.

This is an outcome we must prevent. Progressive educators and voucher or charter supporters of good will could lead the way by calling a truce, reaching out to one another, and searching for common ground. Their joint agenda could focus on returning the control of public schools to teachers and the people they serve with the intent of supporting higher levels of achievement for all students. An emerging national effort to create and protect small schools demonstrates how this can be done.

> Using the inclusive pronoun "we," he identifies a way for people formerly at odds to work together.

Over the past several years, educators associated with the Cross City Campaign for Urban School Reform, a foundation-supported coalition of school reformers in several major cities, have been showing how to establish and run small schools that are both effective and affordable. The Annenberg Rural Challenge, a school reform project supported by the Walter J. Annenberg Foundation, has been achieving

> Relies on research and logical appeals to build his ethos.

similar ends in non-urban districts around the country. In cities such as New York, Chicago, and Philadelphia, educators and activists are creating small schools where teachers, parents, and students play a major a role in shaping their schools' mission, curriculum, and educational practices. In rural areas, they are fighting to keep remaining small schools from being consolidated and asserting their right to determine educational standards based on community values and needs. In each instance, organizers are developing and maintaining the forms of supportive and positive relationships encountered in the best private schools. These public schools are delivering what the advocates of vouchers and charters want.

Research studies since the 1980s have tracked the impact of small schools on the experiences of students, teachers, and families. Reviews of these studies by Kathleen Cotton and Robert Gladden report that:

- Students in small schools are less alienated than those in large schools and less likely to cut classes, drop out, or engage in violent or disorderly behavior.

- More students in small schools participate in extracurricular activities.

- Students attending small schools are more likely to pass their courses, accumulate the credits needed to graduate, and go on to college; they also score as well or better on standardized tests as students in large schools.

- Parent involvement in small schools is higher than in large schools.

- Small schools are not necessarily more expensive than large schools.[1]

Selects research results likely to appeal to voucher supporters, who care about academic excellence, fiscal responsibility, and orderly behavior.

These findings offer educators important research support for what many, if not most, have long believed: that small schools do indeed enhance the learning of all students. As small schools activist Michelle Fine writes, "Now that we know small schools produce the optimal conditions for accountability and equity, policy makers have a moral obligation to provide such settings for all youth, especially those who have least benefited from public education to date—those who are poor or working class, and children of color."[2]

Chooses a quote that uses an emotional appeal to support his call for smaller schools.

The research also offers educators an opportunity to make common cause with parents and citizens attracted to vouchers and charters, by showing that there is a way to meet the educational needs of their own children, create more effective schools, and do so without debilitating public education.

The task now is for adversaries in educational debates about choice and equity to bridge their differences and create more of the kinds of public schools we know will work—schools that are small, personally supportive, linked to their communities, intellectually vital, and available to all students.

ENDNOTES

1. Kathleen Cotton, *School Size, School Climate, and School Performance* (Portland, OR: Northwest Regional Educational Laboratory, 1996); Robert Gladden, "The Small School Movement: Review of the Literature," in Michelle Fine and Janis Somerville (editors), *Small Schools, Big Imaginations: A Creative Look at Urban Public Schools* (Chicago: Cross City Campaign for Urban School Reform, 1998).

2. Michelle Fine, preface to *Small Schools, Big Imaginations*, p. v.

APPLY

Practice connecting counterclaims to your thesis

Now that you've learned about how creating common ground can actually strengthen your argument, try some of the strategies we've discussed in this section with your working thesis and those five counterclaims you already identified in Section 12.1.

Write a sentence for each counterclaim in which the counterclaim appears in a dependent clause and your point appears in the main or independent clause. A pattern for this sentence might look like this:

Dependent clause   Comma   Main clause
         | | |
Although [counterclaim says…], [my point is stronger because…].

Chapter 12 Project
Revise your draft to use evidence more effectively

In Chapter 12, you've identified parts of your research draft that need more—or more effective—support, learned about the importance of addressing counterclaims in your argument, and practiced strategies for doing so. This is your chance to use what you've learned to revise your draft and create a more effective argument. Go for it!

For the Chapter 12 project, we invite you to revise your draft from the Chapter 11 Project to use evidence even more effectively. Perhaps your revised draft will include information that provides important context or background information. Maybe in the revision process you realized that you simply needed more evidence for your claims, so now you want to add that. For some of you, additional evidence will help you boost your ethos or credibility. And of course, your new evidence could help you address counterclaims. Maybe, just maybe, your revised draft needs to include new evidence that fulfills multiple "jobs" for sources that you learned about in Chapter 11. Whatever your situation, revise your draft to maximize your use of sources to support your argument.

13

Pulling It All Together in a Final Portfolio

13.1 Understand the value of a writing portfolio

The term *writing portfolio* may be new to you. In this section, we'll explain the concept and help you understand the benefits of putting together a final portfolio of your writing.

What is a writing portfolio, and why do I need one?

A portfolio is a collection of related items that have been carefully chosen to represent the person who produced the portfolio. Visual artists often have portfolios to show potential employers the style of their art or their experience using different kinds of artistic media, such as watercolors or oil paints. Musicians might put together a compilation of their best songs to send to a producer with the hope of getting a recording contract.

A writing portfolio, then, contains carefully selected pieces of written text that represent the best work that you've produced in a writing course. Typically, it contains an opening reflective statement, which you'll learn more about in Section 15.3, and your revised, best writing from the course.

Showcasing your best work in a portfolio is a great way to create a sense of accomplishment at the end of your writing course. Sometimes turning in one

314

writing project after another without taking time to look back and reflect on how they all fit together can feel like a runner charging forward over a series of hurdles or obstacles. If the aim is just to get those hurdles behind you, you usually don't take time to stop and see the bigger picture. A final portfolio allows you to look back at writing you produced earlier in the course, revise it using skills and concepts learned later in the course, and reflect on your learning.

REFLECT

Compare your potential writing portfolio to a personal collection you've compiled

To think more deeply about putting together your end-of-course writing portfolio, we want you to consider other times in your life when you've curated — selected and organized — a collection of related items. In some cases, those curated collections are of physical items: seashells picked up at the beach, toy dinosaurs, or Lego mini figures. But other collections might not be physical items. Maybe you have favorite stories you like to tell, music to share with friends, a look you've pulled together by making choices about how you want the individual pieces to represent you, or a group of friends that you've deliberately chosen to surround yourself with.

Write a paragraph in which you reflect on a past experience of managing a collection that was important to you. How did you decide what was in and what was out? Did your group of favorites ever change over time? What was behind those changes?

UNDERSTAND

See your portfolio as a way to showcase your growth

You might feel anxious about creating a writing portfolio, especially if a big part of your course grade is riding on this major assignment. You might also feel skeptical about doing additional work at the end of the course, after you've already revised your writing assignments several times. We get it. Having a major chunk of your grade rely on something at the very end of the course can feel risky.

But here's the thing: by giving you the opportunity to present your best work, portfolios actually offer you a strong chance for success in your writing course. The writing you can present at the end of a course is always stronger than the writing you could do at the start. Your portfolio gives you a vehicle to showcase that growth.

APPLY

Think about what your portfolio might look like

Your final portfolio will include the best work you've completed for this course. To get started, think about the one piece that you're most proud of and want to include in your final portfolio. Write a paragraph that identifies the piece and explains why you're especially proud of this work. This reflection will come in handy when you write the portfolio opening statement we explain in Section 15.3.

13.2 Use self-assessment to determine revisions needed for your final portfolio

To assess something is to evaluate it or make a judgment about it. Humans are hard-wired to do this all the time. When we're looking to buy a new smart-phone or tablet, for example, we use all sorts of resources to determine which device would be best for us. We read online reviews, we ask friends about their experiences, we check prices, we compare data plans—we consider a lot of information before we make that decision. In this section, you'll learn to apply those critical reasoning skills to your own writing.

What is self-assessment?

"Self-assessment" means turning your evaluative eye on yourself. Self-assessment asks you to consider work that you've done or behavior that you've exhibited and make a judgment about it. That sounds harsh, but it doesn't have to be. You self-assess all the time. For example, after you've had an argument with someone, at some point you probably ask yourself if you went too far. And when you're getting ready for a test or presentation, you ask yourself questions to see if you're prepared.

In terms of your writing, self-assessment means thinking critically about what you've accomplished in this writing course and what you'd like to do better going forward.

> ### REFLECT
>
> ## Consider your earlier self-assessments to see how far you've come
>
> Whether you realized it or not, you've done self-assessment frequently while working through chapters in *The Writer's Loop*. In every chapter, you completed Reflect activities that asked you to stop and consider questions and struggles you were having and achievements you're proud of. Take some time to look back at each Reflect activity you've completed in *The Writer's Loop* to recall the various questions and insights you had as you moved through the semester. As you think about preparing for your final portfolio, choose one or two of those questions or insights and write a reflective paragraph on the progress you've made or what you've learned about yourself as a writer since that original reflection.

UNDERSTAND

Use course learning outcomes to self-assess your writing

What do you remember about the first time you read the syllabus for this course? The truthful answer is often "I can't have more than three absences" or more likely, "not much." We get that. But now it's really important to go back to the syllabus and look for learning outcomes that your instructor included. Outcomes are specific products (essays, homework, projects, etc.) or behaviors (participation in group work, etc.) that students are expected to have completed or demonstrated in their work to pass the course.

Understanding your course learning outcomes can help you plan revisions for a final portfolio. Let's consider a set of learning outcomes that might appear on a first-year writing course syllabus.

Student learning outcomes

By the end of English 101, each student who earns a passing grade will:

1. Show evidence of using peer feedback and collaboration to develop as a writer.

2. Produce writing that focuses on a clear and consistent purpose.

3. Produce writing that fairly and accurately represents the ideas found in credible outside sources.

4. Develop a deeper understanding of their own voice, style, and writing strengths.

To pass this course, students need to demonstrate that they've met each of the four learning outcomes. Let's look at each one individually and think about how a student could demonstrate mastery of each outcome in a final portfolio.

- **Outcome 1. Show evidence of using peer feedback and collaboration to develop as a writer.** To demonstrate your achievement of this outcome, you could point to some of the peer feedback work you contributed or received and discuss how a classmate used that feedback to revise or how you used that feedback to revise your own draft. You might also point to a group discussion that was especially meaningful for you.

- **Outcome 2. Produce writing that focuses on a clear and consistent purpose.** To demonstrate your achievement of this outcome, you could point to some of the projects you completed in Chapters 2, 3, 5, 6, 7, 9, and 12. Draw examples from those projects that illustrate how you used your rhetorical understanding of purpose and the related concepts of audience, genre, tone, and context in your work.

- **Outcome 3. Produce writing that fairly and accurately represents the ideas found in credible outside sources.** Here you can draw on any writing you've completed that includes outside sources you've determined are credible according to the C.R.A.P. test discussed in Section 8.2.

- **Outcome 4. Develop a deeper understanding of their own voice, style, and writing strengths.** In the "Reflect" activity you recently completed, you looked back to all the reflective writing you've done in this course. In Section 13.3, you'll learn about how to document this reflective work in the opening statement of your final portfolio.

Now, take a moment to look at your course syllabus and locate the learning outcomes for this course at your school. Sometimes they're called "goals" or "objectives," but they're generally a list of what you should have accomplished by the time you finish the course. Read through them and think about how you can use work you've completed in the course to demonstrate that you've met each outcome. Equally important, think about which outcomes may still be a little out of reach. Knowing what you need to continue to work on to improve your writing after you leave this course is an important takeaway.

UNDERSTAND

Review previous instruction and feedback to make revision decisions

As you're making revision decisions for work that will be included in your final portfolio, it's important to reread your existing drafts with an open mind. Be proud of the good work you've done, but also read critically to find areas in your drafts that need improvement. And definitely consider feedback from classmates and your instructor to help you revise.

Each chapter in *The Writer's Loop* has valuable information that could help you make revision decisions. We encourage you to review the table of contents and notice chapter material that speaks to writing issues that you want to address in your revisions. For example, if you think some of your paragraphs need more support, loop back to Section 6.3 or all of Chapter 11. What if you believe you need to tweak a thesis statement? Try looking back at Section 1.2 or all of Chapter 10.

More specifically, though, we invite you to review Chapters 4 and 12 because they address revision more closely than other chapters in *The Writer's Loop*.

As you review these chapters, think about how you can apply the instruction in them to the projects you want to revise for your final portfolio.

APPLY

Use your instructor's criteria to plan revisions

Before you complete your portfolio, it's important to understand how it will be evaluated. Your instructor will likely provide you with guidelines outlining the expectations for your portfolio; be sure to read them carefully. Below is a sample of the grading rubric we offer our own students. As you'll see, we don't assign a grade to each of the individual papers, ▶

essays, and other writing projects inside the portfolio (the "texts"). Instead, we focus on how well the portfolio works as a whole.

Portfolio Rubric

A = The portfolio fully meets all portfolio requirements and texts inside offer appropriate responses to their original assignments. In each piece, the main purpose is stated clearly (via a title or thesis statement) and strongly supported through credible evidence. Texts are appropriate for the audience and show originality in details, word choice, and approach to the assignment. Writing is clear, engaging, and free from distracting sentence errors.

B = The portfolio meets portfolio requirements and texts inside offer appropriate responses to the original assignment. In each piece, the main purpose is stated (via a title or thesis statement) and supported with credible evidence. The text shows an understanding of audience expectations. Writing is generally clear and engaging, though there may be a few minor problems that are distracting.

C = The portfolio adequately meets portfolio requirements and texts inside respond adequately to their original assignments. In each piece, a thesis or main point is present, but it may not be sufficiently focused or supported. Some problems with organization, style, tone, or mechanics are also present.

D = The portfolio is incomplete or otherwise does not meet portfolio requirements. Texts inside show some evidence of attempting to meet assignment requirements but have significant problems with purpose, audience, organization, thesis support, word choice, style, and/or mechanics.

F = The portfolio is incomplete, and texts show no evidence of attempting to meet assignment requirements.

After studying the portfolio guidelines and grading criteria from your instructor and rereading your drafts, consider where and how you want to spend time revising to make sure your portfolio meets your instructor's expectations. Make some notes about your plans for revision, including specific drafts you'll revisit and particular issues you need to address in them.

13.3 Create the portfolio opening statement

Almost there! In this section, you'll learn how to write a new and really important part of your portfolio—the opening statement.

Understanding the current rhetorical situation

Congratulations! You've worked hard and you're almost finished with this college composition course. To get to that finish line, you need to consider one more rhetorical situation: you are writing to your instructor near the end of the course to convey your final thoughts about your performance in the course. What might this opening statement look like? The Chapter 13 Project will give you specific guidelines to follow, but generally documents like this make the following rhetorical moves.

- **Announce your purpose.** State early in the piece that you are introducing your portfolio and reflecting on how you've met the requirements of the course.
- **Respond to your audience.** This is a statement from you to a real audience—your instructor. Connect with your audience by recalling meaningful moments from this course and acknowledging the specific criteria your instructor expects you to meet.
- **Build your ethos.** Go beyond simply stating that you've met the learning outcomes for the course. Include excerpts from your writing or reference particular pieces in the portfolio or memorable moments from class to illustrate that you have really addressed these outcomes.
- **Understand the genre.** Teachers use a variety of formats for this kind of opening statement. Follow the format your instructor has given you, whether it's a letter, a memo, a reflective essay, or other genre.

REFLECT

Identify how you'd still like to grow as a writer

As you consider how you will compose this reflective piece, it's helpful to think not only about how much you've accomplished but also about where and how you wish you'd made more progress. After all, becoming ▶

a stronger writer is a lifelong process. Knowing what you'd like to improve about your writing is important for setting future goals. Write a paragraph that reflects on the parts of your writing or your writing process that you will continue to work on moving forward.

UNDERSTAND

How to write your opening statement

A good way to learn about this genre that may be new to you is to examine a model of it. Below we've listed the prompts an instructor asked her composition students to address in a reflective opening statement in the form of a letter. Following the list, you'll see the letter Carson Cook wrote in response to these prompts. You'll see that Carson uses his teacher's guidelines as an organization strategy for his letter.

Prompts for opening statement/reflective letter

1. Open with a general statement about what you will take away from this course.

2. You completed several assignments that built upon one another as we moved through the semester. Discuss how you navigated that process, including obstacles you encountered along the way, to get to your final portfolio.

3. Discuss an aspect of the course that you believe helped you become a stronger writer.

4. Reflect on what you did that led to some writing successes as well as things you might do differently going forward.

Carson Cook, Portfolio Opening Statement

Dear Professor Pool,

Paragraph addresses prompt 1.

I've enjoyed taking your class this semester. I feel this class has not only improved my writing skills but also helped unlock my passion for writing. I've always enjoyed reading and writing and always done well in English class, but this class helped me realize just how valuable these skills are.

Looking over all my assignments, my research project is the one that presented the greatest challenges for me. I discovered my topic early on and without much difficulty, but I had trouble finding credible academic sources. I had to try lots of different key words and search engines to find relevant sources, and it took more time than I expected. I think I procrastinated too long on the annotated bibliography, and when I found myself running out of time, I ended up including sources that weren't the best support for my argument. Therefore, I had to do additional research before my first draft, and my final paper includes many new sources that weren't in my annotated bibliography.

As I wrote my annotated bibliography the structure of my paper became clear to me. I knew the order I wanted to talk about things and I made a sort of outline with my sources. With that outline, writing the actual paper was fairly easy. Once I begin writing, it usually flows easily. I struggle more with the tedious things like formatting and citations. I also really enjoyed the final presentation. I thought I did a good job communicating my information and I had a nice PowerPoint presentation.

Two paragraphs address prompt 2.

My favorite part of the class was the peer review workshops. It was very helpful for me to get feedback on my assignments and to help other students with their work. Furthermore, I really enjoyed doing it. Next year I am working in the library writing center. I have you and your class to thank. Not only did you write my recommendation, but my experience in peer reviews made me interested in applying for the job in the first place.

Paragraph addresses prompt 3.

I am very grateful for that. You opened my eyes to how much I enjoy writing.

Paragraph addresses prompt 4.

I've actually learned a good deal from this class—definitely more than I thought I would at the beginning of the year. I made some mistakes that I would like to avoid in the future. For example, some of the assignments I didn't take seriously. I didn't always put forth my best work because I underestimated the time required, or I prioritized other things. Maybe I thought those assignments were too easy for me. I've realized that I can always improve my writing. I can always continue to grow. I will still work on the issues that plagued my papers, such as wordiness, clarity, and variety of sentence structure. I know I need to give myself more time to revise, so I should always start early. I may always struggle with these things, but being aware of the issues is still worthwhile.

Sincerely,
Carson Cook

APPLY

Write your portfolio opening statement

You've just studied one student's experience using his instructor's guidelines to compose his portfolio opening statement. Now it's your turn. As you think about what you'll include in your opening statement, consider the following questions:

- How do you want to introduce your portfolio to your instructor? Would it be helpful to review what pieces are actually in the portfolio?

- What changes do you see in yourself as a writer from the beginning of the course until now? Pull some example excerpts from your early drafts and/or revised projects to illustrate those changes.

- What has changed about your writing habits or practices? For example, do you rely on peer feedback more than you have in the past? Or do you build in more time for revision than you have previously done?

- What are you most proud of about this portfolio? Consider pointing to a specific piece of writing or discussing part of your writing process that gives you a sense of accomplishment.

- What is still difficult about writing that you want to continue working on after this course? After all, improving writing is a long-term, recursive, ever-looping process.

With these questions in mind, write a draft of your reflective opening statement in the form of a letter to your instructor.

Chapter 13 Project
Create a final course portfolio

For this project, you will create a writing portfolio that showcases your best work from this course. Read through the drafts of writing projects you've completed in this course and choose three to four pieces you believe could represent your best work once they are carefully revised. If you completed the Section 13.1 Apply activity, you've already begun this process. Congratulations! You're so close to submitting your final portfolio!

You'll need to take four important steps to finalize your portfolio:

1. Carefully proofread the work you want to submit in your portfolio.

2. Review the opening statement you drafted in the Section 13.3 Apply activity, which will introduce your portfolio to your instructor. Make sure it meets all of your instructor's guidelines and that you have proofread it carefully.

3. Format your portfolio according to your instructor's directions. Pay attention to details such as headings, page numbers, and citations as you finalize the formatting.

4. Submit your portfolio according to your instructor's directions.

APPENDIX
Understanding Academic Citation Styles

....

A.1 Learn why and how academic writing cites outside sources

....

This section explains the reasoning behind citing outside sources in academic writing and introduces you to the two most common citation styles used by academic writers: MLA (Modern Language Association) and APA (American Psychological Association).

Understanding citation as a central part of academic writing

To cite an outside source means to quote someone else's writing or otherwise refer to their ideas in your own draft. Academic writers cite their sources for a variety of reasons, including the following:

- **To shore up their credibility.** Citing another smart, reputable writer is a way to say "See, it's not just me who thinks this!"

- **To avoid plagiarism by clearly acknowledging the writing or ideas of others.** It's only fair to give credit where credit is due. Citing your sources signals where your ideas stop and another person's begin.

- **To direct readers to original sources so they can follow up.** If a reader is really intrigued by something you cite, they'll have all the information they need to go look up that text and read it in full.

Understanding different styles of citation

Dozens of academic styles have been developed to meet the specific needs of different fields. For example, AP style was developed by the Associated Press for use in journalism and CSE style was developed by the Council of Science Editors for use in scientific fields. As you get deeper into your major, you'll learn the ins and outs of the style that's expected in your field. For now, we're going to focus on the two styles that are most widely used in first-year college courses: Modern Language Association (MLA) style and American Psychological Association (APA) style.

MLA style tends to be used in English and foreign language classes, and APA style is most often used in social science courses such as psychology and sociology. The different needs of these fields account for some of the general differences between MLA and APA citations. For instance, APA citations tend to emphasize the source date because in psychology and the social sciences it's important to cite the most up-to-date research. In contrast, MLA citations tend to emphasize the name of the author who created the source.

Section A.2 provides basic guidelines for citing several common types of sources. Specific guidelines for citing many types of sources can be found in the *MLA Handbook,* 8th edition (2016), and the *Publication Manual of the American Psychological Association*, 6th edition (2010), both of which you can find at your college library. Your instructor might also assign a writing handbook or another resource for you to use. Automatic citation methods such as EndNote and the auto-citations available via your library's databases can be really helpful, but use them with caution. As with spellcheckers, technology can be a big help, but it's not right 100 percent of the time. You'll want to check any auto-generated citation models against the format provided in an instructor-recommended resource. If you have questions, you can always ask a librarian, your instructor, or a tutor at your school's writing center.

Citing sources within your draft and at the end

In academic writing, source citations must occur in two places: within the text of the paper and in a complete list of sources at the end of the paper.

1. **In-text citations** are used within the text of your paper to indicate to your readers when you are borrowing words or ideas from a source. They are sometimes called *parenthetical citations* because some of the information gets put in parentheses. In the example sentences below, the underlined information forms the in-text citations.

   ### MLA Style

   According to <u>Dweck</u>, people who have a growth mindset believe they can change their basic traits, such as intelligence (<u>7</u>).

   People who have a growth mindset believe they can work to change their basic traits, such as intelligence (<u>Dweck 7</u>).

   These citations tell readers that the ideas are paraphrased from the source written by Dweck and that the information can be found on page 7 of that source.

   ### APA Style

   According to <u>Dweck</u> (<u>2016</u>), people who have a growth mindset believe they can work to change their basic traits, such as intelligence.

   This citation for a paraphrase tells readers that the ideas are from the source written by Dweck, published in 2016.

   <u>Dweck</u> (<u>2016</u>) explains that the "*growth mindset* is based on the belief that your basic qualities are things you can cultivate through your efforts, your strategies, and help from others" (<u>p. 7</u>).

   In APA style, page numbers are cited for quotations but not for paraphrases.

2. **A list of sources** at the end of your finished text, starting on a separate page, provides readers with complete publication information (authors, titles, publishers, URLs, and so forth) for all the sources you cited in the body of your text. This information enables readers to find and read your sources for themselves, if they want to. In MLA style, this list is called Works Cited; in APA style, it's called References. Even if your draft includes only one outside source, you still need to list it on a Works Cited page or references list. Entries for the source in our in-text citation examples would look like this:

MLA Style

> Dweck, Carol S. *Mindset: The New Psychology of Success*. Ballantine Books, 2016.

APA Style

> Dweck, C. S. (2016). *Mindset: The new psychology of success*. New York, NY: Ballantine Books.

Keeping track of sources as you write

If an academic text includes in-text citations, readers know to expect a list of sources at the end. But how do you make sure all your outside sources are included in that list? It helps to keep a running list of all your sources as you collect them and begin using them in your draft. But in the end, it's about rereading your draft carefully, noting all the outside sources that appear in the text, and making sure each one is represented correctly both in an in-text citation and in your Works Cited page or references list.

A.2 Understand MLA style

MLA style is the citation format sponsored by the Modern Language Association. It is typically used by people in the humanities, such as English, theater, and foreign languages. In this section, you'll learn how to create in-text citations and a Works Cited page using MLA style. For additional guidelines, see the *MLA Handbook*, 8th edition (2016), or another resource recommended by your instructor.

Creating in-text citations using MLA style

An in-text citation provides readers with abbreviated information about a source so that they can find it on your Works Cited page. Typically, you'll include at least the name of the author, plus a page number if one is available. If the source is digital, page numbers may not be available.

Let's look at some examples to see how MLA in-text citations work. First, let's say you wanted to use the following quote—or part of it—from a *RollingStone .com* article by Stephen Pearce in your draft:

Everything Is Love is the refreshing final chapter in a trilogy of albums that includes Beyoncé's unburdening 2016 odyssey *Lemonade* and Jay-Z's 2017 conscience-stricken apologia *4:44*, glimpses inside a strained marriage from both sides.

The complete entry for this source on your Works Cited page would look like this:

Pearce, Stephen. "Review: The Carters' 'Everything Is Love'
  Splendidly Celebrates Their Family Dynasty." *Rolling Stone*,
  19 June 2018, www.rollingstone.com/music/albumreviews/
  beyonce-jay-z-carters-album-everything-is-love-w521705.

You'd have several different ways to integrate and cite that source in your text, so let's consider some options.

Sample In-Text Citation	How It Works
<u>Pearce writes</u>, "*Everything Is Love* is the refreshing final chapter in a trilogy of albums that includes Beyoncé's unburdening 2016 odyssey *Lemonade* and Jay-Z's 2017 conscience-stricken apologia *4:44*, glimpses inside a strained marriage from both sides."	"Pearce writes," at the beginning of the sentence is an example of a signal phrase. (See Section 11.2 Understand for more information on signal phrases.) In this case, a page number or numbers in parentheses do not appear at the end of the sentence because this source is digital and doesn't have numbered pages.
Powerful music is often autobiographical, as <u>Pearce notes</u> in his review of Beyoncé and Jay-Z's album *Everything Is Love*.	Here, the citation "Pearce notes" occurs inside the sentence, using only the author's last name, as that's the first word in the full citation on the Works Cited page. No page numbers are needed because none exist in the original source.
Beyoncé and Jay-Z's album *Everything Is Love* has been reviewed very positively, with one critic calling it "refreshing" (Pearce).	Because the author's name isn't mentioned in the sentence, it has to appear in parentheses at the end of the sentence. Notice that the period comes *after* the parentheses.

Now, let's look at a print source and see how in-text citations can change a bit when you have page numbers to work with. Consider the quotation below from an article in *Time* magazine called "Coffee's Climate Crisis" by Justin Worland. It appears on page 42 of the magazine.

> While rising temperatures have caught many industries flat-footed, coffee companies have responded in force, bolstering their presence on the ground in coffee-growing countries like Costa Rica, Ethiopia and Indonesia. . . . [T]hey work with small farms to help them adapt to changing conditions, providing seeds, monitoring production and suggesting new agricultural practices.

The complete entry for this source on your Works Cited page would look like this:

Worland, Justin. "Coffee's Climate Crisis." *Time*, 2 July 2018, pp. 40-45.

You'd have several different ways to integrate and cite this source, too, so let's consider some options. Specifically, we'll examine where to place the author's name and page number in your in-text citation.

Sample In-Text Citations	How It Works
Coffee companies are trying to stay ahead of climate change. As Worland notes, "Instead of just purchasing coffee, they work with small farms to help them adapt to changing conditions, providing seeds, monitoring production and suggesting new agricultural practices" (42).	The author's name appears in a signal phrase inside the sentence, so it doesn't appear in the parentheses at the end of the sentence. Only the page number is included there. Notice that the period always follows the closed parentheses.

Sample In-Text Citations	How It Works
Coffee companies are trying to stay ahead of climate change: "Instead of just purchasing coffee, they work with small farms to help them adapt to changing conditions, providing seeds, monitoring production and suggesting new agricultural practices" (Worland 42).	In this version, the author's name isn't mentioned in the sentence, so it must be included in the parentheses at the end of the sentence. Notice that the page number is also included, with no comma or other punctuation separating the author's last name from the page number.
Unlike some industries, the coffee industry is using innovative techniques to stay ahead of climate change (Worland 42).	This example uses a paraphrase instead of a quotation. Because the paraphrase distills the original message of the quotation, it's important to add a citation after the sentence that includes the author's name and the page number of the passage that you're paraphrasing. Notice again that the period comes after the parentheses.

What if this source didn't have an author or a page number? In that case, you would use a shortened form of the title in your in-text citation, like this:

> Unlike some industries, the coffee industry is using innovative techniques to stay ahead of climate change ("Coffee").

Creating an MLA-style Works Cited list

In MLA style, at the end of your text, the complete list of sources uses "Works Cited" as a heading. It refers to the works you are citing in your writing.

Information to include.   MLA expects student writers to convey specific information about a source by listing nine "core elements" that are relevant to virtually all sources. As you build your MLA citation entries, the table "Elements of MLA-style citations" may help you recall the order of information and the specific punctuation that follows each element, either a comma or a period. Not all sources have all nine core elements, so skip an element for any given citation if that element doesn't apply to your source.

Elements of MLA-style citations

Author.	"Author" is the person or entity that created the source. List the author in this format: Last name, First name followed by a period.
Title of source.	Use the title on the title page of the specific source you're using. Put titles of self-contained sources (books, journals, websites) in *italics*. Put titles of sources that appear as part of a larger source in "quotation marks." Think about essays within a book, articles within journals, or pages on a website. Capitalize all the main words in the title.
Title of container,	Containers are larger venues that contain the source. Academic journals and databases can be containers for articles. Websites can be containers for blog posts, videos, articles, etc.
Other contributors,	If a person other than the author participated in creating this source—perhaps as an editor, director, narrator, or illustrator—acknowledge that person here. Many of your sources will not have other contributors.
Version or edition,	If multiple versions of the source exist (such as editions), indicate the version of your source. Version is another core element that is not always needed.
Volume and issue numbers,	If the source is part of a multivolume, multi-issue, or multi-episode larger work, list its number. For journals, abbreviate "volume" as "vol." and "number" as "no." Separate volume and number with a comma.
Publisher,	The publisher is the organization or company responsible for making the source available.
Publication date,	Publication dates will include at least the year, and, in some cases, also the date, month, or season. Write the publication date with the day of the month first, then month, then year. Months are abbreviated.
Location of source.	Location information tells readers where the source can be found. The location format is often page numbers, a DOI (digital object identifier), or a URL.

Formatting the Works Cited page. Follow these guidelines to format your list correctly.

- Double space and use an easy-to-read font, as you have already done for the rest of your paper.
- Start the Works Cited page on a new page at the end of your paper.
- Center the heading *Works Cited* but do not put it in italics or boldface and do not put quotation marks around it.
- Start each entry at the left margin and use a hanging indent of one-half an inch to indent the second and subsequent lines of each entry.
- Alphabetize the list by the first word of each entry, which is usually the author's last name.
- Italicize the titles of books and journals. Put titles of shorter works, such as articles or book chapters, in quotation marks.
- Capitalize all the important words in titles and subtitles.

For examples of correctly formatted Works Cited pages, see the student essays that appear throughout *The Writer's Loop*.

Formatting the entries. The examples below illustrate expectations for citing frequently used types of sources. Pay close attention to the order of elements, capitalization, and punctuation.

1. Book by one author

> Bowker, Gordon. *James Joyce: A New Biography*. Farrar, Straus and Giroux, 2012.

2. Book by two authors

> Stiglitz, Joseph E., and Bruce C. Greenwald. *Creating a Learning Society: A New Approach to Growth, Development, and Social Progress*. Columbia UP, 2015.

3. Book by three or more authors

> Cunningham, Stewart, et al. *Media Economics*. Palgrave Macmillan, 2015.

4. Two or more works by the same author

> García, Cristina. *Dreams of Significant Girls*. Simon and Schuster, 2011.

> ---. *The Lady Matador's Hotel*. Scribner, 2010.

5. Author with an editor or translator

> Ferrante, Elena. *The Story of the Lost Child*. Translated by Ann
> Goldstein, Europa Editions, 2015.

6. Chapter from an anthology

> Sayrafiezadeh, Saïd. "Paranoia." *New American Stories*, edited by Ben
> Marcus, Vintage Books, 2015, pp. 3-29.

If using two or more selections from the same anthology, list a full entry for the anthology and brief entries for the selections.

> Eisenberg, Deborah. "Some Other, Better Otto." Marcus, pp. 94-136.

> Marcus, Ben, editor. *New American Stories*. Vintage Books, 2015.

> Sayrafiezadeh, Saïd. "Paranoia." Marcus, pp. 3-29.

7. Multivolume work

> Stark, Freya. *Letters*. Edited by Lucy Moorehead, vol. 5, Compton
> Press, 1978. 8 vols.

8. Article from a journal

> Tilman, David. "Food and Health of a Full Earth." *Daedalus,* vol. 144,
> no. 4, Fall 2015, pp. 5-7.

> Butler, Janine. "Where Access Meets Multimodality: The Case of
> ASL Music Videos." *Kairos*, vol. 21, no. 1, Fall 2016, kairos
> .technorhetoric.net/21.1/topoi/butler/index.html.

9. Article from a database

> Coles, Kimberly Anne. "The Matter of Belief in John Donne's Holy
> Sonnets." *Renaissance Quarterly*, vol. 68, no. 3, Fall 2015,
> pp. 899-931. *JSTOR*, doi:10.1086/683855.

10. Article in a magazine

> Kunzig, Robert. "The Will to Change." *National Geographic*, Nov. 2015,
> pp. 32-63.

Wilmot, Claire. "The Space between Mourning and Grief." *The Atlantic,* 8 June 2016, www.theatlantic.com/entertainment/ archive/2016/06/internet-grief/485864/.

11. Article in a newspaper

Bray, Hiawatha. "As Toys Get Smarter, Privacy Issues Emerge." *The Boston Globe*, 10 Dec. 2015, p. C1.

Astor, Maggie, and Karl Russell. "After Parkland, A New Surge in State Gun Control Laws." *The New York Times,* 14 Dec. 2018, https://nyti.ms/2Gqqqcy.

12. Website

Halsall, Paul, editor. *Internet Modern History Sourcebook*. Fordham U, 4 Nov. 2011, legacy.fordham.edu/halsall/index.asp.

The Newton Project. U of Sussex, 2016, www.newtonproject.sussex .ac.uk/prism.php?id=1.

13. Short work from a website

Enzinna, Wes. "Syria's Unknown Revolution." *Pulitzer Center on Crisis Reporting*, 24 Nov. 2015, pulitzercenter.org/projects/ middle-east-syria-enzinna-war-rojava.

14. Blog post

Eakin, Emily. "*Cloud Atlas*'s Theory of Everything." *NYR Daily*, NYREV, 2 Nov. 2012, 6:00 a.m., www.nybooks.com/daily/2012/11/02/ ken-wilber-cloud-atlas.

15. Podcast

McDougall, Christopher. "How Did Endurance Help Early Humans Survive?" *TED Radio Hour,* NPR, 20 Nov. 2015, www.npr .org/2015/11/20/455904655/how-did-endurance-help-early -humans-survive.

16. Online video

> Nayar, Vineet. "Employees First, Customers Second." *YouTube*, 9 June 2015, www.youtube.com/watch?v=cCdu67s_C5E.

17. Infographic or other visual   Include the type of visual at the end of the entry: chart, table, graphic, map, and so forth.

> Brown, Evan. "15 Golden Principles of Visual Hierarchy." *DesignMantic*, 15 Oct. 2014, www.designmantic.com/ blog/infographics/15-golden-principles-of-visual-hierarchy. Infographic.

A.3 Understand APA style

APA style is the citation format sponsored by the American Psychological Association. It is generally used by people in the social sciences, such as psychology and sociology. In this section, you'll learn how to create in-text citations and a references list using APA style. For additional guidelines, see the *Publication Manual of the American Psychological Association*, 6th edition (2010), or another resource recommended by your instructor.

Creating in-text citations using APA style

An in-text citation is an abbreviated form of the full citation of an outside source that appears on the reference page. Using APA style, typically you'll include at least the name of the author and the date of publication in an in-text citation.

Let's look at some examples to see how APA in-text citations work. First, let's say you wanted to use in your draft the following quote—or part of it—from a *RollingStone.com* article by Stephen Pearce:

> *Everything Is Love* is the refreshing final chapter in a trilogy of albums that includes Beyoncé's unburdening 2016 odyssey *Lemonade* and Jay-Z's 2017 conscience-stricken apologia *4:44*, glimpses inside a strained marriage from both sides.

The complete entry for this source in your references list would look like this:

Pearce, Stephen. (2018, June 19). Review: The Carters' *Everything Is Love* splendidly celebrates their family dynasty. *Rolling Stone*. Retrieved from https://www.rollingstone.com/music /albumreviews/beyonce-jay-z-carters-album-everything-is -love-w521705

You'd have several different ways to integrate and cite that source, so let's consider some options.

Sample In-Text Citations	How It Works
Pearce (2018) writes, "*Everything Is Love* is the refreshing final chapter in a trilogy of albums that includes Beyoncé's unburdening 2016 odyssey *Lemonade* and Jay-Z's 2017 conscience-stricken apologia *4:44*, glimpses inside a strained marriage from both sides."	The simple announcement of the author's last name at the beginning of the sentence is an example of a signal phrase. (See Section 11.2 Understand for more information on signal phrases.) After the author's last name, the year of publication appears in parentheses. No page number is listed with this quotation because this source is digital and doesn't have numbered pages.
Powerful music is often autobiographical, as Pearce (2018) notes in his review of Beyoncé and Jay-Z's album *Everything Is Love.*	Here, the citation occurs inside the sentence using the author's last name with the year of publication following in parentheses. No page numbers are needed because none exist in the original source.
Beyoncé and Jay-Z's album *Everything Is Love* has been reviewed very positively, with one critic calling it "refreshing" (Pearce, 2018).	Because the author's name isn't mentioned in the sentence, it has to appear in parentheses at the end of the sentence along with the year of publication. Notice that a comma is included between the author's name and the date, and the period comes *after* the parentheses.

Now, let's look at a print source to see how in-text citations can change a bit when you have page numbers to work with. Consider the quotation below from an article in *Time* magazine called "Coffee's Climate Crisis" by Justin Worland. It appears on page 42 of the magazine.

> While rising temperatures have caught many industries flat-footed, coffee companies have responded in force, bolstering their presence on the ground in coffee-growing countries like Costa Rica, Ethiopia and Indonesia... [T]hey work with small farms to help them adapt to changing conditions, providing seeds, monitoring production and suggesting new agricultural practices.

The complete entry for this source in your references list would look like this:

Worland, J. (2018, July 2). Coffee's climate crisis. *Time,*
     pp. 40–45.

You'd have several different ways to cite this source within your paper, so let's consider some options. Specifically, we'll examine where to place the author's name, year of publication, and page number in your in-text citation.

Sample In-Text Citations	How It Works
Coffee companies are trying to stay ahead of climate change. As Worland (2018) notes, "Instead of just purchasing coffee, they work with small farms to help them adapt to changing conditions, providing seeds, monitoring production and suggesting new agricultural practices" (p. 42).	The author's name and publication date appear in a signal phrase inside the sentence, so this information doesn't appear in the parentheses at the end of the sentence. Only the abbreviation "p." and the page number are included there. Notice that the final period always follows the closed parentheses.

Sample In-Text Citations	How It Works
Coffee companies are trying to stay ahead of climate change: "Instead of just purchasing coffee, they work with small farms to help them adapt to changing conditions, providing seeds, monitoring production and suggesting new agricultural practices" (Worland, 2018, p. 42).	In this version, the author's name and the date aren't mentioned in the sentence, so they must be included in the parentheses at the end of the sentence. Notice the pattern inside the parentheses: Author-comma-year-comma-p.-page number. Again, the final period appears after the parentheses at the very end of the sentence.
Unlike some industries, the coffee industry is using innovative techniques to stay ahead of climate change (Worland, 2018).	Because this example uses a paraphrase instead of a quotation, APA style does not require a page number for the in-text citation. The citation includes only the author's name and the date, separated by a comma. Notice that the period comes after the parentheses.

Creating an APA-style references list

The complete list of sources in APA style has "References" as a heading. It refers to the works you are referencing in your writing.

Information to include.   Entries in an APA-style list of references usually include the following information in this order.

Elements of APA-style citations

Author.	"Author" is the person or entity that created the source. List the author in the format Last name, First initial followed by a period.
Publication date.	Enclose the publication date in parentheses followed by a period outside the parentheses. If the source has a month, day, and year, list the year first, followed by a comma, then the month and the day: (2018, December 14). Do not abbreviate months. ▶

Title of source.	Use the title on the title page of the specific source you're using. Put titles of books in *italics*. Capitalize only the first word of the title and subtitle and any proper nouns. Do not italicize or use quotation marks around titles of shorter works such as essays within a book, articles within journals, or pages on a website.
Title of larger work.	If the source appears within a larger publication, such as a magazine, journal, or newspaper, put that title in italics next, followed by a comma.
Volume and issue numbers,	After journal titles, put the volume number in italics, followed by the issue number (not italicized) in parentheses and a comma.
Page numbers.	Include the page numbers followed by a period.
Place of publication:	For books, list the city and state of the publisher, followed by a colon.
Publisher.	The publisher is the organization or company responsible for making the source available.
Retrieval information.	If you found the source in a database, give the DOI if one is available. Otherwise write *Retrieved from* and include the URL of the journal's home page. If you found the source on a website, write *Retrieved from* followed by the URL. Do not add a period at the end of the DOI or URL.

Formatting the references list. Follow these guidelines to format your references list correctly.

- Double space and use an easy-to-read font, as you have for the rest of your paper. Throughout your paper, including a running head on each page that contains a shortened version of the paper title on the left side and the page number on the right side.

- Start the references list on a new page at the end of your paper.

- Center the heading *References* but do not use italics, boldface, or quotation marks.

- Start each entry at the left margin and use a hanging indent of one half inch to indent the second and subsequent lines of each entry.

- Alphabetize the list by the first word of each entry, which is usually the author's last name.

- Italicize the titles of books and journals. Do not put titles of shorter works such as articles or book chapters in quotation marks.
- In titles of journals, capitalize all the important words. In titles of articles and books, capitalize only the first word of the title and subtitle and any proper nouns.

Sample of an APA-style references list

IMMIGRATION   7

References

Abdou, L. H. (2016). The Europeanization of immigration policies. In A. Amelina, K. Horvath, & B. Meeus (Eds.), *An anthology of migration and social transformation: European perspectives* (pp. 105–119). Cham, Switzerland: Springer.

Gonzales, A. R., & Strange, D. N. (2014). *A conservative and compassionate approach to immigration reform: Perspectives from a former U.S. attorney general.* Lubbock, TX: Texas Tech University Press.

Regan, M. (2010). *The death of Josseline: Immigration stories from the Arizona-Mexico borderlands.* Boston, MA: Beacon Press.

Renaud, B., & Renaud, C. (2015, October 8). *Between borders: America's migrant crisis* [Video file]. Retrieved from https://www.youtube.com/watch?v=rxF0t-SMEXA

Formatting the entries.   The examples below illustrate expectations for citing frequently used types of sources. Pay close attention to the order of elements, capitalization, and punctuation.

1. Book by one author

Yanagihara, H. (2015). *A little life.* New York, NY: Doubleday.

2. Work by two to seven authors

Hurtley, F., Roberts, L., Ray, L. B., Purnell, B. A., & Ash, C. (2015). Putting off the inevitable. *Science, 350*, 1180–1181. https://doi .org/10.1126/science.aad3267

3. Work by eight or more authors

Datta, S. J., Khumnoon, C., Lee, Z. H., Moon, W. K., Docao, S., Nguyen, T. H., . . . Yoon, K. B. (2015). CO_2 capture from humid flue gases and humid atmosphere using a microporous coppersilicate. *Science, 350*, 302–306. https://doi.org/10.1126/science.aab1680

4. Two or more works by the same author

Coates, T. (2008). *The beautiful struggle*. New York, NY: Spiegel & Grau.

Coates, T. (2015). *Between the world and me*. New York, NY: Spiegel & Grau.

5. Author with an editor or translator

Piketty, T. (2014). *Capital in the twenty-first century* (A. Goldhammer, Trans.). Cambridge, MA: Harvard University Press. (Original work published 2013)

6. Chapter from an anthology

Abdou, L. H. (2016). The Europeanization of immigration policies. In A. Amelina, K. Horvath, & B. Meeus (Eds.), *An anthology of migration and social transformation: European perspectives* (pp. 105–119). Cham, Switzerland: Springer.

7. Multivolume work

Palmer, S., & Gyllensten, K. (Eds.). (2015). *Psychological stress, resilience, and wellbeing: Vol. 2. The measurement of stress*. London, England: Sage.

8. Article from a journal

Terry, C. P., & Terry, D. L. (2015). Cell phone-related near accidents among young drivers: Associations with mindfulness. *The Journal of Psychology, 149*, 665–683.

Eavers, E. R., Berry, M. A., & Rodriguez, D. N. (2015). The effects of counterfactual thinking on college students' intentions to quit smoking cigarettes. *Current Research in Social Psychology*. Retrieved from https://uiowa.edu/crisp/

9. Article from a database

Lyons, M. (2015). Writing up: How the weak wrote to the powerful. *Journal of Social History, 49*(2), 317–330. https://doi.org/10.1093 /jsh/shv038

10. Article in a magazine

Paris, W. (2015, March/April). The new survivors. *Psychology Today, 48*(2), 66–73, 82.

Bensman, D. (2015, December 4). Security for a precarious workforce. *The American Prospect*. Retrieved from http://prospect.org/

11. Article in a newspaper

Saul, S. (2015, December 6). Colleges pile renovation costs onto the plates of students. *The New York Times*, pp. 1, 18.

Roberson, K. (2015, May 3). Innovation helps address nurse shortage. *Des Moines Register*. Retrieved from http://www .desmoinesregister.com/

12. Short work from a website If you refer to an entire website, don't list it in your references. Simply give the URL in parentheses within the text of your paper.

Centers for Disease Control and Prevention. (2012, November 9). *Arthritis help for veterans*. Retrieved from http://www.cdc.gov /features/arthritis-among-veterans/index.html

13. Blog post

Costandi, M. (2015, April 9). Why brain scans aren't always what they seem [Blog post]. Retrieved from http://www.theguardian.com /science/neurophilosophy/2015/apr/09/bold-assumptions-fmri

14. Podcast

Abumrad, J., & Krulwich, R. (2015, August 30). *Remembering Oliver Sacks* [Audio podcast]. Retrieved from https://www.wnycstudios .org/shows/radiolab/

15. Online video

Renaud, B., & Renaud, C. (2015, October 8). *Between borders: America's migrant crisis* [Video file]. Retrieved from https://www .youtube.com/watch?v=rxF0t-SMEXA

16. Infographic or other visual

Brown, E. (2014, October 15). 15 golden principles of visual hierarchy [Infographic]. *DesignMantic*. Retrieved from http://www .designmantic.com/blog/infographics/15-golden-principles -of-visual-hierarchy

Acknowledgments

Abe Aboraya. "Orlando Paramedics Didn't Go In to Save Victims of the Pulse Shooting. Here's Why." *WMFE*, September 26, 2018, http://www.wmfe.org/orlando-paramedics-didnt-go-in -to-save-victims-of-the-pulse-shooting-heres-why/91562. Copyright © 2018. Reprinted by permission of WMFE.

Alaska Department of Law. "Alaska Attorney General Announces Settlement with Uber over Data Breach" (press release). September 26, 2018. Modified and reprinted by permission of the State of Alaska.

Hannah Brencher. Excerpt from *If You Find This Letter: My Journey to Find Purpose through Hundreds of Letters to Strangers.* Copyright © 2015 by Hannah Brencher. Reprinted with the permission of Howard Books, a division of Simon & Schuster, Inc. All rights reserved.

Elizabeth Chamberlain. Excerpt from "Buy-It-Yourself: How DIY Got Consumerized." *Harlot*, Issue 14, 2015. Copyright © 2015 by Elizabeth Chamberlain. Reprinted by permission of the author.

Sharon Cohen. "Today's Protests Rely on the Masses" (original title: "Today's Protests: Many Voices, Social Media, Not 1 Leader"). *AP News*, June 22, 2018, https://www.apnews .com/44defd2105f04da891c5ae98062a8fcb. Copyright © 2018. Used with the permission of the Associated Press.

Malaka Gharib. "When Is It OK to Wear the Clothing of Another Culture?" Copyright © 2018 National Public Radio, Inc. Originally published on NPR.org and used with the permission of NPR. Any unauthorized duplication is strictly prohibited.

Craig Gundersen. "The Potentially Negative Consequences Associated with the Healthy, Hunger-Free Kids Act." *Policy Matters*, University of Illinois, August 12, 2014, http:// policymatters.illinois.edu/the-potentially-negative-consequences-associated-with-the -healthy-hunger-free-kids-act/. Copyright © 2014. Reprinted by permission.

Sean Keane. "Don't Obsess Over Your Follower Count" (original title: "Twitter CEO Jack Dorsey Says You Shouldn't Obsess Over Your Follower Count"). *CNET.com*, November 12, 2018, https://www.cnet.com/news/twitter-ceo-jack-dorsey-says-you-shouldnt-obsess-over -your-follower-count/. Used with the permission of CNET.com. Copyright © 2018. All rights reserved.

Ed Kromer. "Growing Social Movements through Reason, Not Disruption" (original title: "Reason, Not Disruption, Is the Most Effective Means of Growing a Social Movement"). November 30, 2015, from the website of the Foster School of Business, University of Washington, https://foster.uw.edu/research-brief/reason-not-disruption-is-the-most -effective-means-of-growing-a-social-movement/. Copyright © 2015 by the Foster School of Business, University of Washington. Reprinted by permission.

Carson Long. "The 'Death' of the English Language: Or How Language Will Never Die." From *A Long Look At*, https://alonglookat.wordpress.com/2015/04/17/the-death-of-the-english -language-or-how-language-will-never-die/. Reprinted by permission of the author.

Christine Martorana. "Death: The End We All Have to Face(book)." *Harlot*, Issue 13 (2015), http://harlotofthearts.org/index.php/harlot/article/view/215/164. Copyright © 2015. Used by permission of the author.

Index